Inter-Firm Alliances

The phenomenon of inter-firm alliances represents an important shift in the organizational practices of companies. Increasingly, firms are focusing on their *core* competencies, which has meant that *complementary* competencies must now be obtained from other firms. Today, the art of managing such alliances is a condition for survival and success.

This volume examines the factors which influence the nature and extent of inter-firm alliances. The discussion takes in alliances between buyers and suppliers, between competitors, between firms in different industries, against the background of developments in international business. On the basis of an inventory of different forms of alliance, the author defines rigorous criteria for choosing one. A set of tools is then developed for the design and analysis of governance of relations, as well as for establishing, developing and terminating an alliance.

Inter-Firm Alliances combines 'resource-based' views, transaction-cost analysis and institutional economics to develop an original and comprehensive theory of inter-firm alliances and a coherent method for managing them. The theory is illustrated and elaborated with real-life detail from a variety of international case studies. Both as a theoretical guide to evolving organizational practice and as a manual for successfully governing inter-film alliances, this volume will be a precious resource for students and researchers in business and international management studies.

Bart Nooteboom is Professor of Industrial Organization in the Faculty of Management and Organization, Groningen University, The Netherlands. He has published widely in the fields of industrial and business economics.

Inter-Firm Alliances

Analysis and design

Bart Nooteboom

To Rogers,

In gratitude for his interest,

Bart

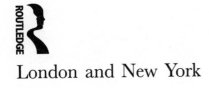

London and New York

First published 1999
by Routledge
11 New Fetter Lane, London EC4P 4EE

Simultaneously published in the USA and Canada
by Routledge
29 West 35th Street, New York, NY 10001

Typeset in Baskerville by
The Florence Group, Stoodleigh, Devon
Printed and bound in Great Britain by
MPG Books, Bodmin, Cornwall

British Library Cataloguing in Publication Data
A catalogue record for this book is available
from the British Library

Library of Congress Cataloging in Publication Data
A catalog record for this book has been requested

ISBN 0–415–18153–4 (hbk)
ISBN 0–415–18154–2 (pbk)

Contents

Figures

Tables

Preface

This book is an outcome of ten years of research and teaching on inter-firm relations. Earlier versions of parts of it have appeared in various journals and books. The journals were: *Journal of Evolutionary Economics*, *Technology Analysis and Strategic Management*, *Small Business Economics*, *Organization Studies*, *Academy of Management Journal*. The books were published by Edward Elgar and Routledge, and were selections of conference papers from conferences of the European Association for Evolutionary Political Economy (EAEPE) and the European Management and Organization in Transition (EMOT) programme financed by the European Science Foundation. I am indebted to many anonymous referees of those publications.

The empirical studies referred to in Chapter 5 were conducted in collaboration with Niels Noorderhaven of Tilburg University and Hans Berger of my own University of Groningen, both in the Netherlands, and I thank them for their cooperation. The studies were partly funded by the Netherlands Foundation for Scientific Research (NWO).

My greatest debt is without doubt to Oliver Williamson: his work has provided a solid basis and a source of inspiration. He has personally stimulated me by demanding precision for concepts such as 'competence' and 'trust' before they can be accepted as legitimate extensions to transaction cost theory.

Introduction

This introduction presents the purpose of the book and discusses its scope. To offer a guide to the reader, it gives an overview of the content of chapters. To help the reader to position the book in the literature, it summarizes the theoretical perspective taken.

SCOPE AND PURPOSE

'Alliance' is a broad term capturing many forms of inter-firm cooperation that go beyond mere market transactions. It includes 'vertical' alliances between buyers and suppliers (subcontracting), 'horizontal' alliances between competitors and 'diagonal' alliances between firms in different industries. It covers the whole range of forms from incidental cooperation between independent firms, through licensing, more systematic and lasting forms of cooperation, equity swaps and equity joint ventures all the way to mergers and acquisitions. This book addresses the full range of alliances.

The purpose of the book is to provide theoretically well founded and empirically tested tools for the analysis, diagnosis and (re)design of alliances. The analysis requires theory. It forms the basis for design of an alliance and for diagnosis of performance and problems, leading to adaptation (redesign). Diagnosis and design require a practical orientation, which takes into account the variety of conditions and goals that are relevant for the choice of alliance form and for its 'governance'. The term 'control' may overly suggest that one can direct and constrain partners from the perspective of the one-sided interest of some 'principal'. The term 'governance' aims to express that there are multiple interests, and that the challenge is to achieve a viable and fruitful balance of interests and power. Rather than viewing an alliance as a zero-sum game, it considers opportunities for achieving mutual benefit (so-called 'win–win' situations). This book does not employ the 'principal–agent' perspective, because it imposes one-sided influence and direction, which in alliances is generally inappropriate and counter-productive.

Providing both theoretical depth and a practical orientation, the book is aimed at both academics and practitioners. The book is not about operational matters of partner selection, legal form, financial planning and control, tax issues, human resource management or planning. It focuses on strategic issues of the goal and form of alliance and their 'governance'. The leading issue is: how to create mutual advantage and to manage risks of dependence and mutual adjustment between alliance partners, in the light of their goals and outside conditions of technology, markets and other institutions. How does one deal with organization 'between market and hierarchy'; with relations between firms that are formally separate and autonomous but factually interrelated and dependent on each other?

The book takes a dynamic perspective, in a double sense. First, it incorporates issues of innovation and learning. The potential of inter-firm alliances is fully realized and their management can be properly understood only if innovation and learning are taken into account. Second, it looks at alliances as forms of organization that cannot be established once and for all, but require careful set-up, development, adaptation and, last but not least, judicious disengagement when the need arises. Not only the advantages of alliances and networks should be considered, but also their possible negative effects in raising entry and exit barriers that create obstacles for efficiency and innovation. Therefore we need to consider both set-up and break-up.

Several forms of alliance involve more than two partners (such as consortia, associations, franchising), but even when they do not they are generally embedded in wider networks of firms and (semi)governmental organizations. This book does not aim to give a systematic account of networks and gives most of its attention to the management of bilateral relations. However, it does also look at alliances with multiple partners and at some of the implications of the embedding of alliances in wider networks, such as risks of spillover and the role of third parties in the design and governance of bilateral relations.

An overview of the content of chapters is given below, to provide the reader with some guidance for selecting parts of the book for reading and perhaps for teaching. The theoretical basis of the book is interdisciplinary: combining insights from economics, sociology and cognitive science, which it aims to integrate into a coherent theoretical framework. In view of the importance of the theoretical perspective, and to allow the reader to position this book in the literature, a further elaboration of the theoretical perspective is given in the final section of this introduction.

OVERVIEW

The book starts with a discussion of theory (Chapter 1). It aims to extend transaction cost economics (TCE) with a social exchange perspective, and to integrate both in the framework of the 'resource' or 'competence' view of the firm. This entails a shift from static analysis of efficiency to a dynamic perspective of innovation and learning. This requires a theory of knowledge and learning, and the chapter summarizes a constructivist theory of knowledge that can be seen as an attempt to contribute to fulfilment of the research programme of the Austrian school in economics. Inclusion of a social exchange perspective entails that trust and the social embedding of relations is incorporated, but the possibility of opportunism and its implications are retained. While trust does go beyond calculative self-interest, it should not be blind. An extensive discussion of trust is given to clarify this issue. Chapter 1 includes a summary of TCE, which can be skipped by the informed reader. But it also discusses criticism of TCE, extends the theory and gives an account of effects of scale in transaction costs. This is relevant for relations between small and large firms and for government policy. An appendix gives a detailed analysis of the notion of 'specificity', which plays a key role in transaction cost economics. In view of debates in this field, and the importance of the guidance from theory, the theoretical perspective of the book will be elaborated a little in the following section.

Chapter 2 gives a discussion of the background: the business environment in which alliances appear. It discusses why and how the importance of cooperation between firms has increased over the past years, as a consequence of developments in technology, world markets and resulting conditions of competition. This chapter is mostly descriptive rather than analytical. It discusses developments in technology (innovation) and markets (globalization) that form the background and indicate the need for inter-firm alliances. In particular, it gives an assessment of the effects to be expected from information and communication technology (ICT). It summarizes the different purposes that alliances may serve in that context. It concludes that in view of developments in international markets and competition (globalization), firms need to outsource as many activities as possible, so long as that enhances rather than detracts from core competence. In particular, rather than claiming to have full competence in all dimensions of their products and production processes, firms should make use of the specific complementary competencies of suppliers, not only in production, but also in the processes of research and development. Rather than making blueprints of required inputs that are 'thrown over the wall' to suppliers, there should be 'early supplier involvement' in the design process (Helper 1991; Lamming 1993). But also in horizontal relations, with competitors and in diagonal relations with firms in other industries, one should look for complementary competencies or other resources, opportunities to share costs, or to gain market entry.

Chapter 3 gives an inventory of the different forms of alliance that are available 'between market and hierarchy', in a two-dimensional scheme that distinguishes forms according to the degree to which claims on profits and decision rights are concentrated or dispersed. It analyses goals and conditions that affect the choice of form. Illustrations are given from the alliance literature. In two appendices, a game-theoretic analysis is given of the conditions for cooperation and of the optimal number of partners in a trade-off between learning and spillover.

Chapter 4 forms the central chapter of the book. It develops the notion of the 'governance' of inter-firm relations. Governance is aimed at the joint creation of value and the control of relational risk concerning the achievement of that value, the distribution of that value, the set-up, development and break-up of an alliance. The chapter develops a process and control model of alliances to be used for diagnosing, (re)designing and managing an alliance. It is based on the synthesis of the competence view, transaction cost economics, theory of knowledge and learning set out in Chapter 1. The model consists of a scheme of interrelated factors which play a role in inter-firm relations. It provides a tool for the analysis of benefits and risks of dependence, and instruments to reduce risks. It offers the basis for a systematic assessment of interaction between alliance partners and possible actions for influencing dependence. This yields an inventory and a typology of strategies for the governance of inter-firm relations. The model can serve as a method for firms to 'audit' (analyse, review and improve) their relations. It also provides the basis for further scientific research of the paths of development of relations. It is used to assess more systematically than in Chapter 2 the effects to be expected from ICT. In an appendix, by way of illustration and experiment, the method is applied to marriage relations. We have considerably longer experience with marriages, in different cultures and conditions, and the metaphor may yield new ideas for alliances.

Chapter 5 discusses developments in buyer–supplier relations and results of empirical studies designed to test the theory of governance set out in Chapter 4. These studies show how the concepts of the theory can be measured and effects of 'instruments' for governance can be tested. The method set out in Chapter 4 is also used for an analysis of different 'generic' systems of supply in Europe, the USA and Japan, of the development of 'lean supply' and implications for business and government. As an example, the perspectives are discussed for introduction of such principles in the construction industry. A more formal analysis of the generic systems of supply is given in an appendix, where the viability of systems in different 'possible worlds' is investigated in terms of the game-theoretic notion of a Nash equilibrium.

Finally, Chapter 6 gives conclusions, by pulling together the main themes and results from the book, and discusses implications for policy and avenues for further research.

PERSPECTIVE

To arrive at a good analysis, diagnosis and design of alliances, depending on their purpose and conditions, a theoretical perspective is needed which draws from different traditions. These are indicated below and discussed in more detail in Chapter 1.

The central purpose of alliances is to utilize complementary resources of different firms. In view of this, the leading perspective is the resource (competence or capabilities) view, which has developed from the work of Penrose (1959) but gained momentum more recently (see, for example, Lippman and Rumelt 1982 and, for a survey, Foss and Knudsen 1996). Whenever possible, in order to achieve a profit and evade or beat the competition, firms aim to distinguish their products from those of competitors, on the basis of firm-specific resources that cannot immediately be copied. In view of this, differences between firms are crucial and the notion of the 'representative firm' from traditional economic theory, which is assumed to represent an entire industry, is rejected as fundamentally misleading. Firms differ in their competencies due to the fact that these are embedded in organizational structure and 'communities of practice' and are partly 'tacit', so that there are greater or lesser and more or less durable obstacles to their 'spillover' to potential competitors.

To understand the role of alliances for the utilization of complementary competencies and to take into account the importance of learning in the purpose and development of alliances, a theory of knowledge and learning is needed. This book employs a 'social constructivist' theory of knowledge and, while it is not the purpose of the present book to expand on theories of organizational learning, a summary is given in Chapter 1.

Transaction cost economics, as developed mainly by Oliver Williamson (1975, 1985) is useful to deal with relational risk ('hold-up'), due to opportunism and dependence as a result of 'specific investments'. But the theory needs to be transformed to fit the competence-based view and to allow for trust next to opportunism. A social exchange perspective is included to deal with this. A discussion of the theory and its extensions, including the notion and role of trust, is given in Chapter 1.

Explanations of alliances in the literature focus on the trade-off between the perceived advantages of full ownership, market contracts and intermediate positions (Contractor and Lorange 1988; Osborn and Baughn 1990; Hagedoorn 1993). There has been a tendency to ascribe alliances to simple causes. The purpose of a firm or market conditions were supposed to determine the choice of the type of alliance. Accumulating experience and research show that the causality of alliances is more complex and we need concepts to deal with this complexity. It was already indicated above that the design of alliances depends at least on: the participants, their competencies, their purposes and external conditions. In social sciences causality is complex. In an explanation of activities performed by people we can consider different types of cause. This is also discussed in Chapter 1.

As will be discussed in Chapter 2, competition has increasingly become a race to the market with new products. It is no longer a matter of choosing between price, quality and innovation: firms must excel in all of them at the same time (Bolwijn and Kumpe 1989). To survive, firms must set high standards of production as well as innovation and concentrate on competencies at which they excel (Prahalad and Hamel 1990). But not to miss out on important resources they must complement their competencies with those of other firms, in some form of alliance. Alliance partners can be suppliers, customers, research institutes, (semi)governmental institutions, but also (potential) competitors. The crucial difference between 'vertical' cooperation between suppliers and users and 'horizontal' cooperation between competitors is that in the second case there is more chance of substitution between their products; of a 'zero-sum game' where one partner's profit is the other partner's loss. In vertical cooperation there is more complementarity; an easier 'win–win' situation. That is why one will sooner see a merger or acquisition, rather than an alliance between partners that remain independent, in areas where rivals compete directly, with the same product in the same market (Bleeke and Ernst 1991). But potential rivals can often cooperate in different products or with similar products in different markets, or in setting a joint standard for a new product or technology, or in the development of new generic technology needed for a new class of products whose costs and risks cannot be carried by any single firm.

A famous case is the cooperation between Sony and Philips in setting the standard for the compact audio disc. While Philips and Sony cooperated in the setting of the CD, in other markets they kept on competing and they resumed competition in CDs once they had jointly set the technical standard. This cooperation was based on their learning from the debacle in the market for videorecorders: they both had superior products (Betamax of Sony and video 2000 of Philips), but the competing VHS system (JVC, Matsushita) won by achieving a breakthrough in market acceptance. This type of effect obtains especially in markets with 'network externality', where the usefulness of a piece of equipment depends on how many others have equipment of the same technical standard. The VHS system won due to a better fit to market demand in the supply of the software (video tapes) that was compatible only with the VHS standard built into the hardware (recorders): length of play for recording baseball games and more extensive distribution of recorded tapes for hire. This gave a head start in the market, with supply according to the technology reinforcing itself, so that a consumer choosing an alternative from Sony or Philips ran an accelerating risk that the supply of appropriate software would fall back and stop.

Concentration on core competencies implies that firms must purchase or contract out more,[1] even activities which are 'sensitive' in the sense that they must satisfy specific demands and are crucial for the quality of one's performance and competitive position; even if there is a danger that in such cooperation there is a risk that one becomes dependent on the partner or a risk that knowledge that is part of one's own core competence 'spills over' to the partner and from there to direct competitors. As a result, high demands are imposed on partners and on one's ability to 'govern' the relationship in order to cope with these risks. This yields issues of control which are complicated because they entail strategic interaction and a balancing of mutual interest and dependence. As summarized at the end of Chapter 4, there are five basic paradoxes of cooperation that one needs to solve. As a result, a crucial competence of management now is its ability to design and manage a good 'architecture' of relations inside and outside the firm (Kay 1993).

Countries also compete for positions in world markets. Good infrastructure, supply of production factors, access to innovative and demanding customers, suppliers and supporting industries give competitive advantage to nations (Porter 1990). Thus, the issues discussed in this book are relevant not only for business but also for government. A discussion of issues for government policy is given at the end of Chapter 5.

To the extent that cooperation is aimed more at the development of new products or processes (innovation, learning), the need both for cooperation and for mutual interaction and adjustment increase. As discussed in Chapter 1, this is accompanied by investments that are 'specific' to the relation: elsewhere, in the switch to another relation, they no longer apply and a novel investment needs to be made before the old one is recouped. In other words: the investment is 'sunk' in the relation. This makes one dependent on the relation and hence on the partner, who may be tempted to take advantage of this and rearrange the distribution of the added value of the relation to his or her advantage. This is the 'hold-up' problem analysed in transaction cost economics (TCE).

This raises the issue of 'governance': what exactly are the causes of dependence, what risks ensue and what options does one have to protect against them. There are different views on this. One extreme is an idyllic image of enduring cooperation based on mutual trust and an equitable sharing of costs and benefits. Another extreme is a sinister image of exploitation of slave labour in sweatshop firms by ruthless principals. Reality ranges between these extremes, with significant differences between countries, industries and economic conditions. During the latest slump in the car industry, for example, suppliers were throttled. Whatever trust had been built up before, leading suppliers to accept the risk of specific investments for the sake of close, joint innovation, was destroyed. One can wonder whether this was wise in the long term, but the pressures of short-term competition to take out the problems on suppliers were apparently too high to resist.

1 Theory

This chapter discusses the theoretical perspective taken in this book. An attempt is made to unify the 'resource' ('competence' or 'capability') view, a constructivist theory of knowledge and a social exchange perspective in a theory of inter-firm relations that goes beyond transaction cost economics to include a dynamic perspective of innovation and learning and to take into account trust next to opportunism. The resource perspective is summarized and extended with a constructivist theory of knowledge, which includes a discussion of the role of 'tacit' knowledge and 'cognitive distance' between firms. Transaction cost economics is criticized and extended. For the extension with a dynamic perspective, use is made of the theory of knowledge and learning. The extension with trust requires a detailed discussion to come to grips with that slippery notion. Attention is next given to the 'multi-level' problem. Knowledge and trust are ordinarily associated with individuals; how do we bring them to the level of organizations? Finally, the multiple causality implicit in issues of inter-organizational relations and social science in general is made explicit.

RESOURCES

This book employs the resource (competence or capability) view. According to that view, the firm is made up from a number of resources, embodied in various forms of capital (financial, human, social, commercial), which to a greater or lesser extent are specific to the firm, i.e. cannot be immediately copied by others. Resources can be classified into assets, competencies and positional advantages (Stoelhorst 1997). Assets are subject to legal ownership and contracts. Competencies and positional advantages are not easily subject to property rights and can be invisible (see Itami 1987).

Competencies include technical, cognitive, motivational, organizational and communicative abilities. Competencies can reside on the personal level, in the form of knowledge, skill and relational competence, but related to the latter, motivation and morality can also be included. 'Morality' includes norms and values of conduct that the individual holds, his degree of commitment to them and susceptibility to ethical appeals (concerning loyalty, justice, truthfulness). On the aggregate, interpersonal level of 'communities of practice' (Brown and Duguid 1991) within an organization, entire organizations and even networks of organizations, there are assets and positional advantages, but also competencies. Competencies on the level of an organization or network would include institutions and patterns of knowledge exchange and transformation. Institutions are defined as environments and arrangements which limit and guide conduct (North and Thomas 1973; North 1990). They include practices, procedures, rules and technical standards, as well as cultural entities such as prevailing norms and values of conduct, goals, role models, rituals. Among other things, they may serve to guide relations with other organizations, and are then part of firm-level relational competence. Organizational competencies in the form of 'patterns of knowledge exchange and conversion' refer to the way in which knowledge is converted from tacit to documented knowledge, absorbed from documented into tacit knowledge, transmitted, pooled, shared and recombined in novel combinations (see Nonaka and Takeuchi 1995). Relational competencies on the individual level enhance learning. Relational competencies on the individual level, supported and guided by relational competencies on the organizational level in the form of guiding institutions, yield positional advantage in the form of efficient access to resources of other organizations. Positional advantages further include product–technology–market combinations, access to materials, distribution channels, political acceptance, brand loyalty and reputation.

Relational competencies form the core subject of the present book. They constitute an ability to 'govern' relations, by selecting and implementing appropriate modes of governance, inside the firm and between firms. As will be discussed extensively, modes of governance include four basic classes of instruments: hierarchical fiat and control, contracts and monitoring, motivation on the basis of self-interest (including mutual dependence, posting of hostages, reputation mechanisms), trust-based motivation and loyalty. Which mix of instruments is appropriate depends on the goals and conditions of an alliance. In some cases highly trust-based, intensive forms of cooperation are appropriate, in other conditions arm's-length impersonal transactions are apt.

The competence perspective has implications for the notion of entrepreneurship. According to Schumpeter's theory, an entrepreneur builds a firm on an innovation which consists of 'novel combinations', causing 'creative destruction' of existing practices, thus exerting a force away from equilibrium between supply and demand. According to Walras' theory, an entrepreneur performs 'arbitration' between supply and demand: by filling 'holes' in the market he exerts a force towards equilibrium (which does not imply that equilibrium will actually be reached). Most other theories of entrepreneurship, including Kirzner's (1973) theory of entrepreneurship as 'alertness', also see it as equilibrating, in the sense of bringing supply and demand together by utilizing novel possibilities to satisfy demand. But the debate on whether entrepreneurship is equilibrating or disequilibrating is misleading, if the very process of utilizing existing opportunities yields the basis for discovering and creating novel opportunities by novel combinations (Nooteboom 1999). The resource perspective suggests that the role of an entrepreneur is to establish a configuration of resources that are to some extent specific to the firm whereby he earns a rent. This activity is equilibrating in the sense that it uses existing opportunities, and disequilibrating in that it constantly looks for novel combinations which cannot immediately be copied. This is not so far from the Schumpeterian notion. Schumpeter recognized innovations not only in technology but also in finding or developing new sources of materials, new markets and new forms of organization. According to the resource perspective, entrepreneurship would include, for example, relational competencies, especially when there is no adequate institutional basis for markets: no adequate legal system to support contractual governance and no well-developed capital markets. Then entrepreneurs have to develop networks of contacts to gain access to resources and to manage them.

Birley *et al.* (1991) found that in Italy entrepreneurs spend significantly more time on the set-up and maintenance of networks of personal contacts than in Sweden, Northern Ireland and the USA. One would expect this to a much greater extent in former communist countries that have not yet developed the institutions needed for a market economy, particularly if the networks of policymakers from the communist 'nomenclatura' are still intact and have an interest in preventing the emergence of market institutions.

The present classification of resources is related to the classification into economic, social and cultural capital. Economic capital includes assets and most of the competencies. Social capital consists of positional advantages based on relations with other organizations. Cultural capital consists of symbolic capabilities to produce new meanings and goals, or institutions in the sense of limiting and guiding conduct.

Resources cannot all be instantly copied by other firms because they are to some extent inscrutable or subject to 'causal ambiguity' (Lippman and Rumelt 1982): even if a would-be imitator can observe activities, this does not yet imply that he can understand them. Resources and especially competencies, can be difficult to understand and imitate because the knowledge involved is to a greater or lesser extent tacit (not documented) and embodied in the heads and hands of people, in teams, organizational structure and procedures and organizational culture. It is particularly such unique capabilities of firms, in addition to market structure (concentration, price elasticity, entry barriers), that yield a profit. As novelty develops into common practice, it becomes less tacit and can be more easily imitated, so that entrepreneurs are driven to develop and implement novelty to maintain profits.

For reasons that will be discussed later in Chapter 2, firms need to utilize complementary resources from other firms, in both a static and a dynamic sense: in a static sense for the efficiency of current production, typically because other specialized firms can make products at a greater scale and therefore more efficiently; in a dynamic sense for developing their own resources, i.e. for learning, because others have firm-specific competencies of development that are complementary to one's own. Increasingly, alliances are formed not just for static efficiency but also for learning (Mody 1993). To understand this we require a theory of learning.

KNOWLEDGE AND LEARNING

Traditional mainstream economic theory implicitly employs a theory of knowledge which one can label as 'naive realism': people observe the world as it is and therefore have the same information and knowledge, once they make the expense of getting the information (search costs). Next, they are capable of processing the information to acquire the knowledge involved in it and to make rational choices.[1] Austrian economics has from the start (Menger and subsequently von Mises and Hayek) given more attention to problems of information and learning, with its perspective of the market as a discovery process (Caldwell and Boehm 1992; Foss 1994; Vaughn 1994). While this may align with recent interest from mainstream economics in asymmetric information and search costs, the crucial difference lies in Austrian subjectivism: not only preferences differ between people, but also knowledge of technology and market opportunities. Different people not only want different things but also think different thoughts. The discovery process of the market entails shifts in both knowledge and preferences. In a sense, the present book aims to contribute to the fulfilment of the Austrian programme. The constructivist theory of knowledge set out below implements such subjectivism.

Herbert Simon pointed out that cognitive capacity is too limited to allow for such all-encompassing ('synoptic') rationality. And then it is efficient to develop routines to deal with standard conditions, so that scarce capacity for rational evaluation can be turned to novel or non-standard issues. Without such capacity for routine behaviour, we would not be able to turn our attention to novelty. Emotions serve to set the agenda for attention: through emotion, danger calls the attention of rational evaluation (Simon 1983). But routines entail a risk: they may become second nature to the extent that we cannot deviate from them even if conditions require it. Note that this problem is more urgent to the extent that the environment is more complex and variable. Complexity enhances the need for routines, but variability increases the risk involved.

There is a familiar distinction between data and information: data become information only when they are absorbed to receive meaning in one's existing

structure of knowledge. In communication, the sender transforms information ('signified') into data ('signifiers'), which then need to be transformed
back into information by the receiver. This is the process of signification.
Observation and the use of information requires 'absorptive capacity' (Cohen
and Levinthal 1990). This may be a problem for several reasons.

First, absorptive capacity may be limited. For an understanding of this we
turn to a 'social constructivist' theory of knowledge (Nooteboom 1992a), which
is inspired in part by the work of Piaget (1970, 1974). As recognized by the
philosopher Kant, we do not observe the world as it is 'in itself'. To put this
in a more sophisticated way, we have no way of judging the extent to which
our thought is consistent with the real world, since we cannot descend
from our mind, so to speak, to see how it is hooked onto the world. We can
confront our views, interpretations and evaluations with those of other people,
within the constraints of language and we can monitor the perceived success
and failure of our actions based on them. This gives us some basis for revising
our thoughts, but at no time can we judge its truth in terms of correspondence
with the world as it is in itself. We perceive, interpret and evaluate our world
according to categories of thought which develop from interaction with the
world and communicative interaction with people. This view is subjectivist in
the sense that cognitive categories are idiosyncratic. But subjectivism is limited
and extreme relativism is evaded, by processes of interaction between people
and their physical and social environment, which yields some commonality of
cognition to the extent that it has developed in a shared environment.
Intelligence is 'internalized action' (Piaget 1970, 1974).[2] This view aligns with
Hayek's insight that 'the knowledge that informs economic decision making is
discovered through the actual activities of market participants' (Vaughn 1994:
121). If the constructivist perspective is valid, categories of perception, interpretation and evaluation are to some extent dependent on the path of development that an individual (person or firm) has followed.[3] As a result, absorptive
capacity is to some extent idiosyncratic and culturally determined.

In their struggle for survival, firms face a dilemma of exploitation and
exploration (Holland 1975; March 1991), or first order vs. second order
learning (Hedberg *et al.* 1976; Fiol and Lyles 1985), single loop vs. double
loop learning (Argyris and Schön 1978), or learning I vs. II (Bateson 1973).
One of the central tasks of contemporary management is to achieve an
adequate balance between these two forms of learning. Management needs
to explore novel markets, products and technologies, but it also needs to
stop exploration at some point, determine a focus and make a commitment
to exploit current knowledge in production. Indeed, a firm may be seen as
a 'focusing device' (Nooteboom 1992a): a means of bringing people together
on a shared purpose, with a shared view, matched competencies and coordination of action to achieve it. But the risk is that they miss relevant
alterations in conditions that require a change of course.

The constructivist theory of knowledge indicates a deeper problem.
On the basis of their path of cognitive development and the categories of

perception, interpretation and evaluation built from it, they may not be able to perceive and interpret some of the relevant developments. Then they need others, with the benefit of a different perspective, to supplement their limited ability to perceive, interpret and evaluate relevant developments. Elsewhere (Nooteboom 1992a) I proposed the notion of 'external economy of cognitive scope' (EECS). If knowledge depends on categories of thought which develop in interaction with the physical and social environment, then thought is path-dependent and idiosyncratic. People will be able to understand each other only to the extent that they have developed their categories in a shared environment and in mutual interaction. It also entails that there are things that one simply cannot see and interpret in the way that others can. Therefore, not to miss out on the perception of relevant opportunities and threats one needs to tap into the complementary cognition of others. This entails scope in the sense of complementarity, the scope is cognitive and it is external. It is essential that the external source has a sufficiently different cognitive history to yield non-redundant cognition: hence 'external economy of cognitive scope'. Summing up: to solve the dilemma of exploration and exploitation, where for exploitation a firm serves as a focusing device, in a complex and changing world the firm requires partners for external intelligence for the purpose of exploration.

COGNITIVE DISTANCE

For learning, partners should on the one hand have sufficient 'cognitive distance', i.e. possess different cognitive categories, to be able to capture knowledge that one could not have captured oneself, but on the other must be sufficiently close, in cognition and language, to enable meaningful communication. If effectiveness of knowledge transfer is the product of novelty and intelligibility, this yields some optimal intermediate cognitive distance, as illustrated in Figure 1.1.

Figure 1.1 reflects Granovetter's (1982) notion of the 'strength of weak ties', which have the advantage of yielding more novelty or 'non-redundance', but understanding may be complicated by lack of shared experience. In particular, when knowledge is tacit, strong ties, based on enduring and intensive interaction, may be needed. Strong ties are also needed when innovation is systemic, i.e. needs to be 'in tune' with changes in other activities. On the other hand, strong ties may have the disadvantage not only of adding little novelty, but also of generating too much personal interaction and loyalty, to the detriment of productive work, criticism and flexibility.

Tacit knowledge is knowledge that is implicit rather than explicit and cannot be documented. The notion of tacit knowledge is generally attributed to Polanyi (1962, 1966, 1969), but is implicit in Hayek's notion of 'specific knowledge' and became explicit in his essay 'Competition as a discovery procedure' (Hayek 1978; see Vaughn 1994: 122). From experience

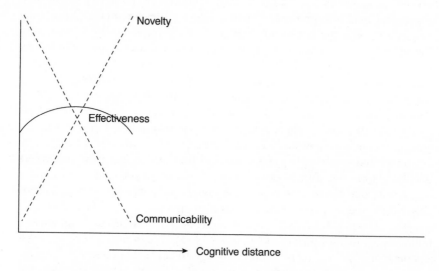

Figure 1.1 Cognitive distance.

we know that a certain practice works, but we cannot explain and prescribe how. In fact, there are two conditions of tacitness (Nooteboom 1998b). One condition is that the practice is so new and experimental that we cannot yet tell where its boundaries of application lie, what different forms are available and which forms should be applied in what conditions. A second condition is that after it has been developed and implemented extensively the practice becomes so routinized and automatic, as part of a skill rather than explicit knowledge, that is has almost become 'second nature' and no longer subject to critical reflection. This relates to the earlier discussion of the need for routines due to bounded rationality, as argued by Simon.

The distinction between tacit and documented knowledge is closely related to the distinction between 'procedural' and 'declarative' knowledge (Cohen 1991; Cohen and Bacdayan 1994). Procedural knowledge constitutes an ability or skill to perform some activity. Declarative knowledge constitutes explicit knowledge of facts, causal relations, etc. The one can be possessed without the other; one can ride a bike without being able to explain how. Procedural knowledge tends to be retained longer than declarative knowledge. Having learned a foreign language, later one can often recognize whether a sentence is well-formed without recalling the grammatical rules for sentence formation (Cohen and Bacdayan 1994). Then one can say that one knows the grammar in the procedural but not in the declarative sense.

Corresponding to the distinction between procedural and declarative knowledge, there are different ways of obtaining (learning) or transferring (teaching) a practice. When knowledge is documented, one can learn declaratively, by studying a blueprint, formula or standard operating procedure.

With tacit knowledge one needs to learn procedurally, as an apprentice, by imitating observed behaviour of one or more 'masters' in a 'community of practice' (Brown and Duguid 1991) and trying it out in practice, subject to correction by that community. Typically, an 'exemplar' is exhibited, which the would-be adopter can try to imitate. Exemplars are often provided in the form of typical cases or role models. In economic theory a famous exemplar to clarify economy of scale by specialization is Adam Smith's pin factory. Role models play an important part for artisans, entrepreneurs and scientists. Exemplars play a role in culture, where they take the form of heroic stories, myths and symbols.

It is not intended to suggest that any given bit of knowledge is either entirely tacit or entirely documented. On the contrary, every bit of knowledge always has some degree of tacitness, but this may be more or less. One reason for an irreducible residue of tacit knowledge is simply that in communication one cannot keep on asking for definitions or justifications, including definition or justification of the terms of definition or justification. At some point one has to take the terms of discourse for granted. That is where knowledge remains tacit.[4]

It was indicated before that information (signified) expressed in language by a sender becomes mere data (signifier) for the receiver, who then has to transform the data back into information. We noted that the receiver may not have the absorptive capacity to do so. Now it is noted that in the transformation of information to data, in a speech act performed by the sender, some tacit knowledge is always lost. Next, the receiver's cognitive categories that enable absorption will add tacit knowledge. Information sent is never identical to information absorbed. This is how misunderstanding can arise. To the extent that knowledge is more tacit, its transmission is more problematic: too much gets lost in signification; in the transformation of information to data and vice versa. Under cognitive proximity, cognitive categories are similar, due to interaction and common experience, so that signification is similar and less tacit knowledge is lost in communication.

A further problem of tacit knowledge, in the form of routines that have become second nature, is that it can form an obstacle to absorption. If an existing practice has become routine, to the point of developing into 'second nature', one may no longer even be aware of it and the justification of current practice appears to be self-evident. An alternative practice may be inconceivable. The transfer of knowledge may then require that one first makes existing tacit knowledge explicit, before it can be criticized and replaced. On the part of the supplier of an innovation, this may require a skill of intellectual 'midwifery' ('maieutics') to elicit from the receiver an awareness of the basis of established practice.[5]

Summing up: whenever tacit knowledge is involved, the dynamic transaction costs of transferring knowledge are high, for two reasons. First, it requires close interaction on the spot and involvement in a community of practice. Second, it encounters problems of absorptive capacity due to lack of awareness as a basis for criticism of existing practice, so that maieutics is needed.

Knowledge tends to be tacit particularly in small firms, for two reasons (Nooteboom 1994). First, for the smaller volume niche markets to which small firms typically need to seek recourse, with tailor-made products, technology often is more craft-like and thereby tends to be more tacit. Second, in small firms coordination and supervision of production can be more informal, oral and direct, requiring less knowledge codified in blueprints, written procedures, explicit models, etc. This enables small firms to be flexible and to offer relatively high levels of motivation, which is part of their competitive advantage. But tacitness does also yield the obstacle indicated here. This explains why often the transfer of technology to small firms is notoriously difficult and the proposals of academics are deemed impractical. As a result, consultancy concerning the adoption of novel technology by small firms often requires maieutics. This typically takes the form of sitting around a table with entrepreneurs who are sufficiently similar to make sense to each other and sufficiently different not to be direct competitors and by comparing their practices to make them explicit. The effectiveness of knowledge transfer to small firms increased greatly when it was conducted in the form of transferring people as carriers of tacit knowledge rather than formal knowledge embodied in programmes.

Generally, when firms grow large, with the need and opportunity of delegation and specialization of different activities in different departments, procedural knowledge with its direct, face-to-face visual and oral coordination and communication no longer suffices. Ways of doing things must be made explicit and explainable, i.e. must be turned into declarative knowledge and documented to form instructions and standard operating procedures across departments or subsidiaries. In other words: transformation into declarative knowledge and codification is required for diffusion over large distances and many people.

The relevance of all this to alliances is as follows. For reasons indicated here and elaborated in Chapter 2, an important purpose of alliances is learning. Even if it is not intended, learning will occur which will affect what partners need and can offer each other, the perspective, the balance of dependence and thereby the development of the alliance (Makhija and Ganesh 1997). Furthermore, the degree to which knowledge is tacit and the cognitive distance needed for learning have implications for the form of the alliance and its governance. Tacitness of knowledge depends on how novel it is and on the size of firms. These implications for alliances will be discussed in later chapters.

TRANSACTION COST THEORY

Alliances entail problems of coordination and mutual dependence. These have been studied, in particular, in transaction cost economics (TCE), as developed mainly by Oliver Williamson (1975, 1985). Chiles and McMakin (1996) distinguished two perspectives in TCE. The first is a long-term evolutionary perspective, where objective transaction costs determine the survival of the fittest governance forms. The second is a short-term managerial choice perspective, where managers act on subjective costs which are based on varying perceptions and evaluations of risk. The latter explains why firms in similar circumstances may make different make-or-buy trade-offs. This book takes the latter perspective.

The behavioural assumptions of TCE are that rationality is bounded and that people may be opportunistic. While people aim to be rational, their capacity to do so is limited, due to two types of uncertainty: behavioural uncertainty concerning the intentions and competencies of transaction partners and environmental uncertainty concerning conditions that may affect the execution of agreements and the outcomes of cooperation. As a result, closed contracts that foresee and regulate all possible eventualities are impossible. Not everybody is equally opportunistic, but the possibility of opportunism exists and prior to a relation one does not know to what extent it may arise. Even the perpetrator of opportunism himself may have had neither the intention nor the expectation to be opportunistic. Opportunism is defined as 'interest-seeking with guile'. This includes actions against the interest of a partner and against the letter or intent of an agreement, when the occasion presents itself, where necessary with the aid of lies or concealment of the truth. The possibility for this follows from the unpredictability of conditions and asymmetric information.

Williamson (1985: 1) defined a transaction as 'transfer across a technologically separable interface'. This includes transfers within an organization. A transaction is an event which takes place during a process of exchange, in which the transaction has a past and a future. Here, it is preferred to define the transaction as the moment at which agreement is established and ownership rights are transferred. Such rights include either claims to profit or decision rights, or both. When it is restricted to decision rights it can still apply within organizations.

In the process of exchange one can distinguish three stages: Contact, Contract and Control. Before the arrangement of a contract or other agreement arises one must find a transaction partner. This entails search costs on the part of the user and marketing costs on the part of the supplier. Search costs are associated with becoming aware of a need and the possibilities for fulfilling it, searching for fitting solutions and alternatives and their evaluation. Marketing costs form the mirror image of this: the research of latent or manifest needs among potential customers, possibilities to satisfy them, development of specifications, tests and search for entry to customers. In the Contract stage there are costs of preparing and concluding a contract or other type of agreement, as much as possible in anticipation of possible problems that might occur after transaction, in the control stage. In the Control stage there are costs of monitoring the execution of the agreement, 'haggling' about it, problem solving, renegotiation and adjustment of the agreement, enforcement and application of sanctions, litigation and possible loss of 'specific investments' and 'hostages' if the relation breaks.

Costs of contract and control arise especially when parties become dependent upon each other due to costs of switching to a different partner. In particular, these obtain when the transaction entails 'specific investments' that are worth less or nothing outside the alliance (Williamson 1975), so that they would need to made anew with a different partner.

A classic example of a specific investment is the die in which a part of a car (door, hood) is stamped into shape. It has the shape of the part and is therefore as 'specific' as anything can get. It is also expensive because it is large and made of hard, durable material to survive the force of stamping and maintain a constant shape. The investment in the die is not recouped until a large number of items are stamped, which requires a minimal number or duration of production. If production is stopped, the die has no more than scrap value.

Transaction specific investments can occur at both user and supplier. There are three kinds of transaction specific investments: 'site specificity', 'physical asset specificity', 'human asset specificity'. Williamson further recognized the category of 'dedicated assets': expansion of capacity only to serve a given partner.

Some examples of site specificity are: infrastructural facilities (roads, pipes and ducts, homes, shops) for labourers of a remote mining facility; supply of heat from a factory's cooling water to adjacent homes (due to rapid loss of heat in transport); a warehouse or production facility 'on the doorstep' of a customer, to provide 'just in time' supply. Examples of human asset specificity are: hiring or training dedicated to specific demands of the partner. That can yield a problem not only for the firm, but also for the employee. When he has to invest in firm-specific knowledge he gets more tied to the firm and the employer can take advantage of this.

Transaction costs due to specific investments yield a reason for integrating activities within a single firm, which offers better control of opportunism and uncertainty (Williamson 1975), because of administrative fiat in obtaining information to judge actions and in imposing solutions, which goes far beyond what one could achieve in a court of law on the basis of a contract with an outside, independent partner. TCE predicts that there should and will be more integration to the extent that there are more specific investments and uncertainty is greater.

An example is the following. For a transport firm, electronic data interchange (EDI) is of great importance to conduct 'tracking and tracing' of the flow of goods. If the form of the messages is specific to the firm and requires dedicated software that is subject to frequent modification, then one would expect the firm to maintain its own development and maintenance of the software.

Integration can be achieved through sales of assets, a merger or acquisition, or an equity joint venture (In the following, 'joint venture' refers to 'equity joint venture'.) But a non-integrative, contractual alliance between different firms has advantages over integration: more 'high-powered incentives' in separate firms that are responsible for their own survival, economies of scale in production by specialized firms (Williamson 1975) and greater flexibility in the configuration of complementary competencies or assets. However, such alliances raise complicated issues of 'governance', in 'hybrid' forms of organization 'between market and hierarchy' (Williamson 1991), to deal with the fiduciary risks of dependence and corresponding problems of coordination and problems of spillover (Kogut and Singh 1988).

An important issue is the extent to which dependence due to specific investments is symmetric between partners. When a supplier engages in specific investments, this not only makes him dependent but also his buyer. When a break in supply occurs the buyer will not have an immediate substitute of equal quality and cost. It will take an alternative supplier time to set up specific investments and meanwhile the buyer will either face a discontinuity of supply or will temporarily have to accept a product which does not fit his requirements, i.e. has lower quality. Also, apart from physical assets, a buyer will need to make adjustments in procedures, organization and knowledge to adapt to the specialized product, assets or competencies of the supplier which also constitute specific investments. At least he will have to invest in specific knowledge of the supplier's procedures, people involved, etc. However, there is no guarantee that dependence due to specific investments is symmetric. Generally, the weight of specific investments, in a variety of resources, including both physical and human resource assets, tends to be higher on the supplier's side. A further more formal analysis of specificity is supplied in Appendix 1.1.

There are several means to reduce the risk of one-sided dependence due to specific investments. One is to restrict chances for opportunism by contract, e.g. by forcing the partner to continue transactions until the cost of investment has been recouped. Another is to have the partner participate in the ownership of the investment, but to do this the partner may in turn demand guarantees against the misuse of such safeguards, e.g. that the investment is indeed specific and not used for transactions with others. There may also be an exchange of 'hostages', defined as things that are of value only to the giver and not the keeper, so that the latter is not tempted to keep the hostage even if the agreement is honoured. Another is to reduce the partner's incentives or inclination to utilize opportunities for opportunism. These can impinge on the partner's self-interest or on his sense of loyalty. This may include reputation effects: if the partner gets known as unreliable, it will jeopardize future transactions. Chapter 4 will analyse different forms of 'governance' in much more detail.

Generally, the cost and delay of setting up and maintaining elaborate schemes of governance between two partners ('bilateral governance') are substantial. When the transaction involved is small or infrequent, the benefit is not worth the cost. One will prefer to keep contracts simple and engage a trusted third party to act as an arbitrator ('trilateral governance'). The classic example is an architect who arbitrates in transactions between a builder and a supplier of building materials.

CRITICISM AND EXTENSIONS

An extension of TCE is to consider effects of scale in transaction costs. If transaction costs differ between large and small firms, this is important for inter-firm relations; it needs to be taken into account when large and small firms form alliances. There are effects of scale on both sides of a transaction relation: a small firm as supplier and as a customer (Nooteboom 1993b). Search costs are higher for a small firm due to a lack of staff support in marketing, legal matters, personnel, finance and accounting. This also yields restrictions in the stages of contract and control, because it makes the set-up costs of governance expensive relative to the size of the transaction. Therefore, in relations with small firms, use will more often be made of an outside arbitrator to settle conflicts, instead of detailed contracts and formal procedural agreements ('trilateral governance'). In a small firm as object of investigation or control, costs are higher due to a greater degree of tacitness of knowledge. There are fewer formal, documented sources of information, which makes small firms more inscrutable. One needs to extract the required information from the minds of people, or deduce it from their actions, which can be difficult due to 'causal ambiguity'. That is also why small firms are often unattractive customers for consultants.

This is further enhanced by the fact that small firms are more diverse than large ones, for two reasons (Nooteboom 1994). First, as a motivational or 'final' cause, they have more diverse goals of entrepreneurship: not necessarily maximum profit or growth, but also independence, going their own way, maintenance of a traditional life or way of doing things, staying small and informal or wanting to try out things which are rejected in large firms. Second, as a conditional cause which makes this possible, small firms exist more on private capital and are therefore less subject to the rigours and criteria of success imposed by capital markets ('corporate governance'). Connected with this, they are not subjected to an outside supervisory board, which leaves more room for idiosyncratic goals and ways of doing things.

The inscrutability and diversity of small firms yield problems in the stages of contract and control. There is less formal documentation as a basis for contracts or other agreements and for monitoring compliance with them. Note that here there is a double effect. First, there is an effect of scale in setting up a contract and a monitoring system. Second there is less documented information to use for it.

Given a certain size per transaction, a smaller firm has fewer transaction partners and therefore less spread of relational risk. One can try to improve this by taking a larger number of partners, with a smaller transaction per partner, but that is often not attractive due to the effects of scale in transactions because of minimum set-up costs of contact, contract and control. A small firm may also burden the partner with a greater risk of discontinuity due to default. A smaller spread of commercial risk across multiple products and markets raises the risk of default for smaller firms. Small firms may also raise the suspicion that they are opportunistically engaging in 'hit and run': going for a fast profit with an unreliable or bad quality product, or a product without future support and leaving the market when the damage becomes evident. In other words; small firms may lack the discipline of reputation. To eliminate such suspicion, the small firm may need to demonstrate that it is committed to the longer term and may need to point to the existence of exacting partners who can be expected to be critical and competent in judging the reliability of the small firm.

A relatively minor point of criticism of TCE is that it suggests that specific products require specific investments; when one tailors a product to special needs one needs to make investments that can cater only to those specialized needs. But the more formal analysis of specificity in Appendix 2.1 shows, as is also fairly obvious without such analysis, that to the extent that technology is flexible an investment can, by definition, be used to produce a range of differentiated products. For example, a programmable workbench for machining metal can yield parts of a variety of shapes and functions without the operator needing to adapt his skill. Software for designing and testing virtual prototypes of machines, cars or airplanes by means of computer simulation yields much greater flexibility for a range of different designs than old-fashioned physical prototypes subjected to 'real' testing (such as testing the aerodynamic properties of a car in a wind tunnel).

A more fundamental point of criticism of TCE is that it does not incorporate the resource-based perspective. Like traditional economics it adheres to a naive theory of knowledge and competence, with the assumption that technology is accessible more or less 'off the shelf' to anyone who pays the price. From the perspective of the theory of knowledge employed in this book, a firm may need to contract some good or service from outside simply because it is not capable of providing it, or may need to produce it because the resources needed do not exist elsewhere. Furthermore, they need outside partners to obtain 'external economy of cognitive scope'. This makes a large difference: greater uncertainty, in the sense of a more complex and variable environment, increases the need for such outside sources, contrary to the prediction of TCE that greater uncertainty will yield more integration into the firm.

Williamson recognized that when activities complement each other and cannot well be separated (non-separable 'economy of scope') this also provides an argument for integration within a single firm. But the importance of teamwork is neglected, particularly in complex technical systems which require fine-tuning of complementary competencies, especially when these involve much tacit knowledge. Then it is not always possible and efficient to regroup teams for every new project. The largest unit that Williamson could envisage on grounds of inseparable scope was a symphony orchestra. But think of the assembly of aeroplanes and networks of service in consulting and finance, where increasingly one needs to provide the service at remote locations, as customer firms progressively spread their activities across the world. Apart from efficiency of production there is also scope in a strategic sense.

Philips company is a user of chips (semiconductors) as components in many kinds of consumer electronics. A compact disc player, for example, requires a combination of mechanics, laser technology, electrotechnology, control technology and informatics. Should Philips make its own chips or contract them from specialist producers? The production of chips constitutes high tech surface technology, to affect at a microscopic level the conducting properties of a silicon disc by means of sophisticated physical and chemical processes. This does not seem to fit with Philips's core competencies so it seems reasonable to have it contracted out. But there are three complications: two strategic ones and one as a result of 'economy of scope'. The first strategic issue is that the world-class producers of chips are the same Japanese companies that compete with Philips in the market for consumer electronics. Should one become dependent for supply on one's main competitors? The second complication is that the development of technology and markets is very rapid and new products often arise from novel combinations of existing technologies. Frequently one needs to react fast to novel opportunities: the 'window of opportunity' is narrow and closes quickly. For this reason one may need to maintain competence in an area in which one would surrender within a static situation. The complication of scope is connected with this: during the merging of technologies in consumer electronics the quality of product and process may require involvement in those component technologies which perhaps can only be maintained by remaining active in their development and use.

One of the two main criticisms of TCE is that it offers at best 'comparative statics' in the analysis of different governance structures in different situations. It is not dynamic in the sense of including issues of innovation, as Williamson (1985: 143) admitted: 'the study of economic organisation in a regime of rapid innovation poses much more difficult issues than those addressed here'. Since currently firms labour under such a 'regime of rapid innovation', it is of critical importance to gain more insight. This was also recognized by Williamson (1985: 144): 'new hybrid forms of organisation may appear in response to such a condition (regime of rapid innovation) ... Much more study of the relations between organisation and innovation is needed.' Hence, the attention of this book is focused on innovation and learning and the development of the theory of transactions needed to incorporate them.

The second main criticism concerns the lack of a role for trust in TCE. Traditionally, approaches from economics have focused on the role of self-interest and opportunism. The threat of opportunism has to be taken into account and instruments to constrain opportunism are based on coercion by means of contracts and monitoring compliance (Williamson: 'legal ordering'); on incentives such as participation in the ownership of specific investments (yielding a balance of dependence); restraint of opportunism to safeguard future profits from cooperation (Axelrod 1984; Heide and Miner 1992); a reputation mechanism, or posting of hostages (Williamson: 'private ordering'). While in his earlier work Williamson (1975) recognized the relevance of 'atmosphere', he did not further develop this notion (Williamson 1985). He posited that trust makes sense only if it goes beyond calculative self-interest (1993) and since he sticks to the economic perspective of calculativeness, there is no room in his view for any role of trust.

But this raises doubts not just about the plausibility or acceptability of TCE, but of its consistency. Williamson granted that not everybody is opportunistic; that different people are opportunistic to different degrees. The crux of his argument was that prior to a relation one cannot judge the degree of opportunism and hence one should take its possibility into account.

But if there is a reputation mechanism, and Williamson would certainly not deny that such mechanisms are important, then one may have an idea of someone's opportunism prior to a relation. This is the point of a reputation mechanism. Furthermore, as a relation develops one will obtain more information on the partner's inclination towards opportunism, so that in time governance may be adjusted to take this into account. And what is trust other than an assessment of a limited risk of opportunism? The progression of a transaction relation in time is also of the essence in TCE, otherwise the problem of specific investments would not obtain. Specific investments are problematic precisely because one cannot recoup them in a single transaction. This is how such investments create the dependence that causes the risk of 'hold-up'. Therefore if time is of the essence, one should also consider its implications for the possibility of learning more about the partner's degree of opportunism and the possibility that inclinations towards opportunism change as the relationship develops. The view in this book is that trust is indispensable and this merits a further discussion.

THE ROLE AND MEANING OF TRUST

While in TCE there is a one-sided emphasis on opportunism, in other research traditions, notably the work of the IMP (Industrial Marketing and Purchasing Group), trust is a central variable (Håkansson 1982, 1987, 1989; Johanson and Mattson 1987). But in that perspective, trust appears to be pervasive to the point of ignoring the role of self-interest and the temptations of opportunism. In various other studies trust has been found to be the glue that keeps business partners together (Barber 1983; Palay 1984; Killing 1988; Lorenz 1988; Berger *et al.* 1995; Noorderhaven 1995, 1996; Nooteboom 1996; Nooteboom *et al.* 1997).

The perspective taken in this book is that trust as well as its limits due to opportunism play a role and that trust is a relevant dimension of governance in addition to coercion and incentives (see Buckley and Casson 1988).

Trust is not only a condition that can limit transaction costs, but may also form part of the utility of a relationship. According to social exchange theory (Blau 1964), in addition to an economic dimension (extrinsic utility), exchange and cooperation often have a social dimension (intrinsic utility). Economists tend to think of value in exchange as something that exists independently from the transaction. As formulated by Murakami and Rohlen (1992: 70): 'The value of the relationship itself is typically ignored and the impersonality of the transaction is assumed.' In intrinsic utility, the exchange process itself matters, as does the economic surplus and its sharing that the exchange yields. This was also recognized by Buckley and Casson (1988). People may prefer to transact on the basis of trust and its sources: ethics, kinship, friendship or empathy. Social exchange relies more on unspecified, implicit obligations which depend on shared systems of meaning, belief and ethics. The idea that exchange includes non-contractual elements goes back (at least) to Durkheim. But this book attempts to evade both the over-socialized view of sociology, according to which conduct is directed by social programming, and the under-socialized view of economists, according to which people act autonomously (see Etzioni 1988).

The economic relevance of trust is that it economizes on the specification and monitoring of contracts as well as material incentives for cooperation and reduces uncertainty (Arrow 1974; Jarillo 1988; Bradach and Eccles 1989; Hill 1990; Powell 1990; Bromiley and Cummings 1992; Berger *et al.* 1995; Casson 1995; Gulati 1995; Chiles and McMackin 1996; Nooteboom 1996; Nooteboom *et al.* 1997). This not only makes transactions cheaper and, on the basis of social exchange theory, more agreeable, but also yields greater flexibility. With detailed formal contracting, it is more difficult (slow and costly) to modify terms when conditions change. It yields a straight-jacket for action which can be very constraining especially when the goal of the relation is innovation: the development or implementation of novelty. Then virtually by definition one cannot foresee what duties are to be regulated and what returns are to be shared. Furthermore, detailed formal contracting can start a relationship on a footing of mistrust which inhibits the development of trust and may yield a vicious circle of regulation and mutual constraint.

Apart from its own worth, trust pays. It does so by lowering costs of search (Casson 1995) and monitoring, because trusting people are less secretive and more readily supply information (Zand 1972). Trust reduces costs of contracting and control because it lowers fears of opportunism (Bradach and Eccles 1989) and accepts more influence from the partner (Zand 1972). In the case of trust, people will deliberate and renegotiate on the basis of give and take ('voice') rather than walk out ('exit') when conflict arises (Hirschman 1970, 1984; Helper 1990; Nooteboom 1997b).

But trust also carries the risk of betrayal. Trust is a complex, slippery concept and we need to be more precise about it. It can be interpreted broadly and more narrowly. As a broad concept, trust can be defined as follows.

- To trust is to accept or neglect the possibility that things will go wrong.

This definition is consistent with many given in the literature. It ties trust closely to the notion of risk in the sense of the possibility that things go wrong (not the economist's definition of risk as the variance of a probability distribution of returns), as is customary in the literature (Luhmann 1988; Chiles and McMackin 1996; Nooteboom 1996). Note that it leaves open the question of for whom things go wrong: the bearer of trust or someone for whom he has concern. I can trust that things do not go wrong for you. The definition also leaves open a wide range for the object of trust, that to which trust is extended: goods, people (including oneself), social systems (such as firms, economies, legal systems, governments), nature or God. Thus we can speak of consumer confidence in the economy, for example. When extended to people it is usual to call this *behavioural trust*. Thus it also leaves open the cause of things going wrong, by accident or by design.

By including both 'acceptance' and 'neglect' of the possibility of things going wrong, the definition also includes both *cognitive and affect-based trust* (McAllister 1995), as follows. To 'accept' trust is to conduct an explicit, rational evaluation of the probability of things going wrong and the ensuing implications. 'Neglect' of the possibility of things going wrong may be based on habit or routine. Certain actions in certain contexts never went wrong, and we lose awareness of that possibility as long as observed conditions and actions remain within a certain zone of tolerance (Parkhe 1993; Gulati 1995; Nooteboom *et al.* 1997). Trustworthiness is often taken for granted until violated. Such non-rational routine behaviour is rational when the capacity for evaluation is limited, as Herbert Simon explained long ago. Between calculation and habit, Uzzi (1997) proposed the use of the notion of a 'heuristic': quick and parsimonious rules for choosing action on the basis of observation. Such rules arise from trial and error, survive on the basis of their success and are thereby close to the notion of 'routine'. Neglect may also be based on naivety, or on unwillingness to face risks due to fear. It may be based on cognitive dissonance related to friendship or kinship: one does not want to contemplate the possibility of opportunism on the part of friends or family. Particularly in the latter case, trust is to a greater or lesser extent based on affect. But also ethics based trust can be related to affect: emotions connected with the notion of justice or decency. Emotional closure to reason, while not rational in its operation, is rational in its consequences to the extent that it yields credible commitments that lift people from prisoners' dilemmas (see Frank 1988).

The definition may be compared to the famous definition from Deutsch (1962, quoted in Zand 1972):

- Trusting behaviour consists of actions that (1) increase one's vulnerability (2) to another whose behaviour is not under one's control (3) in a situation where the penalty one suffers if the other abuses that vulnerability is greater than the benefit one gains if the other does not abuse that vulnerability.

This definition limits damage to the bearer of trust, limits the object of trust to people one deals with and assumes that possible damage exceeds possible gains. For the purpose of studying transaction relations, this is a very useful definition.

A distinction has been made between trust and *confidence* (Luhmann 1988). This distinction does not exist in all languages, e.g. not in Dutch. Trust is associated with choice and confidence with the inevitable. Trust refers to relations we choose to engage in and when things goes wrong we can blame our judgement. Confidence refers to the continuity of the natural and moral order: nature, God, the government, the legal system. If things go wrong we cannot blame our judgement. The distinction seems related to North's distinction between institutional environment ('the system') and institutional arrangements for specific circumstances (North and Thomas 1973). To the extent that one is inevitable to oneself, one can speak only of self-confidence. But if there is no unitary identity of the self and there are several selves that can oppose each other, as in problems of 'weakness of the will', one may speak of trusting or mistrusting oneself. Thus it makes a difference to say that one has no confidence in oneself or to say that one does not trust oneself. Here, confidence is a special case of the more general notion of trust. Note that confidence in social systems and behavioural trust in people can connect: behavioural trust may be based on the expectation that the trusted person is susceptible to norms and values that are part of the 'institutional environment' and this is at the same time confidence in the robustness and 'tightness' of the social system.

Trust has been defined as a *subjective probability* that something will not go wrong (Dasgupta 1988; Gambetta 1988a; Mayer *et al.* 1995). This is an appealing idea and ties in well with the notion that trust is intimately related to risk (in the sense indicated above). But it seems to imply that trust is always calculative, if subjective probabilities are seen to be conscious and obeying the customary axioms and calculation rules of ordinary probabilities. Trust can also be based on routine, lack of awareness, naivety or emotional or ethical commitment. In other words, the basis for trust can be implicit or tacit. And it is doubtful that tacit subjective probabilities make sense.

Summing up: the general notion of trust, according to the first definition, has many ramifications and forms. We have so far seen the following: behavioural trust (the object is individual people); confidence (the object is an encompassing, inevitable social or natural system); explicit/rational trust (in terms of subjective probabilities); tacit affect- or routine-based trust. But there are more ramifications.

What is the object of trust: to what can it be extended? The difference was indicated between trust in people (behavioural trust) and trust in social or natural systems (confidence). How about trust on an intermediate level: trust in organizations? How can a firm be the object of trust and how would that relate to behavioural (individual) trust? How is it produced? Organizations do have characteristics and these appear in organizational culture, reputation, membership of industry associations, networks of suppliers, customers, (executive or supervisory) directors, research institutes and the like. The relation between the organizational and the individual level arises in the assignment of people to roles and the conditions and directions given for playing these roles, in the form of organizational structure, procedures and culture. Particularly important for the perception of trust are the public conduct of the firm's leadership and roles that connect with partners: 'boundary spanners and gatekeepers' such as purchasers, marketers, negotiators, staff exchanged or combined in joint teams. This would suggest that organizational trust is a constellation of behavioural trust, with organizational structure and culture acting as institutions that limit and guide the behaviour of staff. Thus it goes beyond any simple 'aggregate' of behavioural trust. Where trust is based on self-interest, one can meaningfully speak of an organization's objective 'self'-interest, apart from attitudes of staff, in terms of survival conditions in the market. These include the intensity and type of competition, orientation of the capital market and efficiency of reputation mechanisms. Intense price competition and an orientation of the capital market towards short-term profits favours short-term opportunism rather than long-term cooperation. Quality competition favours cooperation and a longer term perspective. Summing up: on the organizational level one can speak of 'system' trust, going beyond behavioural trust, in terms of organizational structure, culture and survival conditions.

A crucially important distinction in behavioural and organizational trust is between *competence trust* and *intentional or goodwill trust* (Barber 1983; Nooteboom 1996). If I say that I do not trust someone with my car, I may mean that I doubt her driving abilities (competence), or I may mean that I expect her to be careless or to steal my car (intentions). If someone does not honour her commitment, it may be from incompetence, *force majeure* or from opportunism, and what action is appropriate depends on that. If someone cannot do something, you may help. But if someone does not want to do something that would be a waste of time and one should improve motivation or exert control. The complication is, of course, that if someone defects by opportunism she will claim *force majeure*. One may often be unable to establish which is the case: *force majeure*, incompetence, neglect, opportunism. Thus, limits in competence and intention demand different action, but cannot always be distinguished.

Note that behavioural trust is more encompassing than intentional trust. Behavioural trust can be based on intentional trust, but also on other factors (such as a failure to recognize unilateral dependence). The existence of intentional trust cannot be inferred from the presence of behavioural trust alone (Craswell 1993; Kee and Knox 1970; Noorderhaven 1996).

One should not forget that trust involves surrender to risk and can have disastrous consequences. As argued by Zucker (1986), trust does not always enhance efficiency. Its production can be very costly and when it is embedded in institutions it can limit flexibility and obstruct innovation. Once it becomes a 'rule of the game' it may have to be followed, even when detrimental to efficiency. This raises the question of whether perhaps a trust-based economy meets obstacles in radical innovation (Nooteboom 1997b). On the other hand, Hill (1990) argued that, since trust economizes on transaction costs, trust-based societies have a competitive advantage and will prevail in the evolution of global competition. This presumes that such a society can prevent the entry of opportunists which may break down the domestic ethic of trust, but if one does not open one's borders in this way one may be ostracized from world trade (Nooteboom 1997a).

Table 1.1 Sources of cooperation

	Macro	*Micro*
Egotistic	Coercion or fear of sanctions from some authority (God, law)	Material advantage or 'interest'
Non-egotistic	Ethics: values, norms of proper conduct	Bonds of friendship, kinship or empathy

Source: Williams (1988).

What are the sources of trust? Williams (1988) proposed a scheme for the determinants of cooperation, which is reproduced in Table 1.1. These are also sources of trust. The macro sources, which apply beyond any specific exchange relation, relate to North's notion of 'institutional environment': ethics, God, the law. The micro sources relate to 'institutional arrangements': sources that one might use in specific relations.

Williams (1988) argued that none of these sources alone suffices and that, in cooperation, some mix will always be operative, while no universally best mix, regardless of specific conditions, can be specified. Often, trust based on friendship or kinship will not suffice as a basis for cooperation. Conversely, material self-interest and coercion are seldom sufficient as a basis for cooperation. One needs trust on the basis of non-egotistical sources to the extent that one cannot fully control the partner's conduct by threat and reward (see Deutsch 1962, quoted in Zand 1972).

If we consider the conscious, explicit and rational (rather than the tacit, habitual) side of intentional trust and identify this with a subjective probability that the partner will not behave opportunistically, without further qualification, then anything that contributes to such subjective probability would belong to trust; anything that restrains the partner in his opportunistic conduct. This would include the direct control that one may exercise over conduct by contract, monitoring or threat (coercion). It would also include motives of self-interest that restrain the partner, such as the preservation of reputation (Weigelt and Camerer 1988), expectation of future rewards from cooperative conduct in the present (Telser 1980), or the desire to protect 'hostages' (Williamson 1985).

This can create tricky misunderstandings. If someone says that she can be trusted, then assuming that she is sincere and not engaging in strategic signalling, she can mean that she will cooperate as long as it is in her interest, or she can mean that even if things go against her interest she will try to remain loyal and do her utmost to help solve problems. She may not be sincere and profess her trustworthiness only to keep you from securing safeguards against the opportunism that she intends (such as a 'godfather' professing his trustworthiness to his rivals).

Thus, it is useful to distinguish between a wide and a narrow concept of trust. The wide concept includes all sources of trust. The narrow concept would go beyond self-interest. We trust someone in the narrow sense if we believe that he is likely to cooperate, even if he is not coerced to do so and has no direct material interest. Following Nooteboom (1996: 993) this is defined as follows.

- To have trust in the narrow sense, or 'real' intentional trust, is to accept or neglect the subjective probability that a partner will not utilize opportunities for opportunism even if it is in his interest to do so.

An argument for using this narrow or 'strong' notion of trust is that it corresponds more closely to commonsense intuitions of trust. Is it really a matter of trust when you expect someone to conform to agreements out of self-interest or coercion? It is proposed here that you 'really' trust someone when you are willing to forego guarantees on the basis of coercion or self-interest. Only then does trust economize on transaction costs.

THE PRODUCTION, ASSESSMENT AND LIMITS OF TRUST

If trust is associated with the neglect or acceptance of the possibility that a partner will not cooperate, then optimism, positive experience or naivety increase trust. Trust therefore varies among agents, even under similar circumstances. A zero probability means blind distrust. The problem is that because it prevents us from cooperation, we miss the opportunity to build trust on the basis of successful cooperation and zero trust remains zero (see Gambetta, 1988b). On the other hand, if on the basis of a non-zero subjective probability of cooperation by the partner one enters cooperation, the probability will be adjusted on the basis of experience. If we put subjective probability in a Bayesian process of adaptation, it increases with positive experience. However, negative experience is likely to have a greater impact: when trust is betrayed, it may take a long time to build up again. If trust is blind, in the form of a 100 per cent subjective probability, it is likely to cause disappointment sooner or later because few partners will be able to resist every 'golden opportunity' for defection, when the reward for betrayal is too high to be resisted. But positive experiences with a relationship plus an expansion of its scope will enhance a favourable perception of probability of cooperation.

Zucker (1986) made a distinction between different modes of trust 'production', which is complementary to the different sources in Table 1.1. These are given in Table 1.2.

The following may not be clear. If institutions include norms and values of conduct, then they are first of all part of macro sources of cooperation: the institutional environment. But such norms and values might also be built up in specific relations, on the micro level, in which case they become part of institutional arrangements. One can debate whether they are then part

Table 1.2 Modes of trust production

Basis	Examples	Connection with Table 1.1
Characteristics	membership of family, community, culture, religion	All sources
Institutions	Certification, professional standards, benchmarking, intermediaries	Macro
Process	Loyalty, commitment, friendship, habituation	Micro

Source: Adapted from Zucker (1986).

of non-egotistic sources of ethical conviction or of egotistic ones of social control and enforcement. Sydow (1996) also considered this issue and arrived at an interaction between trust in wider social systems and trust in specific relations: process-based trust builds on prevailing customs and norms.

Zucker (1986) argued that in the USA characteristics related to family and (local, ethnic or religious) community and process-based trust in ongoing relations have been increasingly eroded. Communitarianism was replaced by individualism and the vacuum had to be filled by means of institutional based trust. A similar argument was developed by Fukuyama (1995).

What, more precisely, is the relation between trust and opportunism, between self-interest and loyalty? There is no trust in mainstream economics. Williamson came close to accepting the notion of trust with the notion of 'atmosphere' in his earlier work (1975), but this did not reappear in later work. Williamson (1985, 1991) did recognize the effect on transaction costs of 'the larger context in which transactions are embedded', which seems similar to the notion of 'institutional environment'. But this is connected with the assumption that it applies equally to all actors in a given context or national culture. It does not serve to distinguish between alternatives of governance structure ('institutional arrangements') within that context. This is not adequate for two reasons (see Nooteboom *et al.* 1997). First, the susceptibility to values and norms (which we take to be part of the institutional environment) is likely to differ between individuals within a national culture and between organizations, as part of organizational culture, so that their impact may vary within national boundaries (see Noorderhaven 1995). Second, institutions in the sense of norms, values and habits of conduct may not be exogenous to a transaction relationship and may partly develop within it, as part of process-based trust (Ford 1980).

There is an inconsistency in Williamson's argument concerning opportunism. The argument is explicitly not that everybody is opportunistic all the time, but that people are more or less opportunistic more or less of the time. Since prior to transaction one does not know how much and how often, one should take into account the possibility of opportunistic conduct.

But the argument implies variation in opportunism between people, which is subsequently ignored.

There is also an anomaly of time. On the one hand, time is of the essence for the problem of specific investments: the problem is that in order to recoup an investment made now, one needs repeated transactions in the future. On the other hand, the assumption of opportunism is based on the argument that prior to transaction one does not know the extent of the partner's opportunism. One problem with this is that it negates the possibility of a reputation mechanism, which Williamson accepts elsewhere. The second problem is that if time is relevant, with ongoing transactions to recoup specific investments, it is also relevant for learning about the partner's inclination towards opportunism. Furthermore, in time inclinations towards opportunism may change.

In Williamson (1993) the issue of trust in institutional arrangements is squarely confronted. Williamson proposes that if trust does not go beyond calculative self-interest, it adds nothing to conventional economic analysis and should be discarded as superfluous and confusing. This is reasonable. But if trust does go beyond calculative self-interest, Williamson argues, then it is blind trust, which is ill-advised and will tend not to survive. It should be reserved only for family or other loved ones. There are two problems with this.

First, action can be non-calculative without being blind. One can and one does act partly on the basis of routines, and in view of limited cognitive capacity this is a necessity. In this book this is called 'habituation'. Such action is non-calculative, because it is non-reflective. But it is not blind, in the sense that it has a rational basis: it is based on experience that it works, before it becomes a routine. In other words it is inevitable that we take certain aspects of the behaviour of others for granted. One reason was given before: to question everything is to get bogged down in an infinite regress of suspicion and questioning. The second reason is that reliance on routine is rationally warranted in view of persistent success and lack of disaster in the past.

Second, to go beyond calculative self-interest logically one can go beyond calculativeness, which is the option that Williamson considers; or one can go beyond self-interest which is an option that Williamson ignores. To go beyond self-interest is to take into account the interests of others, even if this may to some extent damage one's own interests. I propose that people are willing to do this to some extent, although this varies between people. This behaviour is based on the non-egotistic sources of cooperation recognized by Williams (Table 1.1): the institutional environment of norms and values and institutional arrangements based on bonds of friendship, kinship or habituation.

But Williamson is no doubt right in saying that trust should not be blind, because there are limits to trustworthiness. To say that to a greater or lesser extent people will remain loyal to a relationship, even if there are opportunities for opportunism and it is advantageous to utilize those opportunities, does not imply that this resistance to temptation is boundless. Perhaps the cynic is right who says that everyone has his price. After all there are degrees of temptation, from small advantage to sheer survival. Firms in more competitive markets will succumb to temptation sooner than those in markets with lesser pressure of competition.

The deeper the trust and trustworthiness, the greater the resistance to temptation, but even the strongest may succumb to a 'golden opportunity'. When relying on trust, the art is to find out how far one can go; to assess when the partner's resilience to temptation is tested too much. How far will partners go in trying to solve problems that affect their interests before they defect? Some will go further than others and this will depend on the wider culture (institutional environment), bonds of kinship, habits and routines or bonds of friendship built up in a relationship (institutional arrangements, characteristics and process-based trust).

So, the fact that trust is limited does not eliminate that it allows for limited contracts and monitoring, thereby yielding cheap governance, flexibility in relations and a basis for further developing trust.

But in what sense, or to what extent, can trust be produced or installed? There may be a basis for trust prior to the setting up of an alliance, founded on shared norms or rules, reputation or existing bonds of kinship or friendship. Some institutions, such as systems of certification or legal systems, can be developed on the basis of some rational design, though this often takes a long time. One can select a partner on the basis of his or her characteristics, such as being a member of a family or community. But one cannot simply buy into characteristics-based trust. One can marry into a family and become a member of some communities, but entry selection can be strict and again it can take considerable time. Process trust of building loyalty on the basis of growing familiarity, habituation, friendship and shared norms and expectations can be facilitated, in the sense that one creates conditions for its growth, but it cannot be purchased and installed by the pound. To 'produce' process trust is as paradoxical as to order spontaneity: if it worked it would not be real. Process trust is as much the outcome of a relationship as the basis for it. As indicated by Hirschman (1984), trust, unlike most economic commodities, may grow rather than wear out by usage. Sydow (1996) approached this from the perspective of Giddens's structuration theory: to the extent that process trust is already available it provides the basis for a relationship. It is reproduced in the relationship, if it goes well and may be deepened to provide the basis for further extension.

In the attempt to create conditions for process trust to develop, detailed contracts can be destructive. They demonstrate mistrust, which engenders mistrust, so that mistrust becomes a self-fulfilling prophecy (Macauley 1963, Zand 1972). But how then does one begin a relationship if there is no prior basis for trust in the institutional environment, or in selection on the basis of characteristics, while self-interest does not suffice to prevent risks of opportunism, perhaps because the relationship is or may develop into a zero-sum game? In such a situation, how can one do without contracts? A relationship between strangers will tend to start tentatively, with small steps that do not demand detailed contracts and whose success generates more competence trust and more intentional trust through habituation and the emergence of relation-specific norms and values, empathy and perhaps friendship. It is not unlike courtship prior to marriage (Nooteboom 1994). This metaphor of marriage is explored further in the appendix to Chapter 4.

Intermediaries can perform important roles in the development of trust relations (Sydow 1996; Nooteboom 1998b). If X has both competence trust and intentional trust in Y and Y has intentional trust in Z, then X may rationally give intentional trust in Z a chance. X needs to feel that Y is able to judge well and has no intention of lying about his judgement.

If blind trust is unwise, trust is often a step-by-step process of building mutual trust and one can observe little more than people's actions. How does one assess the intentional trustworthiness of a partner from his actions? It shows itself best in loyalty under adversity. It is especially important to assess whether it is intrinsic or extrinsic, because in the first case loyalty is an internal goal, while in the second case it is a means to pursuing self-interest. The first does not require monitoring and the second does. The first is based on ethics and conscience, on norms and values, on emotions of friendship or kinship, or on the enjoyment of trusting relations. The latter is based on quid pro quo, lack of opportunity for opportunism, dependence or fear of reputational loss (Deutsch 1973). Connected with this, Deutsch also recognized the notion of 'focus', with three possibilities: focus on results for the other; on warrantable effort (is one seen to be doing one's reasonable best); or on doing as one is told. Is one genuinely trying to cooperate or is one intent only on legitimizing one's actions?

So, when a supportive action by X is observed, how does one judge what lies behind it? The following sequence of questions can be an aid to assessment (adapted from Deutsch 1973):

1 Was the outcome intended by X, or was it an unintended result of his action?
2 Did the action entail significant risk to X?
4 Was X aware of the risk and was it neglected out of impulsiveness?
5 Did X attach a positive value to this risk, out of masochism, sensation, (self) image?
6 Did X have a choice or was the action dictated by compulsion or conformity?
7 Was it out of confidence in the system rather than a positive evaluation of the situation?
8 Was it out of enlightened self-interest?
9 Was it out of enjoyment of trust relations?
10 Was it out of ethics, friendship or kinship, habituation?

Deutsch noted that power can have an adverse effect on trust. If one is very powerful, there is more suspicion that the people subjected to that power are trustworthy only because they have no choice.[6] In the case of absolute power, the hypothesis that this is the case can never be rejected. This is how the powerful become suspicious. The problem with this is that mistrust tends to feed upon itself even more than trust does. (Mis)trust by X tends to engender (mis)trust on the part of Y, which justifies and deepens X's (mis)trust. But while trust can be falsified because it leads to reliance on others which can be disappointed, mistrust cannot because it blocks the trusting action that might disprove it.

MULTI-LEVEL THEORY

Learning and trust are concepts that are ordinarily applied to individuals. Since the focus of this book is on relations between organizations, the question arises as to what is the relationship between the conduct of individuals and firms. As argued by Ring and van de Ven (1994), they are related by the roles that individuals are assigned within organizations. Conduct 'qua persona' is restricted and guided by organizational roles. Alignment between the two can be a problem. If cooperation is founded on trust based on personal bonding, problems may arise concerning the exigencies of organizational roles. Personal loyalty may deviate from organizational interest and may even lead to corruption or embezzlement. The development of personal ties that are too strong may need to be prevented by the turnover of personnel across roles. Conversely, personnel change may lead to a breakdown of relations based on personal trust. Such considerations should be part of governance.

Organizations provide an environment for people to learn and this individual learning is contributed to the organizational practices in which they participate. Nooteboom (1998b) modelled this interaction in terms of organizational 'scripts' as patterns of collective action. A script constitutes an organizational order into which people contribute their activities, within certain restrictions that ensure the needed coherence and consistency between actions and define organizational roles. In this process of interaction between people in an organization, there is 'knowledge conversion' between tacit and explicit knowledge (Boisot 1995; Nonaka and Takeuchi 1995). There are cycles of exploitation and exploration (Nooteboom 1998b) in which individuals can explore novelty while staying within the constraints of their organizational role to ensure ongoing exploitation. Latitude for such exploration is a source of both error and innovation. But it would be going too far to discuss this process in detail here.

Concerning trust, the relation between the organizational and individual levels is as follows. First, if trust is indeed interpreted as a subjective probability assigned to conduct, it can logically apply to a subjective probability held by an individual with respect to the conduct of an organization in terms of the decisions it takes. Of course, this subjective probability may, at least in part, be based on experiences and perceptions of individuals in their organizational roles and corresponding organizational constraints at the partner organization. Thus one can deal with trust in terms of relational risk with respect to the partner organization, as perceived by an individual who enacts the relation with the partner organization. Trust between organizations is thus connected with attachments between 'boundary spanners' between firms in the form of friendship or kinship bonds (Seabright *et al.* 1992). Such bonds are associated with the notion of 'habitualization' (Nooteboom *et al.* 1997). Trust requires familiarity and mutual understanding and, hence, depends on time and context, habit formation and the positive development of a relationship. Repeated interactions lead to the formation of habits and the institutionalization of behaviour (Berger and Luckmann 1966; Zucker 1986). Case study research has borne out that in industrial buying relations buyers display a strong tendency to persist in the use of existing suppliers (Woodside and Möller 1992). Survey research confirms the importance of habitualization (Gulati 1995; Nooteboom *et al.* 1997).

CAUSALITY

Repeated use has been made of multiple types of causality: actions of people; their motivations; resources, methods, technology and knowledge; conditions affecting their use. These are implicit in TCE and have been used in the theory of knowledge and learning and in the explanation of the variety of conduct in small businesses. The concept of multiple causality goes back to the philosopher Aristotle, with his notions of efficient cause (agent), material cause (input), final cause (goal or purpose), formal cause (modus operandi), exemplary cause (model to imitate), conditional cause (external conditions affecting the other causes); in other words: who, with what, why, how, when?[7]

'Conditional causes' reflect contingencies: opportunities and restrictions in the environment of firms such as physical infrastructure (including infrastructure for communication), market structure (including present competition and entry barriers), schooling and institutions. North (1990: 3) defined institutions as 'the humanly devised constraints that shape human interaction' and form the 'rules of the game' needed to limit transaction costs. They constrain but also guide behaviour. North distinguished between formal and informal institutions. Formal institutions include commercial, legal and technical norms and standards. Informal institutions include culturally determined and transmitted behavioural rules and practices. In alliances, conditional causes include restrictions on entering markets, owning property, hiring personnel, repatriating profits from abroad, minimum 'local content' in production abroad, etc. They also include facilitating agencies such as banks, legal firms and consultants. Conditional causes vary between countries and cultures.

'Efficient' causes constitute agency: people or organizations taking action. In alliances these include the partners or more generally the agents involved. 'Final' or motivating causes attract agents ('pull'), or force them to adopt a practice ('push'). When two sides engage in cooperation, their motives and purposes need not be the same, but they do need to be aligned to some extent to be consistent and preferably mutually reinforcing. 'Material' causes provide the raw materials and other inputs for the practice; in alliances, finance and information. 'Formal' causes enable a practice by providing technology, tools, methods, procedures and organization; in alliances, how to select appropriate forms of alliance and to design effective instruments for their management or 'governance'. If such a method or procedure exists but cannot be spelled out or grasped, perhaps because it constitutes tacit knowledge, a so-called 'exemplary' cause yields a model for us to imitate. This includes 'role models' of people or other organizations. Earlier, exemplars were shown to be needed particularly in the transfer of tacit knowledge. Summing up: in explaining and designing alliances we aim to answer questions of when (conditional cause), by whom (efficient cause), with what (material cause), why (final cause) and how (formal cause, exemplary cause).

This constellation of causes fits naturally with notions of primary processes of production in a firm, or the 'value chain'. Incoming logistics is associated with material cause; technology of production and transformation with formal cause; workers with efficient cause; supporting activities (personnel, legal, management, finance/accounting services) with conditional cause; and stakeholder interests with final cause.

In transactions or other interactions between people they may be tempted to consider each other as instruments, i.e. as material or formal causes. In alliances, as in most if not all other relations, that would be a great mistake: one should constantly be aware that the partner has its own objectives and discretion for action, which may change in time. The bargaining position forms an important conditional cause: it determines how much of one's objectives can be achieved.

When people (efficient cause) for their purpose (final cause) develop technology (formal cause) and make investments accordingly, this creates novel conditions for further action (conditional cause). This can yield path-dependency: a choice between alternatives that initially were equally accessible yields actions whose cumulative effects block a switch to alternatives.

One familiar example is the development of oil-based rather than hydrogen-based motor fuels. As the story goes (Dosi 1984), before consolidation they were equally feasible, but the closure of water wells due to a cattle disease blocked access to sources of hydrogen and this gave an advantage to oil-based fuels. Currently, a hydrogen technology might be more preferable as it is less polluting, but now the installed base of oil technology (expertise, technology and physical assets in exploration, production, manufacturing and distribution) provides a huge economic and political obstacle to switching. To evade this problem, the car industry is currently experimenting with motors that burn gasoline, but next use the resulting water and carbon monoxide to produce hydrogen, in order to burn that too. This achieves less pollution and more fuel economy while preserving the existing installed base of machinery and infrastructure of the oil economy.

During the course of their actions people (efficient cause) may in different ways influence each other's purposes and choices (final cause).

In markets for example, consumers copy each other's choices ('bandwagon effect'), or evade them ('snob effect'). In the diffusion of a new product, early adopters exert a demonstration effect upon potential later adopters ('contagion'). This yields the familiar S-shaped ('logistic') curve of diffusion. Such contagion may occur at a distance or, mostly with stronger effect, in direct contact. It matters to what extent the source of information operates under similar conditions (role equivalence or equivalence in network position; see Burt 1987). The adoption of an innovation depends on its compatibility with the abilities of the adopter (efficient cause), his objectives (final cause), the conditions (conditional cause), possible costs of switching to a different modus operandi (formal cause), availability of the proper inputs (material cause) (see Rogers 1983).

The formal causes (technology) implied by the choices of some people have effects on the choice of others (final cause). An example of this is network externality: the utility of some technology depends on the number of others who choose the same alternative.

The standard example is the telephone. It is useful to the extent that others have a telephone that is compatible, in order to call and be called. Another example is the celebrated case of video recorders. Initially there were three alternatives: Philips's Video 2000 system,

Sony's Betamax and the VHS system of a consortium of other Japanese companies (JVC, Matsushita). The latter system won due to a better fit with market demand in the supply of the software (video tapes) that was compatible only with the VHS standard built into the hardware (recorders): length of play for recording baseball games and more extensive distribution of recorded tapes for hire. This gave a head start in the market, with supply according to that technology reinforcing itself, so that the choice of an alternative entailed an accelerating risk that the supply of appropriate software would fall back and stop. This yielded dominance to VHS, even though technically it was inferior.

The multiple causality discussed here is related to the different kinds of resources and capital discussed earlier. An attempt to specify the relations between them is given in Figure 1.2. Assets and most competencies constitute economic capital and yield material and formal causality. Efficient causality (human resources) is partly economic, partly cultural and partly social. Final causality is primarily cultural: the goals and meanings which people attach to work. Exemplary causality is partly cultural and partly social, since the exemplar is often a role model supplied by network contacts. The comparison illustrates the motive for discussing multiple causality. It enhances the richness as well as the coherence of the concepts of 'resource' and 'capital'.

The purpose of this book can now be characterized as follows: improve insight into the different aspects of causality concerning alliances and to strengthen the formal causes of alliances, the know-how. The aim is to go beyond case studies as 'exemplars' (see Lorange and Roos 1992; Faulkner 1995) and to contribute to the further development of tools for the analysis, choice, design and management of alliances. Chapter 3 considers the motivating causes: the reasons for heightened interest in inter-firm alliances. As an introduction, Chapter 2 first gives a sketch of the conditional causes: the context in which firms operate.

Resources:	Assets, capabilities, positional advantages
Capital:	Economic, cultural, social
Causality:	Material, formal, efficient, final, exemplary, conditional

Figure 1.2 Resources, capital and causes.

APPENDIX 1.1 ANALYSIS OF SPECIFICITY

As proposed in Nooteboom (1993a), 'specificity' in general means something like this: 'to achieve a given purpose there is no alternative to a given means'. Specificity is a two-place predicate: x is specific (with respect) to y. This means that for x to exist there is no substitute for y; y constitutes a necessary condition for x. Or what is logically equivalent: non-y implies non-x. The following notation is introduced: x being specific to y is represented as xy. This allows for strings: xyz means that x is specific to y and y is specific to z. This binary relation of specificity is reflexive and transitive but not symmetric:

- reflexivity: xx
- transitivity: xyz implies xz
- asymmetry: xy does not imply yx

If in xy we substitute $x = a$ (asset) and $y = t$ (transaction), yielding at, we obtain *transaction specific assets*. If the transaction no longer applies (is discontinued), the asset no longer applies (does not fulfil its function). We can experiment with other substitutions for x and y. Consider, for example, that the positions of a and t are reversed: ta. This signifies an *asset specific transaction*: if the asset is not in place, the transaction cannot take place. Due to the asymmetry of specificity this does not necessarily go together with the previous case. The condition that an asset has value only in a given transaction is not the same as the condition that the asset is necessary for the transaction. An asset may be necessary for a transaction while having value in other transactions as well.

Due to the property of transitivity, there can be direct transaction specificity of assets (at), because one or both parties to the transaction have to invest directly in the transaction (costs of search or contract). It can also arise indirectly, with the product as an intervening variable: ap with a = asset and p = product, i.e. a *product specific asset* (the asset cannot be used for other products) and pb, with b = buyer, i.e. a *buyer specific product* (there is no alternative buyer for the product), which together yields ab. This indicates that the asset can be used only for producing for this buyer. In other words, the buyer is a *monopsonist*. This makes the supplier dependent, especially if also sa: the supplier has no other assets, because then by transitivity $sapb$ yields sb: without the buyer the supplier cannot exist. The supplier has countervailing power if also pa: the product is asset specific; the product cannot be produced without that asset. Particularly if also as: the asset is specific with respect to the supplier; so that by transitivity ps: the supplier is the only one who can produce the product. In other words, the supplier is a monopolist. Mutual dependence is further enhanced if also bp: the buyer is a single-product producer, because then $bpas$ yields bs.

Table A1.1 Forms of specificity

No.	x	y	Label	Case
1	Buyer	Product	Prod. spec. buyer	Single product buyer
2	Supp. asset	Product	Prod. spec. asset	Dedicated asset
3	Product	Buyer	Buyer spec. prod.	Monopsony
4	Product	Supp. asset	Asset spec. prod.	Inflexible technology
5	Supp. asset	Buyer	Buyer spec. supp. asset	Transaction spec. asset
6	Buyer asset	Supplier	Supp. spec. buyer asset	Transaction spec. asset
7	Supp. asset	Supplier	Supp. spec. supp. asset	Supplier spec. asset
8	Supplier	Product	Prod. spec. supp.	Single product supplier
9	Product	Supplier	Supp. spec. prod.	Monopoly
10	Buyer	Supplier	Supp. spec. buyer	Captive buyer
11	Supplier	Buyer	Buyer spec. supp.	Captive supplier
12	Buyer	Supp. asset	Asset spec. buyer	Single technology buyer
13	Supplier	Supp. asset	Asset spec. supp.	Single technology supplier

Table A2.1 specifies thirteen possibilities for substituting *a* (asset), *b* (buyer), *p* (product) and *s* (supplier) for *x* and *y* in *xy*, excluding the reflexive substitutions (*xx*, *yy*).

Forms 5 and 6 represent the transaction specific assets of ordinary TCE: one form for the supplier and one for the buyer. They can arise directly or indirectly by transitivity. Form 5 can arise from 2 followed by 3. This is the paradigmatic case: suppliers' assets are specific to the buyer because they are specific to the product, which is specific to the buyer. Note that dependence of a buyer on a supplier (10) can arise in several ways. It can arise from 1 followed by 9: a buyer is interested in a feature offered only by the particular product of a particular supplier. Form 10 can also follow from 6: the buyer is dependent due to supplier specific investments. Form 10 can also arise directly, in case of family ties, personal bonds or lack of information.

Case 1 can be associated with demand differentiation: different buyers want different products. It is important to note that one can have product differentiation without transaction specificity of (supplier's) assets. This is important because it binds the buyer without binding the supplier. A supplier can produce a differentiated value by building it into the product, which often requires high specificity of assets (with respect to the product); or by adding it onto the product in the form of accessories, services, logistic utilities of time, place or assortment, with reduced asset specificity; or by assembling standard components in a specific way, with highly limited asset specificity; or by creating a special appeal or image by advertising, with asset specificity virtually zero. But even for building specialized properties into a product, asset specificity can be limited when the technology is flexible: by definition then a given installation can produce a variety of product forms. One can argue that to the extent that asset specificity is less (potential) competition is higher and there will soon be close substitutes, weakening the dependence of the user. This is not necessarily true, however, due to the possibility of entry barriers. (Potential) competition arises from imitability and this has no necessary connection with asset specificity. A practice is difficult to imitate if it is specific with respect to the supplier's organization (7), not because it is embedded in an asset that is specific with respect to a given customer (6). Such firm specificity of assets, or more generally resources, can be due to patents, but also due to tacitness of knowledge or embeddedness of knowledge in organizational structure, procedures or culture.

2 The context and purpose of alliances

This chapter discusses the context in which alliances occur, such as technology, world markets and competition and the implications for their purpose. It includes the role of scale, scope, experience and learning, information and communication technology, shortening life cycles of products, and pressures towards 'radical product differentiation'. This leads to the conclusion that firms need to concentrate on core competencies, to outsource more activities and use outside partners as sources of complementary knowledge and competence. Alliances serve a variety of additional purposes: to spread fixed costs (in production, distribution, R&D), circumvent entry barriers, achieve speed of market entry, adapt products to markets, acquire sources of materials, components, labour, technology or learning, set market standards, pre-empt or attack competition.

TECHNOLOGICAL DEVELOPMENT

Speed of development has increased in different areas of technology (information, communication, new materials, surface technology, biotechnology, optics, microtechnology) and across the boundaries between them: integration of information and communication technology (ICT); integration of electronics, mechanics (mechatronics) and optics (optotronics). This is yielding ever-new opportunities for novel products and production processes: microelectronics, sensors, robots, designer chemicals and pharmaceuticals, micromachinery, rapid prototyping, computer aided design and testing, computer assisted or even integrated manufacturing. Consider the following illustration.

The production of semiconductors requires sophisticated (miniaturized, uncontaminated and perfectly accurate) technology, with physical and chemical processes for etching micro patterns on the surface of silicon slices and modifying conductive properties in those patterns. Similar technology can also be used for the deposition of thin layers on surfaces for other purposes, such as hardening materials, coating photovoltaic cells or the production of sensors.

ICT has a tendency to reduce transaction costs and thereby increase competition, facilitate inter-firm relations and shift decisions to make or buy inputs for production towards a preference to buy (Nooteboom 1992b). Earlier, a distinction was made between three stages in the process of exchange: contact, contract and control. In the stage of contact, search costs can be reduced and the speed increased by access to detailed data on available products and their quality assessments. Marketing costs are reduced and novel opportunities are offered by access to detailed data on consumer purchases (quantity, site, time, basket of products bought), provided by scanning bar codes at electronic points of payment. These can be related to promotional actions such as advertising and special offers, and those of competitors, to assess their effects. Consumer data are now extended, subject to limitations for reasons of privacy, by means of customer cards, which also record personal data on gender, age, family size and composition. These facilitate the composition of personalized buyer profiles, in order to make tailor-made sales offers.

In the stage of contract, use can be made of information services on credit ratings. There is software to support both standard and tailor-made offers or contracts. Increased efficiency, speed and quality can be gained by the use of computer aided design and its linkage to cost calculation, production planning and control. There are fast and reliable systems for bookings and payment. In the stage of control, ICT links can be used to monitor logistics ('tracking and tracing'), which facilitate 'just in time' supply, the status of orders, their processing by suppliers and quality control systems of suppliers.

These developments will in some important aspects make distribution channels and other intermediary functions redundant, especially where the product is in the nature of information (e.g. banking, insurance). Often, communication and distribution entail effects of scale: utilization of transport systems, high cost of advertising on national TV. This limits access for small producers. Where such channels can be skipped, e.g. by communication and distribution on the Internet, economies of scale may disappear and novel opportunities may be offered to small firms. On the other hand, the small firms that play a role in distribution functions may be eliminated: in wholesaling, retailing, intermediation in insurance, accountants, etc, but new intermediary functions may appear, as will be discussed in Chapter 4.[1]

ICT is above all a means of internal and external integration. It thereby contributes to linkages between firms and forms of 'organization between market and hierarchy', thus causing a further 'fuzzying' of firm boundaries. Inside firms, rigid multi-level hierarchies make way for more decentralized and fluid structures. Between firms, more or less permanent and all-encompassing forms of integration such as mergers and acquisitions make way for more temporary and partial forms of integration and cooperation.

In Chapter 5 a further analysis is given of the effects of ICT on the governance of inter-firm relations.

SCALE AND SCOPE

Economy of scale entails higher efficiency at higher volumes of a given product. Scope entails higher efficiency due to the pooling and cost sharing of different products. One form of economy of scale is division of labour: because people specialize in a specific part of production they can perform the work more efficiently. This is maximally exploited in an assembly line and is associated with large, hierarchically composed, vertically integrated firms. The system is often termed Fordism after Henry Ford, who introduced the assembly line to the car industry. This source of scale has been subject to considerable erosion because it also detracts from motivation and the value of team work, where workers are able to complement each other, to survey an integral part of the production system and to come up with improvements. This is important to the extent that work becomes more professional and innovative and products become more differentiated or made to measure. 'Business process engineering' has also shown that there can be high losses of efficiency in the transfer of goods, information or customers in process between different stations, due to mismatches, distortions of information and delays in waiting. The term 'post-Fordism' has been used to indicate this departure from Fordism, but there are some misleading simplifications connected with it (Amin 1989; Amin and Dietrich 1991). One is that the effects of scale have disappeared and we are entering a period where the small firm will prevail.

Indeed, in some areas of production, effects of scale and scope have diminished, above all in information technology. This is partly due to the miniaturization of hardware and its reduced sensitivity to location (temperature, dust, vibrations), making it cheaper and eliminating the need for specialized large rooms. It is also partly due to increasing availability of user-friendly and powerful software, eliminating the need for specialized staff to utilize IT. However, Ohmae (1989) argued that since the turn of corporate ICT to (local and wide area) networks, fixed costs have risen again. But there can be some doubt here: threshold expenditures in setting up or participating in a network appear to be small. For a small network one can employ a small network server. Terminals are not expensive and there are many firms providing services of hardware, software and installation.

Another form of scale economy is due to the mathematical fact that the content of a sphere is proportional to the cube of the radius and its surface is proportional to its square, while content yields production capacity and surface is connected with costs of material, weight and air resistance and hence costs of transportation, cleaning and heat loss. As a result, the revenue per unit of cost increases with size. This applies to process industries (oil, chemicals, some pharmaceuticals, some food), but also to trucks and aeroplanes. This cause of scale effects is undiminished.

Another form of both scale and scope effects is due to the presence of fixed 'threshold' costs: due to the fact that productive capacity is not feasible or viable below some minimum level; or due to minimum set-up costs for an installation for physical production, a research facility or some service capacity. Such threshold costs of a service facility include the point of sale at a shop, a call desk, driver of a truck, teacher before a class, specialist support staff in a firm.

Threshold costs have increased dramatically in the research and development of advanced technology and, as a result, in the development and production of many products which employ such technology: semiconductors, aeroplanes, cars, consumer electronics, biotechnology, etc. Consider the following illustration.

Formerly, products in consumer electronics could be made with low fixed costs and cheap labour, in the manual assembly of components in boxes. With the onset of miniaturization, this practice was no longer viable and had to be replaced by the use of robots for assembly, which requires considerable fixed costs. The Dutch aircraft producer Fokker was too small to carry the increasing costs of the development of new models and the maintenance of a worldwide service system. Without a takeover or alliances the firm was bound to go down.

In marketing there are also substantial 'threshold costs': in distribution channels and brand name. In distribution there are the set-up costs of laying a pipeline or track, building a warehouse, building a station or airport, having an attendant at a service point, sending a truck along a certain route. To develop a brand name one must invest heavily in advertising and other forms of promotion. The fixed cost of a national TV advertisement is more easily recouped for a product that is marketed nationwide than for a local product. The need to market a specialized product worldwide, in order to gain sufficient economy of scale to compete, creates the need for a worldwide brand name, with correspondingly higher fixed costs.

Recently, relatively novel effects of scale were reported to arise in the insurance business: novel opportunities arise in direct marketing and telemarketing, but this requires large fixed outlays for hardware, software and the building up of databases.

A special case of scope is the spread of risk across different activities.

One example is sales in different countries, with a spread of risk of exchange rate fluctuations, political conditions, weather, business cycles and their effects on demand. Another example can be found in the publishing of books: the yield of a single book is uncertain and highly variable, so that one needs some minimum portfolio.

In R&D all sources of scale effects can arise together: increasing specialization of research staff, set-up of information networks and databases, efficiency of large installations, need for capital intensive processes due to miniaturization, need to spread risks.

DIFFERENTIATION

The technological developments indicated above enable an increased variety and differentiation of products: by rapid design and testing of products, flexible production and the use of just in time supply to reduce stocks that would otherwise explode with an increase of product variety.

In consumer markets there is a paradoxical development. On the one hand, national tastes and life styles are becoming more similar, due to the ubiquitous sharing of information and recreation on TV, radio, film and the Internet. On the other hand, within nations there has been a movement towards ongoing individualization. This provides market opportunities and hence a motivating cause ('pull') for differentiating products. Due to globalization of markets, one can achieve large-scale and corresponding lower costs, in spite of such differentiation. This raises doubts concerning the proposition of Porter (1985) that there are separate strategies of low cost and differentiation between which firms have to choose. It seems that low cost and differentiation can be, and due to competitive pressure have to be, combined whenever possible.

A further development in consumer behaviour that enhances the trend towards differentiation is the increase of prosperity, which raises consumers to higher levels in Maslow's 'hierarchy of needs'. On lower levels of this hierarchy, physiological needs for food, warmth and shelter are similar between different consumers and therefore less amenable to differentiation. At higher levels of social distinction by 'life styles' and 'self-realization' by spiritual values, preferences are more idiosyncratic. Furthermore, on higher levels differentiation can be achieved more easily, because utility assumes a more abstract, immaterial form (image, atmosphere) or a superficial form (packaging, appearance) that can be differentiated by comparatively cheap means (design, packaging, advertising). Thus, more product dimensions arise (more levels in the hierarchy), and the new dimensions are more idiosyncratic and can be differentiated more cheaply.

A further motivating cause of what Zuscovitch (1994) called 'radical' product differentiation is provided by increased competition: to reduce pressures of price competition by means of product differentiation. This advantage of product differentiation can be explained as follows: by differentiating products to satisfy the specific demands of different market segments, price elasticity is reduced for each segment, which increases profit margins.

> Sometimes products are differentiated down to the individual consumer. During a trade fair in Turin in 1993, Fiat tested computer programmes with which a buyer could choose colour, upholstery and configuration of add-ons, after which the order was sent directly to the factory (*Innovisie*, January 1994).

Summing up: radical product differentiation is enabled by technological developments and increased size of (global) markets and is motivated by individualization of consumer demand and increased competition.

COOPERATION

The developments with which firms are confronted provide opportunities for innovation, but at the same time tend to intensify competition, which puts further pressure on the speed of innovation. As a result, life cycles of products and new product development times are shortening. Competition on world markets has increasingly become like a race where, in order to have a chance of winning, firms must concentrate on their core competencies (Prahalad and Hamel 1990: 81–82) that 'spawn unanticipated products' and 'empower business to adapt quickly to changing opportunities'. Core competencies are further specified as 'the collective learning in the organization, especially how to coordinate diverse production skills and integrate multiple streams of technologies'.

Concentration on core competencies implies that one needs to seek partners that supply competencies which do not belong to one's core but are needed as complementary to it (Porter and Fuller 1986). This yields one motivation for seeking alliances, while remaining careful not to surrender one's core competence to a partner. Radical product differentiation greatly increases the complexity of both input and output markets. To be 'sustainable' (Zuscovitch 1994) firms need to concentrate on core competencies. Having partners also increases flexibility in regrouping core and supplementary competencies. Furthermore, the theory of knowledge discussed in Chapter 1 indicates that one needs partners to complement one's perception, interpretation and evaluation of external developments ('external economy of cognitive scope').

In particular, rather than claiming to have full competence in all dimensions of their products and production processes, firms should make use of the specific competencies of suppliers, not only in production but also in the process of research and development. Rather than making blueprints of required inputs that are 'thrown over the wall' to suppliers, there should be 'early supplier involvement' in the design process (Helper 1991; Lamming 1993).

In total, the advantages of cooperation are as follows. By furthering specialization it yields the advantage of economy of scale. It enables the sharing of risks that otherwise would not be acceptable. It furthers motivation in independent firms that are responsible for their own survival. It yields more flexibility and a greater diversity of sources of competence that can be combined in novel, innovative combinations. Contracting out transforms fixed costs of investment into variable costs of supply. That is one source of increased flexibility. A more or less hidden objective may be cheaper production in small firms with lower remuneration and worse conditions of labour. More fundamental is the flexibility of forming novel combinations of perspectives from firms with different ways of perceiving, interpreting and evaluating opportunities and threats, as already discussed.

In cooperation, both partners will want to maintain several objectives: maximum flexibility and minimum risk of dependence and hence minimum share in specific investments and maximum share in joint added value, while maximizing joint added value as a whole. These objectives are often in conflict: less specific investments will reduce the added value of the relationship; one-sided dependence of the partner will block his cooperation. Thus, a tug of bargaining arises which will in general lead to some compromise between added value, dependence and flexibility.

With respect to such cooperation between firms and the resulting balance of objectives, there are significant differences between different countries. Evidence for such differences in industrial organization is given for buyer–supplier relations in the auto industry between Japan and the USA (Cusumano and Fujimoto 1991; Helper 1991; Lamming 1993; but see also Kamath and Liker 1994); buyer–supplier relations in Britain versus Germany (Lane and Bachmann 1996), the printed circuit board industry in Britain versus Japan (Sako 1994); the machine tool industry in the USA versus Germany (Herrigel 1994); patterns and styles of internationalization between British and German multinational enterprises (Lane 1997). Firms engaging in crossborder alliances will encounter such different practices. The causes of such differences lie in customs and other institutions such as legal infrastructure and the basis for trust, which depend on national culture and economic development.

Different institutional environments and arrangements provide for different relations between firms and hence different structures of capitalist economies. In the 'Rhineland' economies of continental Europe (Albert 1993), there is a tendency towards 'network economies', with more or less durable ties between organizations. In Anglo-American economies, firms tend to be more autonomous. In the Dutch policy debate much attention has been given to the role of 'clusters' of complementary firms and industries (Jacobs and de Man 1996), inspired by the work of Porter (1990). Recently, the present minister of economic affairs has elaborated on the view of his predecessor by proposing that his ministry has a brokerage role to play in stimulating the development of such clusters (*Financieel dagblad*, 9 and 10 September 1997). In these matters, a thorough understanding of the governance of inter-firm relations is crucial.

SPILLOVER CONTROL

For a firm, the downside of efficient transfer of knowledge or competence between firms is the risk of spillover: the chance that directly or indirectly, through linkages in networks, part of one's core competence leaks to competitors.

Risk of spillover is determined by several factors. When knowledge is more tacit the risk is lower than when it is codified and the risk is lower to the extent that knowledge is embodied in teams, procedures, organizational structure or culture. Then one may be able to observe what a firm is doing, but fail to grasp the underlying logic and causality ('causal ambiguity', see Lippman and Rumelt 1982). Typically the two go together: tacit knowledge is often embodied in elements of organization (structure, procedures, practices, culture). Typically competence is then embodied in the heads or hands of people, or in practices and routines developed by teams rather than in the form of blueprints or other documents. In that case, exchange may take the form of employees from one company being stationed temporarily at the partner. Spillover might result either from buyouts of such people or teams, or imitation, but this may be hampered by causal ambiguity.

Risk of spillover also depends on the presence of direct or indirect linkages to competitors. Thus the risk is higher, ceteris paribus, in horizontal rather than vertical relations. It depends on the number of partners, because then the chance is higher that there will be competitors among those partners. Spillover can be limited by 'technologies of monitoring'. If one can trace what happens to the competence supplied to a partner, in any subsequent diffusion in the partner's network, one can demand control of diffusion by the partner and monitor his compliance. It is then important to design a technology of monitoring with sharp focus that sorts out what really belongs to the core of one's distinctive competence. If it is too coarse, the ban on diffusion will detract too much from the benefits of competence transfer to the partner.

Spillover further depends on the speed of change. If the technological make-up of products changes more rapidly than it would take for the relevant information to spill over to competitors and be used for imitation, then the problem disappears (Nooteboom 1998c).

Note that spillover can be accidental or intentional. In the latter case it may be related to the use of confidential information as a hostage: information is leaked in retaliation for a breach of contract or confidence. However, it can be impossible to distinguish the source of spillover. Intentional, opportunistic spillover may be covered up by claims of accidents.

INTEGRATION AND DISINTEGRATION

As already suggested, current conditions exert a pressure on firms to outsource more activities. To put this in perspective, let us consider other general arguments concerning the boundaries of the firm, which include more than just those concerning learning and transaction costs already discussed.

As indicated by Langlois and Robertson (1995), in the economic literature there are two approaches towards the boundaries of the firm: from the perspective of ownership and from the perspective of coordination. These are to a large extent inspired by notions from more or less recent streams in economic thought such as: 'property rights', 'nexus of contracts', 'transaction costs', with problems concerning 'incentive alignment', 'bounded rationality' and 'impacted information', problems of 'measurement and monitoring', 'specific assets' with ensuing problems of 'hold-up', etc. Some of these have been discussed in the summary of TCE in Chapter 1.

Ownership is understood as the possession of 'residual rights': rights to revenues after deduction of claims from 'specific rights' allotted to suppliers of capital, labour or services. Coordination is associated with 'hierarchy', i.e. direct control of performance, with an authority to demand information and compliance to agreements which would not stand up in court vis-à-vis an outside firm.

A standard argument in favour of the market, in the form of non-integrated, specialized production in firms under separate ownership and coordination, is that it stimulates effort since one is responsible for one's own survival as a firm and has to compete with alternative suppliers. In other words: the market provides stronger incentives for effort.

Arguments for integrating different activities under unified ownership or coordination are mostly related to the notion of 'complementary assets' or 'economy of scope'. When combined in a unified process, certain products can be produced more efficiently, or certain production factors can be used more productively. Such economy of scope is 'inseparable' if it does not obtain when the assets are separated in some sense. The question is: in what sense, separation in time and/or place, in coordination or in ownership?

In a static setting, i.e. without regard to innovation, integration of activities under unified ownership may be required in the case that assets or products are complementary and the monitoring of performance is problematic. Then, in order to ensure incentives in the utilization of such complementary assets, that party should have ownership in terms of residual rights whose performance is most difficult to monitor by outsiders. With specific rather than residual rights, that party is most tempted to shirk.

Unified coordination of complementary assets, in a 'hierarchy', may be required in a static setting under several conditions. One is the presence of inseparable economy of scope, in the sense that activities can be performed more efficiently under unified coordination than when separated. Note that this does not imply that a complementary asset should also be owned by the coordinating agency. Integration in ownership is required if it is impossible to hire in the complementary factor from an outside firm on a spot basis. This may be so because it is part of the idiosyncratic competence of the focal producer and therefore simply is not available outside. Or less extremely, because of effects of experience (in the sense of the 'experience curve') some continuity in the provision of the factor is needed to realize the economy of scope, or it requires specific investments on the part of the supplier, to ensure consistent coupling with the producer's process. As discussed in the previous section, integration in ownership may be needed if even under integrated coordination monitoring is problematic. In particular, integration may be needed to prevent hold-up (misuse of dependence of the partner) in case specificity of complementary asset yields switching costs that punish exit from the relationship.

In a dynamic setting of innovation, Teece (1986) pointed out that it may be necessary to keep exploitation of an innovation within the firm where it was generated, if there is no other way to appropriate the rents from the innovation: in the case, for example, that there is insufficient patent protection, or insufficient control of compliance to licensing agreements. In other words, integration may be needed to prevent spillover. But it was noted before that risk of spillover may be limited to the extent that the knowledge which one wishes to protect as part of core competence is tacit or is subject to radical speed of change.

Teece (1986, 1988), Langlois and Robertson (1995) and Chesbrough and Teece (1996) pointed out that if different steps of a value adding process are systemically linked, then change in each should be kept in unison with change in contiguous steps. This may require integration under unified coordination, due to 'dynamic transaction costs' (defined as problems and costs of transferring new knowledge to others; or coordinating across different sets of knowledge).

Teece gives the example of replacement of aluminium by plastic composites as a material for constructing aeroplanes. Because of physical and functional connections between parts one cannot replace an isolated aluminium part with a part made out of composites without taking care of repercussions in connecting parts and the balance of the system as a whole.

When change is minor and kept within existing standards for interfaces between the parts, disintegrated change is feasible. But when change is more fundamental and interfaces have to change along with steps, unified coordination is required. However, Langlois and Robertson (1995: 135) recognize that there also is 'a kind of radicalness ... that large organizations do not handle well. For this type of uncertainty, a decentralized network does much better.' When innovation is radical, in the sense that novel combinations are explored, existing systemic linkages are no longer relevant and the argument no longer applies (Nooteboom 1998b).

In fact, we are back to the discussion of weak and strong ties and cognitive distance of Chapter 1. Systemic coherence and tacit knowledge require strong ties, but weak ties are needed for innovation, in order to generate novelty or 'non-redundancy', with 'novel combinations'. The net value of weak versus strong ties depends on a trade-off between the advantages of non-redundancy, greater flexibility and the other advantages of separate firms and the disadvantage of problematic transfer when the knowledge is tacit and/or systemic (not stand-alone). The trade-off favours weak ties to the extent that the innovation involved is more radical. If radical innovation involves novel combinations, the advantage of non-redundancy is more important and the problem in the transfer of systemic knowledge is not relevant because the old systemic coherence is destroyed. Strong ties align with existing systemic connections and thereby obstruct novel combinations. Also, when novel combinations are in order, you take for granted the problem of the difficulty of transferring tacit knowledge in novel contacts because, although the strong ties may provide a better basis for it, these again do not cover the novel connections required. There, one can very efficiently transfer tacit knowledge but it is not innovative. Then it is to be accepted that the build-up of understanding and a joint 'community of practice' is needed, to transfer or connect tacit knowledge between two partners. This constitutes a specific investment which makes partners dependent, entails the risk of 'hold-up' and the ensuing need for governance.

The advantages of integration, with strong ties, and disintegration, with weak ties, can be summed up as follows:

1 Advantages of disintegration:
   • incentives for quality, efficiency and innovation, in order to survive;
   • economy of scale by specialization;
   • flexibility in the coupling, in stand-alone technology, of modules in configurations that fit market conditions;
   • diversity of experience and competence, yielding 'non-redundant' information and opportunities for the exploration of novel combinations, in radical innovation, even if technology is systemic.
2 Advantages of integration:
   • continuity needed to recoup specific investments, when that cannot be achieved in governance between separate firms;

- perspectives for ongoing cooperation to restrict temptations of opportunism, where this cannot be achieved between separate firms;
- cognitive proximity and close interaction for efficient communication and for transfer of tacit knowledge;
- to protect against spillover of knowledge when it is largely documented, is not subject to radical speed of change and cannot be monitored;
- maintain connections when innovation is systemic, not radical but incremental and has not yet progressed so far as to generate standards across the interfaces between elements of the system;
- provide scale and inseparable scope when needed to achieve efficiencies and a wide market reach.

The latter applies especially when innovations are diffusing and, due to new entrants, competition increases and scale and market expansion are needed to achieve low costs and to exploit the innovation.

These considerations are crucial for the choice of the form of an alliance and its governance. For example: where the demands of radical innovation and learning prevail, one can expect a shift away from more integrative forms of cooperation to more disintegrated forms, such as a shift from mergers and acquisitions to equity joint ventures and from the latter to non-equity alliances. This will be discussed more extensively in Chapter 3.

LOCATION

Locational patterns of industry and agglomeration effects have been ascribed to geological factors (natural resources), geographical factors (e.g. population characteristics, infrastructure), cultural factors (e.g. religion), climate and economic factors (e.g. size of market, transaction costs). As early as 1920, Marshall distinguished three economic factors: concentration of related firms offers a 'pooled' market for specialized labour, facilitates the development of specialized products and services and allows firms to profit from externalities in the form of spillovers.

More detailed considerations can be derived from the theory of learning indicated in Chapter 1. They are related in particular to the third factor from Marshall: spillovers between firms. Note a fundamental difference between the notion of 'external economy of cognitive scope' (EECS) discussed in Chapter 1 and Marshall's notion of external economy of learning. The latter refers to spillover, i.e. the speed and efficiency of the acquisition of 'information' as some cognitive commodity that one could have obtained otherwise, but then more slowly or expensively. EECS refers to the filling of gaps that, due to the path dependence and ensuing idiosyncrasy of one's categorial apparatus, could not have been filled (any more than a camel could decide to be a horse). It is not a matter of receiving information but of extending one's absorptive capacity.

ICT enables rapid and cheap collection, dissemination and access of massive amounts of data. As a result, when innovations pass from tacit to documented knowledge they spread quickly across the world. Detailed data on consumer purchases are obtained from bar code scanning at shop check-outs and from remote electronic shopping. Movement of orders, products and payments can be monitored continuously and in minute detail. This enables firms to reduce stocks by tight control of logistics ('just in time' supply).

Will distance ever become totally irrelevant? A crucial question here is whether communication technology will progress so far as to enable the transfer at a distance of tacit knowledge. In Chapter 1 it was argued that such transfer requires 'cognitive proximity' which involves on-the-spot inter-action in a 'community of practice', since it needs not only observation but real-time, 'hands-on' interaction, with demonstration and correction, with multiple media of sight, speech, touch and perhaps even smell. But it is technically feasible to approach this with modern communication technology, as is demonstrated, for example, by remote surgery, where a surgeon oper-ates at a distance through a robot, using a camera which monitors its movements.

In communication at a distance, the question is also whether one knows what one should communicate and with whom. But in 'exploration' of new knowledge, chance encounters play a role and for this one needs more or less unstructured interaction of people meeting each other frequently in a context of roughly shared interest (like scientists at a conference or firms in an industrial district). While this seems to require at least occasional physical proximity, so that spatial distance matters, perhaps the Internet begins to provide such a facility at a distance.

A further reason why distance may still matter is that exchange of knowledge also requires trust. To build up knowledge exchange one must develop common understanding, which to a greater or lesser extent consti-tutes a relation specific investment. As explained in transaction cost economics, discussed in Chapter 1, this yields a need for governance. It was also noted that in innovation it can be highly counterproductive to utilize formal instruments of control, in the form of detailed, legal contracts, proce-dures for monitoring and credible threats of litigation. It is not only difficult and costly, especially for small firms, to handle this instrument. It also threatens to stifle the relations between participants and to block rather than support the required exploration by trial and error. If you do not yet know precisely what cooperation will yield, because you engage in cooperation to develop novelty, you cannot specify precisely the obligations that partici-pants should fulfil. Too detailed and formal contracts may seriously inhibit the growth of trust. Thus, particularly in innovation, one must seek recourse to alternative, more informal mechanisms of control: reputation mechanisms, exchange of hostages and trust. These yield more flexibility and economize on the costs of governance (Nooteboom 1996). In these forms of governance small firms have less of a disadvantage and in some respects even an advantage, compared to large firms. Further, for such forms of governance, distance matters: reputation, trust and bonding are best achieved at small spatial, cognitive and cultural distance. As discussed in Chapter 1, trust is either based on ex-ante shared norms and values, bonds of friendship and kinship, or is built up in a relationship, in what Zucker (1986) called 'process based trust'. The first requires shared culture, the second clan or family membership (Ouchi 1980) and the third is greatly enhanced by local, face to face interaction. Trust is also important when there is risk of spillover in knowledge exchange.

GLOBALIZATION

Recently, there has been much talk of globalization. But the internationalization of business is not a new phenomenon and some authors say that it has been exaggerated (Ruigrok and van Tulder 1995). Indeed, trade streams and foreign direct investment are less now than they were prior to World War I. Even the international financial system is less integrated than it was then. Leading equity fund managers still hold only a minority (11 per cent) in foreign shares. These phenomena can, however, be ascribed to the colonial system that still prevailed at that time. Compared to the 1950s, globalization has increased considerably. But trade streams and foreign direct investment are also still more intense within than between the blocks (Europe, USA, Far East).

Globalization of some phenomenon means that it is becoming more pervasive or coherent (similar, integrated, related) across the world. It can refer to a variety of phenomena: politics, technology, consumer behaviour, firm strategy, markets, trade flows, capital flows. In some areas it has progressed further than in others. It is not inevitable and may recede as well as proceed.

In politics and trade, globalization has been going on for many centuries: in the trading activities of the Chinese, Phoenicians, Greeks, Romans, Normans, Arabs, Venetians, Portuguese, Dutch, British. In politics it has had its fits, starts and setbacks. Milestones were the institution of the League of Nations, its collapse and the subsequent institution of the United Nations, GATT and the World Bank. It is manifested in a range of other international governmental and non-governmental organizations, such as the Red Cross, ILO, FAO, Amnesty International, Greenpeace and Doctors Without Frontiers. It accelerated with the breakdown of the communist system. New markets and sources of competition are emerging across the world. We have moved from two blocks of economic power (the USA and Europe) to three blocks (including the Far East). In the Far East, Japan, Taiwan, Hong Kong and Singapore are about to be followed by other countries in the region. India and Latin America will follow. But the breakdown of the simple polarization between capitalism and communism has led to a variety of forms of capitalism. The increase in globalization has stimulated the search for identity on the basis of language, religion and ethnicity, which yields an increase of differentiation in politics that runs counter to globalization.

Globalization has clearly been spectacular, especially in communication due to its combination with information technology. In firm strategy, globalization is still more a goal or perspective than a reality. There has been an increase in foreign trade and foreign direct investment, but foreign location of research and head offices, foreign recruitment of top management and foreign sourcing of capital are still rare (Ruigrok and van Tulder 1995). In particular, globalization is becoming evident in cross-border mergers and acquisitions and alliances.

The different aspects of globalization are connected according to the multiple causality indicated in Chapter 1. Developments in politics, international law, GATT, WTO and other institutions contribute to conditional causes. Through a process of self-reinforcement, to be discussed presently, globalization stimulates firms to internationalize further, which contributes to 'final' causes of motivation. It opens up new areas of economic activity across the world and thereby contributes to the 'efficient cause' of new players. Information and communication technology contribute to the acquisition of new sources of materials and information. Hence they contribute to 'material causes' and provide novel forms of organization, thus contributing to 'formal causes'. Several more specific aspects are discussed below: technological development, product differentiation, scale and scope.

INTERNATIONALIZATION

Since alliances are often sought for entry into foreign markets, it is useful to review the motives for 'going foreign', as discussed extensively in any textbook on international business (e.g. Daniels and Radebaugh 1995; Griffin and Pustay 1996). A summary is given below.

The first step in internationalization of the firm is usually export and then often 'indirect' export, which entails exporting through a trade corporation or suppling one's product to a customer who then exports it together with his own product ('piggyback'). In direct export one takes care of it oneself, perhaps using a local agent or distributor, before making the step of setting up a sales office. The idea is that one should not take a big step until having first found out via small steps that the process is worthwhile and until one has gained the requisite experience. However, that procedure may be too slow.

A next step is to set up production abroad with 'foreign direct investment' (FDI), or to let another produce the product on the basis of a licence. In Table 2.1 the reasons for foreign investment are grouped on the basis of the resource–competence view. As proposed in Chapter 1, following Stoelhorst (1997) resources are classified in three groups: assets, competencies and positional advantages. Assets can be owned, competencies are embodied

Table 2.1 Reasons for foreign investment, a resource perspective

Type of resource	Reason
Assets: efficiency, scale and scope	
Efficiency	Transportation costs
	Lower production costs (e.g. due to lower wages)
Scope	Spread risk, evade exchange rate risk
Competencies	Access to local competencies or other resources;
Positional advantages	
Marketing	Adapt product to the local market
	Follow the customer
Politics	Circumvent import restrictions
	Political acceptance
Strategy	Pre-empt the competition
	Attack competition in its home market
	Occupy unique resources

in people and organization and positional advantages relate to positions in markets and competition. Ownership and utilization of assets are closely related to goals of efficiency, on the basis of economies of scale, scope or experience.

A well-known reason for efficiency is lower wages. Of course, one should be aware that the real issue is costs per unit of product, so that next to wages one should take into account labour productivity. When a product is heavy or bulky, transport costs are high, which gives a reason for going from export to FDI.

A curious case is Heineken beer. Most brewers produce in the country of destination, because export entails the transport of what is mostly water. Nevertheless, Heineken stuck to export. The reason was the maintenance of the image of a top quality, original product from Holland.

Political reasons include the dodging of import restrictions in the form of quota and duties, restrictions on the repatriation of local profits, demands for a minimum share of added value from local production ('local content')', need to gain the image of a local producer to obtain better product acceptance and access to distribution channels.

A strategic reason can be that one wants to 'pre-empt' a competitor: if he enters the local market one may lose market share. Another reason is that one's main competitor is local and one wants to attack him in his own market in order to weaken his basis for competition elsewhere. A third reason is to block a competitor by occupying a unique source of materials. For example: a producer of aluminium achieved a monopoly by occupying the main sources of bauxite (the main material for aluminium). A fourth reason is that one must follow one's customers in their internationalization, in order to maintain 'just in time' supply or to provide the same service (e.g. in accounting) to foreign divisions as at home.

Toyota started to produce in the USA in order to dodge import restrictions. The Japanese tyre producer Bridgestone had Toyota as its main customer and had to come along. Tyres are expensive to transport. If Bridgestone did not come along, American producers would take over the replacement-tyre market for Toyota and from there perhaps also the new-tyre sales and perhaps even sales in the Japanese home market (Daniels and Radebaugh 1995).

Avoidance of exchange rate risk by local production means that costs and revenues are priced in the same currency, so that one avoids the decline in foreign revenues with respect to domestic costs. Thus revenues are in dollars for several Dutch industries (oil, aeroplanes), while production costs are in Dutch Florins. Thereby they suffered for many years from the appreciation of the Dutch Florin with respect to the dollar. This was one of the problems which brought Fokker Aircraft into trouble.

Reasons of competence include the need of local presence to achieve close understanding of the market and adaptation of a product to local requirements. How important this is depends on whether one chooses a global or multinational strategy. In the first one chooses to maintain a constant product all over the world, with perhaps adaptations only in appearance, advertising, packaging and distribution. In a multinational strategy one adapts the product to local tastes and use conditions. What strategy is best depends on a trade-off between effects of scale, which plead for a global strategy, and the degree to which product differentiation is possible and needed, while taking transportation costs into account. This may yield several production centres in a few different regions across the world, to limit transaction costs and have some proximity to markets, while maintaining sufficient volume to achieve economy of scale.

Differentiability is not only a matter of technology, taste and conditions of use, but also the importance of a constant product to reduce 'search costs', so that on the basis of brand name the consumer can be certain of a fixed quality everywhere. This is important when customers travel across the world, especially when the product is not a physical one that is constant in nature, but a service, which is characterized by a merging of product and production process. The quality of a hamburger greatly depends on its local preparation. Financial, accounting and consultancy services also depend crucially on local staff.

A producer of copying machines (Xerox) sold their American product in Japan until they found out that the shorter Japanese had to climb onto boxes to reach the buttons. McDonalds, on the other hand, takes extreme care to make hamburgers the same the world over, so that anyone anywhere knows precisely what he will get (Lorange and Roos 1992).

MOTIVES FOR ALLIANCES

The developments discussed above are yielding a whole new system of technology, production, organization and markets. A new 'techno-economic paradigm' is being created (Freeman and Perez 1989): a new 'logic' not only of production but also of markets, competition and organization. In this context, the main drive towards alliances is the need to cooperate in order to maintain flexibility, core competence and the incentives that arise from autonomy, while utilizing complementary resources for both efficiency and learning, as discussed above.

Related to this is the need to utilize economy of scale and scope (Ohmae 1989). In principle, one can spread the weight of fixed costs and risks by expanding one's own scale or scope of production; by increasing production volume or by adding products that share the same costs. But the latter strategy of diversification can rapidly be at odds with the need to concentrate on core competencies. There may be other restrictions on the expansion of one's own sales and products. High transportation costs or import restrictions may require local production. Local production by greenfield investment or takeover of a local firm may not be allowed, may not be feasible, or may be too risky.

A third motive is the need for speed: one may need partners because it would take too much time to develop all relevant (non-core) competencies (Lei and Slocum 1990).

Clearly, the choice of partner should match the objective. If a product needs to be differentiated to fit local demand, the partner should have the requisite local knowledge, experience, market acceptance and access to distribution channels to help achieve that fit.

ICT enables the coordination of activities across large distances. This could work in a direction opposite to the trend towards alliances, since it enables coordination of activities within one's own extended firm. But it also enables whatever coordination and communication is needed in alliances. As indicated above, it reduces transaction costs.

An alternative to getting involved in foreign production is to sell a licence to someone else. Arguments for and against this strategy are summarized in Table 2.2.

Table 2.2 Arguments for and against licensing

For the licensor	
For	*Against*
Assets Local volume is not worth own investment	Profit goes mostly to licensee
The product cannot be protected against copying	Lack of control of quality, brand name, sales effort
Competence The activity lies outside core competence Perspective for learning from licensee	
Positional advantage Entry into market is blocked or entails too many risks or investments	Lack of control; danger of creating a competitor

For the licensee	
For	*Against*
No R&D expense and risk	Arrow's paradox of information for assessing value
Profit from knowledge, expertise, contacts of licensor	Contractual limits on operations Risk of obsolescence Ongoing royalty payments

Arrow's paradox of information is as follows: in order to assess what one is prepared to pay for information one needs to have it, but if one has it, one no longer wants to pay. This applies, among other things, to licences. The problem is not insoluble. One partial solution is to pay only a small fixed amount upfront which does not exceed the minimum a priori plausible value and to contract to pay a percentage of revenues or profits derived as its value is proven. However, when this percentage becomes sizeable it detracts from the motivation of the licensee to make the best of it. Another, at least partial, solution is to have the value of the information or licence assessed by a third party who is mutually trusted both in his competence to evaluate its value and his commitment to fair dealing. Thus, an impartial assessment of value can be given to the licensee without the latter actually obtaining the information.

Especially in the pharmaceutical and cosmetic industries we see massive cross-licensing between competitors. How can this be explained? Why give products to competitors that have been developed at high costs of R&D? Of course one does not aim at this, but the outcomes of R&D are often unpredictable and can yield a product that does not fit into the competencies of production, marketing or distribution.

The unpredictability of R&D is called the 'King Saul effect' (Mokyr 1990: 286). Examples are the following. Looking for a better dynamo for bicycle lights, the Philips company hit upon the development of an electric shaver. Gasoline was at first a useless byproduct of deriving lubricants from crude oil, before it was developed into a fuel for the internal combustion motor. Bessemer invented his steel making process while trying to solve the problems of a spinning cannon shell (Mokyr 1990: 116).

The licensing of an unintended and ill-fitting product at least yields some revenue. There is not much harm in giving it to a competitor if it does not compete with one's own products, either because it is not a substitute or because the licence covers countries outside one's distribution area. When there is cross-licensing, dependence and vulnerability to cheating are symmetric, which helps to control them. Both sides benefit from exchanging complementary products, thereby achieving economy of scope in better utilization of distribution channels and a more attractive range of products for consumers.

If licensing is not the preferred option, the next question is whether to seek the help of a local partner rather than going for one's own 'greenfield investment'. The arguments for this are summarized in Table 2.3.

The avoidance of duplication of fixed costs is especially important in process industries, where fixed costs are high and furthermore 'sunk' in the market, thereby creating exit barriers. In such cases, there is a threat of ruinous price competition under conditions of excess supply, because assets cannot be reduced or sold off. Therefore the emergence of excess capacity should be avoided. A problem here is that in some industries (oil, basic chemicals) for strategic reasons governments stimulate domestic production capacity in order to avoid becoming dependent on other nations in times of crisis. This is yet another reason not to create even more excess capacity

Table 2.3 Advantages of the use of a local partner

Assets
Evade duplication of fixed costs

Competence
Use of existing competencies in: knowledge of and access to the local market, local sources of materials, local labour market, distribution channels, trade mark, patents, goodwill or reputation.

Positional advantage
Speed
Eliminate competitor

when entering a country. Some firms, often supported by governments, cooperate to rationalize a process industry with excess capacity by a balanced reduction of capacity. An example is a joint venture between British ICI and Italian Enichem in the PVC industry (Faulkner 1995).

In Table 2.3, 'elimination of a competitor' indicates that one limits competition by cooperating with a local partner who would otherwise be a competitor.

The next chapter investigates the range of alliance forms and ways to choose between them, depending on one's goals and conditions of technology, market and institutions.

3 Forms of alliance

This chapter discusses the variety of forms that alliances can take and develops principles for choosing between them. This choice depends on the goals that the participants have, on outside conditions of technology, market and country. It aims to give a systematic and reasonably complete inventory of goals, conditions, problems and ways to solve them.

FORMS OF ALLIANCE

At the beginning of this book it was announced that the term 'alliance' is interpreted in a broad sense, covering a wide spectrum of forms of cooperation between firms, between the extremes of full integration within a single, centralized firm and fully independent firms engaged in pure market contracting. Usually, the spectrum is indicated along a single dimension of concentration or integration (Contractor and Lorange 1988; Hagedoorn 1993; Osborn and Baughn 1990). But integration has at least two dimensions: financial integration of ownership, entailing claims to profit, and organizational integration, entailing decision rights. This two-dimensional approach was taken before by others (Huyzer *et al.* 1992) and is attempted in Figure 3.1.

Contrary to most treatments, degrees of integration within the firm are also included. Thus, a merger or acquisition can yield an integrated or disintegrated company, in terms of both decision-making and distribution of ownership. The reason for doing this is that networks of firms with strong ties (such as 'industrial districts') can become very similar to a highly decentralized ('virtual') large firm. A 'virtual firm' has a limited but strategically crucial central coordination of dispersed, decentralized activities and considerable dispersion of profit in component activities.

Industrial districts yield attractive properties of 'flexible specialization' (Piore and Sabel 1983, 1984): network structures of partially cooperating and partially competing small firms in research and development, production, distribution and supporting services make optimal use of the motivating force of the market and flexible combinations of products, production units, knowledge, depending on market conditions. It is a constellation of high

The classic example is the fashion firm Benetton. It consists of weak ties between a large number of small firms engaged in the production and distribution of fashion clothing, with rapid adjustment to market signals by ICT linkages between the firms. The strength of Benetton lies not in any particular competence of design or technology of product or production, but in the brand name and the coordination of the information network for speedy adjustment to changes in taste (Lorenzini and Baden-Fuller 1993). Is this an 'industrial district' or a 'virtual firm'?

potential 'dynamic' efficiency, especially in the exploration that accompanies radical innovation (Nooteboom 1998b). Illustrations in practice are the development of microelectronics in 'Silicon Valley' and machine, textile and shoe industries in Northern Italy (Piore and Sabel 1983). The concept of a 'virtual' firm may be seen as the large firm's answer to this. The importance of industrial districts and virtual firms illustrates the importance of relational competencies for entrepreneurship, from the resource perspective, as discussed in Chapter 1.

Here and in the remainder of the book 'joint venture' or 'JV' refers to equity joint ventures (set-up of a novel firm under shared ownership of the parents) and 'NEA' refers to non-equity alliances. A JV provides an intermediate

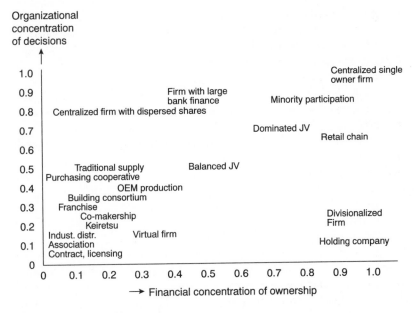

Figure 3.1 Degree of integration.

position between a non-equity alliance and full integration by merger/ acquisition. Non-equity alliances embrace a variety of cooperation, with a wide spectrum of organizational concentration: franchising; more or less contractual cooperation in research or in product development, with joint development of a product between a buyer and supplier (co-makership) as an example, or in production, marketing, distribution or sales; licensing; consortia for building projects or for conducting R&D; associations for advertising, quality programmes, certification, political representation; industrial districts; dealerships, service contracts and sales agents. An NEA can yield different levels of dependence, associated with different heights of exit barriers or switching costs (e.g. due to transaction specific investments, as discussed in transaction cost theory) and this requires different degrees of governance. Licensing yields a more tenuous link through royalty agreements. Cooperatives and franchises centralize some decision rights and distribute rights to profit that are not, however, tradeable on a share market and entail some specific investments, which together yield exit barriers. Consortia also centralize supervision to some extent, which yields some exit barriers, but they generally last for a shorter time. Associations last longer and also have some centralized decisions or supervision, but generally concern only a limited part of participants' activities and interests and exit barriers are generally low. Agreements for management support, training, start-up assistance, maintenance or other services are long-term contracts, approaching market transactions. This book will not go into detail of what tasks are distributed or shared between participants, and how, for all possible forms of cooperation.[1]

The scheme of Figure 3.1 is not quite satisfactory because it is ambiguous: the position of several forms in the scheme is debatable. There are two reasons for this. There are not just two but at least nine dimensions, compressed into two. Most forms of alliance span a range of values along one or more dimensions. The nine dimensions are specified as follows:

1 *Legal form*: limited company, legal partnership, society, foundation, contract. A JV will generally be a company, an association might be a foundation.
2 *Number of participants*: in a JV it is typically two, in a consortium several, in a franchise or association many.
3 *Duration*: a single project, latent relations that are activated for projects as they come along, continuous ongoing cooperation.
4 *Range of joint assets*: a full range as in a JV, or a range focused on some specific activity such as co-makership, or next to no shared assets as in most associations.
5 *Distribution of asset ownership among the participants*: this may be uniform or skewed, as in a balanced versus a dominated JV. A simple measure would be the share of the largest participant.
6 *Range of activities in which cooperation takes place* (Faulkner 1995): a systematic classification would be on the basis of Porter's 'value chain', as practised

by Huyzer *et al.* (1992). Which activities in the primary process (purchasing, incoming logistics, production, outgoing logistics, marketing, service) and secondary, supporting activities (management, personnel, legal, financial, research) do participants share or supply to each other? In an association this is typically very limited, in co-makership it is considerable, in a JV it is extensive.

7   *Intensity of cooperation*: mutual adjustment by dedicated investments, the type and extent of knowledge exchange, frequency of meetings, exchange of staff. This is a very important aspect in the governance of the relationship, as will be discussed below and in Chapter 4.

8   *Distribution of decision rights*: who has decision power over what activities.

9   *Network pattern of relations between participants*: this becomes more salient as the number of participants increases. One pattern is the hub and spoke: a central firm has relations with all others, who have no relations among themselves. That is the typical pattern of an association. Another is that all participants have connections with all others. This might be the case in a research consortium. In the field of network analysis (e.g. Burt 1982) there are several concepts that characterize different properties of network structures, such as 'centrality', 'structural equivalence', 'holes'.

For each form of alliance a profile can now be composed with a score on each of these dimensions.

For example, co-makership usually takes the legal form of contract (for some but often not all of the shared activities), two participants (but it could be more), considerable duration (typically for the life cycle of the product developed), some shared assets, activities aimed at development (specification, design, prototyping, testing, production development, production), intensive interaction in the activity of developing a product, with considerable exchange of knowledge, including tacit knowledge. Decision rights are more or less equally distributed. It goes beyond the usual type of outsourcing (labelled 'traditional supply' in Figure 3.1) where the buyer gives a complete specification of the contribution to be made by the supplier. Different systems of supply will be discussed extensively in Chapter 5. The main point here is that buyer and supplier also cooperate in specification.

A well-known measure of concentration that takes into account both the number of participants and the distribution of their shares is the Herfindahl index (sum of squared shares of all participants), which by definition ranges between zero and unity. To deal with the indicated complexity and yet arrive at the two-dimensional scheme of Figure 3.1, the following approach was taken. For each alliance form, along the two axes the Herfindahl index of concentration was multiplied by the range of assets/activities involved, as a percentage of a 'full range' of a complete company. In terms of Porter's value chain, a full range would include all primary and secondary activities of a typical firm in the industry. This roughly takes into account the dimensions 2, 4, 5, 6 and 8. Thus, legal form, duration and intensity of cooperation and network pattern are not included in Figure 3.1. Another approximation is that for each form 'typical values' are taken rather than the full range that variables might take.

Thus a JV 'typically' involves two participants, but it sometimes includes more. For a dominated JV the case of a 80–20 per cent distribution of ownership was taken and the same distribution of decision rights was assumed. It was also assumed that activities include the full range of primary and secondary activities. Thus, the balanced JV has a value of 0.5 along both axes (equal to the Herfindahl index H) and the dominated JV a value of 0.68 (H).

A merger/acquisition is also assumed to include a full range of activities. In principle, the paradigm case is single ownership and centralized decision-making with $H = 1.0$. But both distributions can be skew, depending on the distribution of share ownership, the distribution of decision rights between share owners and management ('corporate control') and the degree of centralization of the company.

An association typically has a large number of participants (say 100), a very limited range of shared assets (say 1 per cent), but an equal distribution of their ownership (yielding an $H = 0.01$), a more extended but still limited range of activities shared or exchanged (say 5 per cent) and a considerable degree of centralized management (let us say an 80 per cent share of the central administration, with an equal distribution of the rest), yielding $H = 0.64$. Thus it has a value of 0.001 along the horizontal axis and a value of 0.032 along the vertical axis.

A franchise might also have 100 participants, a limited range of shared assets (say 10 per cent), let us say completely owned by the franchiser ($H = 1$), a considerable range of shared activities (say 50 per cent), with most decision rights (including rights of monitoring the effort of franchisees) at the franchiser (say 80 per cent, yielding $H = 0.64$). Its value along the horizontal axis then is 0.1 and along the vertical axis 0.32.

An industrial district might include, say, 10 firms, with a 70 per cent range of shared assets, equal distribution of ownership ($H = 0.1$), 100 per cent range of activities, with equal distribution of decision rights ($H = 0.1$). The value along the horizontal axis then is 0.07 and along the vertical axis 0.1. A virtual firm might differ in that there is a full (100 per cent) range of assets, which is centrally owned for 50 per cent ($H = 0.3$), yielding a horizontal score of 0.3.

Full details of the assumptions and calculations underlying Figure 3.1 are given in Appendix 3.1 to this chapter.

FRAMEWORK FOR CHOICE

The goal of this chapter is to formulate general principles for choosing an alliance form. Subsequently, Chapter 4 will develop principles for the 'governance' of an alliance. To make the analysis tractable, the design of an alliance is treated on two levels: the choice of form and basic structure, as indicated in Figure 3.1, which is treated in the present chapter and a more process oriented analysis of 'governing' the alliance, treated in Chapter 4.

As discussed in Chapter 1, multiple causes should be taken into account, such as: the partners involved ('efficient cause'); their goals for the alliance ('final cause'); the forms and designs available ('formal cause'); the outside conditions ('conditional cause') which affect the desirability and feasibility of goals and forms. The form and structure of the alliance should be chosen or designed according to design principles (D) to yield solutions (S) of problems (P) in achieving a fit with the goals (G) of the protagonists and the conditions (C) of institutions, market and technology. This is illustrated in Figure 3.2.

The framework combines the 'strategy–structure' and the 'contingency' perspectives of organizational theory. It also resembles the 'Structure–Conduct–Performance' scheme of industrial organization economics and takes into account the dynamics of an alliance. There is a mutual influence between the goals and the conditions of a relationship. For example: in the case of innovation, uncertainty is greater than in the case of routine production. The goal may be to deal with institutional restrictions. Conversely, firm strategy may affect the conditions. The arrows from strategy and conditions to design principles and the arrow from design principles to structure

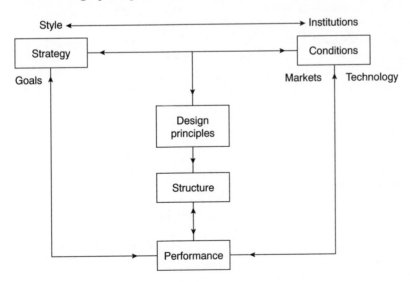

Figure 3.2 Framework for choice.

indicate that design takes strategy and conditions into account, to yield structure. Structure together with strategy and conditions determine performance, which feeds back into them. Structure is adapted in view of performance, performance may lead to novel goals and may affect conditions of market, technology or institutions.

Much prior research has suffered from failures to take into account the interaction between strategy, conditions and structure. Geringer and Hebert (1989) criticized earlier studies of the balance between control and performance of inter-firm relations for failing to take conditions and goals into account.

Examples of studies that took into account the conditions of markets, industries and the developmental stage of nations are Daems (1983), Hagedoorn (1993) and Beamish (1985). The conditions include 'institutions' that limit and guide behaviour and are needed to limit transaction costs, as discussed in Chapter 1. This does not mean that existing institutions always have that effect: they may reflect established interests that increase transaction costs. They include restrictions on entering markets, owning property, hiring personnel, repatriating profits from abroad, minimum 'local content' in production abroad, etc. They also include facilitating agencies, such as banks, legal firms and consultants. They vary between countries and cultures.

An early recognition of the need to take strategy into account in an evaluation of forms of inter-firm relations is due to Franko (1971). Later examples are Porter and Fuller (1986), Bleeke and Ernst (1991), Huyzer *et al.* (1992), Hagedoorn (1993) and Hagedoorn and Schakenraad (1994). Next to explicit goals, strategy includes 'style', such as basic attitudes and preferences towards ways of dealing with relationships: legal versus relational contracting; 'exit' versus 'voice' (Hirschman 1984; Helper 1990); formal versus informal; open versus closed; authoritarian versus deliberational; aggressive versus cooperative; risk aversive versus entrepreneurial.

The position taken here is that one should take into account not only conditions and or goals, but both. The following sections will discuss the elements of the framework: goals, performance, conditions, problems and principles of design to yield solutions.

GOALS

The analysis of Chapter 2 produced a basis for specifying the goals of alliances, in view of developments in technology and markets. It yields the wide range of goals gathered in the literature (Doz 1986; Porter and Fuller 1986; Contractor and Lorange 1988; Kogut 1988; Lei and Slocum 1990; Lorange and Roos 1992; Faulkner 1995). In Table 3.1 they are grouped on the basis of the resource view. As indicated in Chapter 1, following Stoelhorst (1997) resources are classified in three groups: assets, competencies and positional advantages. Assets can be owned, competencies are embodied in people and organization and positional advantages relate to positions in markets and competition.

Ownership and utilization of assets is closely related to goals of efficiency, on the basis of economies of scale, scope or experience. Here, positional advantages are distinguished into two kinds: advantages with respect to gaining access to a market and advantages in strategic manoeuvring with respect to competition. For some goals it is not quite certain where they belong. For example, setting a market standard (Gp10) is classified under positional advantage with respect to competition, but arguably it could also be seen as a positional advantage in market access or even as an asset. Under competencies we make a distinction between gaining complementary competencies in existing technology and in learning and innovation. This is connected with the difference between 'exploitation' of present knowledge or other competence and 'exploration' of new ones, as discussed in Chapter 1. As argued there, the use of alliances for learning and innovation is increasing.

Table 3.1 Goals of alliances

Assets: efficiency, scale and scope

Ga1   To prevent excess capacity

Ga2   Scale: to share the burden of threshold costs (in technology, distribution, brand name) (Ohmae 1989), or to create larger production units

Ga3   Scope: to improve utilization of assets with different products (in R&D, production, distribution, marketing)

Ga4   To share or spread risks: e.g. in R&D or experimentation with a prototype

Ga5   To complement or swap products (e.g. in cross-licensing) (G14)

Ga6   To experiment with a guinea pig

Competencies

Gc1   To the extent that competitive pressure is high and products are amenable to differentiation, one should try to differentiate products

Gc2   In order to have a chance in 'races to market' one should concentrate on core competencies and cooperate with others to achieve benefits of complementary competence in existing technology (exploitation; Porter and Fuller 1986)

Gc3   Insofar as the environment is complex and changing, as in conditions of innovation, one should use outside competencies not only in production but also in the creation of knowledge (exploration)

Positional advantages: market

Gp1   To satisfy governmental restrictions concerning import or 'local content'

Gp2   To satisfy restrictions concerning repatriation of profits

Gp3   To obtain favour for custom of the government, firms or consumers

Gp4   To satisfy political preferences for consortia (e.g. in defence industries)

Gp5   To tailor products to local markets

Gp6   To gain rapid access to inputs (materials, components, labour, services, patents)

Gp7   To gain rapid access to markets of outputs (distribution channels, brand name)

Positional advantages: competition (Kogut 1988; Porter and Fuller 1986)

Gp8   To pre-empt the competition

Gp9   To attack a competitor in his home market

Gp10 To install a cartel or entry barriers

Gp11 To set a market standard

Table 3.2 Goals of joint ventures

Goals	Percentage of mention	Goal in Table 3.1
Ensure or create distribution network	11.3	Gp7
Product development	1.8	
Economy of scale by combining financial means	11.1	Ga2
Knowledge pooling	16.4	Gc3
Productivity increase by merging capacity	4.1	Ga2
Survival of subsidiary	1.0	Ga1?
Preliminary to acquisition	0.4	
Supply of material	9.2	Gp6
Control the market	2.7	Gp10
Disinvestment	1.4	Ga1?
Help to other company	1.2	
Export	4.1	Gp7?
Penetration novel markets/industries	22.0	Gp7
Spread risk	7.4	Ga4
Divide the market	0.6	Gp10
Divide risk	5.3	Gp4?
	100	

Source: Hoekman (1988).

As indicated, these goals have appeared in many empirical studies. One example is a study of the goals of a sample of 512 joint ventures of the ten largest companies in the Netherlands reported by Hoekman (1988, quoted by Huyzer *et al.* 1992), which is summarized in Table 3.2. In the table, the goals mentioned are matched with the goals from Table 3.1.

Economy of scope includes the increased utilization of brand name by taking different products under its umbrella.

> Thus the Swiss watchmakers Swatch moved into spectacles and later even entered cooperation with Mercedes on the development of a small car. The British producer of pipes and tobacco, Dunhill, added aftershave. Nike moved from sports shoes to a line of sports and leisure clothes.

But one should take care that the different products all fit and do not detract from brand identity.

> The Dutch RABO bank years ago wanted to move into consumer credit, but felt that it would detract from its brand identity, which was associated with savings accounts. Therefore consumer credit was offered by a separate subsidiary with a different name ('Lage Landen'). Later,

consumer credit became a normal product within the range of any bank and RABO incorporated 'Lage Landen' under its own name.

Staying with the RABO bank, an illustration of reinforcing the product range by pooling complementary products is the cooperation between RABO, which offered a personal securities investment service through its advisors, and ROBECO, which offered a security investment fund to which consumers could subscribe by phone, without intermediaries. The two were pooled to yield a full line of service.

Economy of scope also includes the sharing and spreading of risks.

Pharmaceutical companies merge to share the risks involved in increasing R&D costs. The development and testing of a new drug takes many years and hundreds of millions of dollars. After a 'new chemical entity' has been patented another twelve years may elapse before it appears on the market as a drug. Eight or nine out of ten drugs do not recover their development costs. The one or two left then must be 'blockbusters' to recover total costs and failure to achieve this means failure of the company. By pooling resources, companies spread this risk and increase the chance of having at least one blockbuster. At the same time, the blockbusters create suspicion of excessive profits in the eyes of the public. Governments, which through medicare systems are the ultimate payers for the drugs, increase pressure on prices. This further increases the need for pooling resources (source: *NRC/Handelsblad* 3 February 1998, on the occasion of a merger announced between SmithKline Beecham and Glaxo Wellcome, which was not actually realized).

An interesting way to classify goals is to relate them to the stage in the life cycle of a product, as shown by Huyzer *et al.* (1992). A well-known complication is that the identification of life cycles is often difficult and highly sensitive to the level of aggregation.

For example, in retailing, since the 1950s, there have been very pronounced, exemplary life cycles in the development of shop types within the food trade (service, self-service, supermarkets, discount stores), but none at all when aggregated to the higher level of food stores (Nooteboom 1984).

Table 3.3 Goals in the life cycle

Innovation	Take-off	Stabilization	Saturation	Decline
Ga6, Ga4 Ga5		Ga2, Ga3	Ga1	
Gc3	Gc2	Gc1		
Gp11 Gp1 to Gp7, Gp8		GP9, Gp10	Gp12	

Furthermore, companies often have different products in different stages of their life cycles, which are often difficult to separate. Nevertheless, such a classification is conceptually interesting and can help to guide managerial decisions. Following the example of Huyzer *et al.* (1992), the goals from Table 3.1 are assigned to different stages of the life cycle, in Table 3.3.

In fact, the attempt to match goals with stages of the life cycle should be part of the wider issue of the relation between goals and conditions, which is the subject of a later section. There, stages in the life cycle are included in wider conditions of market, technology and institutions.

A crucial question concerns the configuration of goals of different participants. Can they be reconciled, are they complementary or, preferably, mutually reinforcing (Grandori 1997)? The following configurations are paradigm cases of successful collaborations and embrace most of the examples discussed in the literature.

- *Technology–design collaboration.* One side has the scientific–technological and the other the application–design capability for a product; for example, university–business collaboration. Another example is the alliance between Honda and Rover, where Honda supplied the technology and Rover the knowledge of British taste and design preferences (Faulkner 1995).
- *Production–product collaboration.* One side has a good product and the other has the appropriate production technology: for example, a Japanese company contributes efficient production to a European product design.
- *Product–market collaboration.* One side has a competence in product and production and the other has access to a market: for example, an American producer requires a Japanese company to access Japanese product and labour markets, such as Xerox which supplied a product to be marketed in Japan by Fuji (Lorange and Roos 1992); a Japanese producer requires a European partner to dodge EU import restrictions, such as Mitsubishi which teamed up with Volvo and the remainder of the Dutch car producer DAF in the joint venture NEDCAR, in the Netherlands.
- *Collaboration in complementary know-how,* In R&D, production, service, marketing: for example, R&D alliances, production consortia.
- *Sharing.* This involves sharing among similar producers costs, facilities and brand name, or the pooling of effort to achieve efficiency, spread

risk or exert power: for example, franchising, purchasing cooperatives, production cooperatives, trade associations.

• *Collaboration between a firm in an emerging industry with one in the industry which it is substituting.* This allows the newcomer to tap existing distribution channels, gives the incumbent firm a stake in the future and reduces resistance to substitution (Porter and Fuller 1986: 334).

PERFORMANCE

Increasingly, the literature has recognized that the measurement of performance is problematic (Geringer and Hebert 1989). Measurement by return on investment (ROI) is difficult due to problems of accounting. Often investments are made by one partner, but the corresponding profit is partly absorbed by the other partner, yielding investments without full returns and returns without investments (Ohmae 1989). Return on sales is better (Hagedoorn and Schakenraad 1994), since it copes with such separation of profits and investments. But financial measures generally are problematic when the objective of collaboration is long-term (e.g. Ga1, Gc1, Gc2, Gc3), so that their realization does not appear in short-time profits; when the objective is risk reduction rather than profit (Ga4); or when it is not directly related to profit (obstructing competition, Gp8, Gp9). Using financial measures can yield a systematic negative bias for Japanese companies, which are less oriented towards short-time profits.

Performance has also been measured by the duration of a relation, but this is problematic because especially non-equity alliances may be designed only for a short duration (Kogut 1988): for example, to set up and complete a project, as in a consortium for building a refinery. A relationship may also be deliberately temporary in order to assess the value of a firm prior to acquisition (Mody 1993).

This has been argued as the reason for a short joint venture in white goods (washing machines and the like) between Philips and Whirlpool: for the latter to have time to assess the true value of Philips' white goods division, in spite of the set-up and governance costs expended on the joint venture.

A relation may also be experimental in that potential is seen for a long-term relation, but it is considered wise to start small as a means of exploration.

In conclusion, it is better to assess the achievement of objectives more widely and to a large extent qualitatively, on the basis of participants' perceived objectives and their realization (Killing 1983; Beamish 1985; Bleeke and Ernst 1991).

CONDITIONS

The proposed conditions are based on the analysis in Chapters 1 and 2, with a distinction between institutions, market and technology. They are listed in Table 3.4.

Institutional conditions yield characterizations of nations or regions. Underdeveloped institutions yield high transaction costs. These can also result from contractual attitudes: a highly legalistic attitude (for example USA), or prolonged processes of consensus creation (Japan, Netherlands). The first is associated with a system of 'exit': when dissatisfied, walk out and sell out. The second is associated with 'voice': when dissatisfied, deliberate in an attempt to save the relation. The first makes for low trust, short-time relations with limited depth and intensity and high costs of legal litigation (Fukuyama 1995), but yields few obstacles to the dynamics of radical innovation. The second makes for high trust, long-term and intensive relations that enhance incremental innovation and diffusion of innovations, but the strength of ties in networks of firms may yield an obstacle to radical innovation (Nooteboom 1998d). When different partners are used to different institutions, particularly when they are not aware of these differences, styles of governance may clash.

The conditions of market and technology characterize industries, technologies and individual firms. The conditions of market and technology are mutually related. To give a few examples: radical and incipient innovation creates uncertainty; in incipient innovation, knowledge tends to be tacit, which creates dynamic transaction costs (costs of transferring or sharing knowledge); under radical innovation benefits of experience become limited.

Table 3.4 Conditions

Institutional
C1   Developed/underdeveloped technical, legal, knowledge infrastructure
C2   Moral order: individualistic/familial/clan/elitistic/religious/social
C3   Contractual attitude: market/relational; legalistic/personal; exit/voice oriented

Market and technology
C4   Degree of uncertainty: complexity (number of items and their relations), variability, radical uncertainty (openness of contingencies), observability of outputs and inputs of efforts from contributors and their preferences
C5   Degree of innovation: zero, incremental, radical ('creative destruction')
C6   Stage of innovation: incipient, breakthrough, stabilization, decline
C7   Type of knowledge and technology: tacit, documented, standardized; systemic, stand-alone; appropriability; share of fixed costs
C8   Effects of scale, scope, experience
C9   Differentiability of products
C10 Intensity of competition, in relation to concentration and degree of mono/oligopoly, price elasticity, entry barriers.

The next sections yield an inventory of problems that needs to be taken into account in the choice and design of an alliance. Problems arise in costs or complications of governance, conditions, mismatch between goals of participants. Three groups of problems can be distinguished: costs and complications of governance, problems of spillover and problems of institutions.

PROBLEMS OF GOVERNANCE

Product differentiation (Gc1) and intensive cooperation in knowledge exploitation (Gc2) and exploration (Gc3) are recognized as goals, but they yield problems that need to be solved. The gravity of these problems depends on the conditions, such as institutions and their effect on transaction costs. The problems of governance are summarized in Table 3.5.

P5 reflects the fact, discussed in Chapter 1, that costs of governance depend on uncertainty. P6 reflects that apart from direct out-of-pocket costs

Table 3.5 Problems of governance

P1 If products are differentiated (C9 and 10) and production technology is inflexible (C7), outsourcing entails specific investments, which yields exit barriers (which may yield a hold-up problem).

P2 To the extent that knowledge is tacit (C7), which is particularly the case in R&D and in small firms, its transfer or linkage requires close observation and interaction or the transfer of teams of staff. If required contributions from collaborators can not be specified, contractual arrangements become difficult. Communication requires close interaction and transaction specific investment in mutual understanding, which yields exit barriers.

P3 When there is (radical) uncertainty of conditions, or when neither outputs of efforts nor inputs of efforts and preferences of contributors are measurable (C4), no ex-ante regulation in contingent contracts is possible (Grandori 1997).

P4 There are other means of governance than governance by contract, as will be discussed in Chapter 4. But they entail costs of set-up, running and maintenance.

P5 To the extent that markets are turbulent (C4), with many exits and entries on markets, and there is rapid innovation (C5), the loss of flexibility is most serious, there is a chance that a more attractive partner appears on the scene and this increases risks of dependence and puts a strain on loyalty in existing relations.

P6 To the extent that ex-ante regulation is feasible, then apart from direct costs there may be opportunity costs of restricting the flexibility of collaboration.

P7 To the extent that competition is more intense (C10), there is greater pressure to utilize opportunities for opportunism, in switching to a new, more attractive partner, or using that opportunity for leverage in bargaining.

P8 To the extent that technology is systemic but not yet standardized (C7), and there is no innovation or innovation is incremental (rather than radical, C6), close coordination of component technologies is required.

there are opportunity costs: by regulating what is to be done one excludes not only undesirable but also desirable alternatives. An excessively control-oriented approach to governance may confirm or create suspicion and thereby ruin the basis for a build-up of trust and loyalty as an alternative basis for cooperation. This point needs some qualification. A modest amount of regulation will not destroy the basis for trust and may indeed help to establish it. P7 is illustrated with the following case.

Some time ago, we approached the company that exploits the Dutch gas reserves to discuss their supplier relations. From experience in the highly competitive car industry, we were explaining our approach to the issue in terms of benefits but also risks of dependence in specific investments due to possible opportunism. In the car industry we had been criticized for talk of 'trust and loyalty in lasting relations of co-makership'. Under the conditions of slump and excess capacity that prevailed at the time, there was cut-throat competition and suppliers were squeezed for the last penny. The people at the gas exploration and production company were puzzled at our parlance of the risk of opportunistic exploitation of dependence due to specific investments. They had very amicable, enduring and loyal give-and-take relations with their suppliers. Of course, they had a monopoly and were under no pressure to do otherwise.

P8 goes back to the discussion in Chapter 2 of systemic as opposed to stand-alone technologies (C7), such as materials (Willinger and Zuscovitch 1988) or telecommunication systems, which require integration across interfaces between components of the system and, in early stages of technology, when standards for such linkages have not yet been developed (C6), this requires close coordination. Furthermore, under incremental innovation (C5) close coordination is needed to keep innovation within the different parts in tune (Teece 1988; Langlois and Robertson 1995). However, the latter argument loses force when innovation is so radical as to exert 'creative destruction' on existing systems of component technologies.

PROBLEMS OF SPILLOVER

There are various problems related to spillover: the transfer of knowledge or other competence to an actual or potential competitor. They are summarized in Table 3.6.

The last problem (P11) may require discussion. It is related to the problem of spillover, but now from the perspective of the partners. The more partners

Table 3.6 Problems of spillover

P9	Risk of turning the partner into a new competitor because of the knowledge or other competence transferred to him, either by design or by accident.
P10	Risk that information given to one's partner spills over to an existing competitor, to the extent that the partner has direct or indirect linkages to competitors, the knowledge is documented, monitoring of spillover is not possible and speed of knowledge change is not radical (as discussed in Chapter 2).
P11	Threat to existing partners: an alliance partner may be a competitor of a partner in another alliance, in a network of cooperative relations and may thus pose a spillover threat to both.

there are, in different activities, the more there exists a spillover threat. Whenever a novel partner is contemplated one should consider the spillover risk presented to existing partners, in order to control the risk of destabilizing existing relations. This is probably why the Japanese *keiretsu* consist mainly of vertical, complementary relations between buyers and suppliers rather than horizontal relations between competitors. Next to the mainly vertical *keiretsu* there are other lateral and partly horizontal groups (*kigyo shudan*), but direct competitors mostly take part in different groups and competition occurs mainly between groups.

PROBLEMS OF INSTITUTIONS

Institutions have an important effect on transaction costs and opportunities for governance. They are summarized in Table 3.7.

In a society without clear laws and regulations, with corrupt, arbitrary or incompetent execution of laws, the importance of personal networks increases and they are expensive to set up. Especially under such conditions, relational competencies form an important part of entrepreneurship, as indicated in Chapter 1 where it was noted that in Italy entrepreneurs spend significantly more time in setting up and maintaining a network of personal relations than in other countries. This indicates a lack of reliable institutions that

Table 3.7 Problems of institutions

P12	When the legal infrastructure (laws, law enforcement, C1) is poor, legal governance may be very expensive or infeasible.
P13	When contractual attitudes are highly legalistic (C3), costs of legal governance may be excessive.
P14	When contractual attitudes are relational or personal and the moral order is familial, clan based, elitistic or religious sectarian (C2), entry barriers are high.
P15	Problems arise when voice-based and exit-based contractual attitudes meet.

seems related to the operation of the Mafia, which implants itself where laws are lacking or derelict. This effect can be expected to a stronger degree in the former communist countries.

Anthony Pagden (1988) gives an analysis of the breakdown of trust in the kingdom of Naples in the seventeenth and eighteenth century, when it belonged to the Habsburg empire of the Spanish King Carlos and later Philip II. The Spaniards opted for a cheap way to hold down the country from a distance by breaking down the social structure and culture of trust. In the Netherlands they had learned that sheer suppression does not suffice. For control from a distance the institutions of a society must be broken down in a strategy of 'divide and rule'. The nobility was divided by creating an upstart nobility that owed its position to the Spanish masters. These were given the task of collecting exorbitant taxes from which they could take a large share for themselves, provided that it be spent on idle, economically useless and politically harmless games such as duelling and defence of personal honour. This destroyed faith in the nobility as the defenders and personification of order and reliability. The characteristic of knightly honour, in contrast with honour in the sense of loyalty to the state, is that it relates to self-respect rather than a sense of community or state. The man of honour is his own law-giver. This contributed to the breakdown of the state. Trust in the state is based on public information on conduct, standards and procedures, so this was abolished. The critical role of the intelligentsia was destroyed by means of mystification and a relaxation of academic standards. Universities were obliged to continue the teaching of Aristotelian logic 'because it never accounted for anything'. Excessive attention to religious ceremony was required. The standards of the legal degree were dropped and it was also awarded as a token of honour to the upper classes, which contributed to the undermining of the legal system. Arbitrary and unpredictable exceptions to legal rules were granted. Through the oversupply of incompetent lawyers their price was lowered, yielding an excess of worthless and inconclusive litigation. The attention of the populace was distracted by frequent public feasts. Social ties were replaced by mutual suspicion and people were thrown back on themselves or close family. Trade became a game of mutual cheating. Exchange was reduced to immediate quid pro quo, without credit or investment. Gambetta (1988b) showed how this breakdown of institutions as a basis for trust in the kingdom of Naples, which included Sicily, allowed the Mafia to insinuate itself, to steal into the holes created by institutional breakdown and to install their perverse order to fill the vacuum. The first evidence of the Mafia as an established order is from 1838. The Mafia is connected with Sicily, but something similar developed in Naples, the Camorra.

Problems resulting from the conditions of institutions as well as those of the market and technology further determine to a large extent which goals of inter-firm relations are relevant. For example:

- When there are institutional problems (P12–15), when there is mismatch between contractual attitudes and institutions, or when there are entry barriers to markets (C10), the need for local partners is particularly strong, in order to enter the market. This is further reinforced when the product is amenable to differentiation (C9). Hence adaptation to the local market and intense competition (C10) stimulate such differentiation (Gc1).
- When the product concerned is not amenable to product differentiation (C9), then the goal of using a local partner for adaptation of the product (Gp5) is not relevant. A global strategy (same product in different countries) may be preferable, particularly if the technology entails economy of scale (C8) and competition is intense (C10). Then the focus shifts to the use of partners to achieve economy of scale or scope (Ga2, Ga3).
- In stable, saturated markets (C5) with high fixed and sunk costs of production (C7), partners may be needed to rationalize the industry (Ga1).
- In a turbulent environment, with radical innovation (C5) in an incipient or breakthrough stage (C6) (yielding radical uncertainty, C4), the focus shifts to the use of partners as varied sources of information (Gc3).

The question now is how the various problems can be solved by the choice of form or design of the alliance.

BASIC DESIGN PRINCIPLES

Several authors indicated that the literature exhibits a pro-governance bias, neglecting the fact that governance can be expensive and bothersome (P1–8) and is not needed when interests are well aligned and no problems of hold-up or free riding occur (Geringer and Hebert 1989; Lorange and Roos 1992; Grandori 1997). As was evident in classical TCE, if there are no transaction costs, a simple market mechanism suffices and no costs of organization or governance need to be incurred. Thus, an important design principle is that control or governance is not a goal for its own sake. One should restrict and focus governance on where it is needed.

Consider, for example, the paradigm case referred to by Grandori (1997) of a consortium for cooperative R&D in which each participant needs to realize his contribution to the full in order to be able to absorb the contribution by the others (Cohen and Levinthal 1990). This is a special case of joint production, which can be represented by a multiplicative structure of returns:

$$r_i = r_j = a.c_i.c_j \qquad (3.1)$$

where: i and j refer to different partners, r = return, c = contribution, a is some parameter. By decreasing one's contribution, one decreases one's own return as much as that of the partner, so that free riding (alternatively called 'shirking') is discouraged. A more detailed model is supplied in Appendix 3.2

But often a relationship will require relation specific investments and then the problem of governance does arise (P1–2). Basic design parameters are the following:

1   Degree of integration.
2   Number of participants: bilateral, trilateral or multilateral (networks).
3   Time perspective: short-time (project), experimental, long-term.
4   Mode of governance:
    • control: bureaucratic or legal regulation and monitoring;
    • loyalty: values/norms, habituation, family, kinship, friendship, clan;
    • value: extent and unicity of partner value;
    • binding: exit barriers, reputation, hostages.

When the base case or benchmark is separate firms, the set-up costs and corresponding exit costs (P1–8), are higher for greater levels of integration. Mergers and acquisitions require the merging of two cultures, with different conditions (e.g. in wage and work) and habits, which can be very risky, costly and lengthy. TCE has neglected the costs of merger and acquisition, because it has neglected that firms form cumulative, path-dependent and therefore, to some extent, idiosyncratic constellations of competence and culture, which may be difficult to integrate. One reason for the interest in JVs and NEAs as an alternative to mergers and acquisitions is the persistent evidence that the latter fail to yield added value as often or more than they succeed (Ravenscraft and Scherer 1986; Scherer 1988; Mueller 1989). Set-up costs are higher for a JV than for a non-equity alliance. They can be higher even than the costs of merger/acquisition, to the extent that in the JV people from different firms, with different cultures and work conditions, are brought together. Additional overhead costs have to be incurred for management and staff. In non-equity alliances, more elaborate governance costs more than simpler forms. As a solution to this, governance should only be instituted where it is needed (D1).

Agreements may of course be needed because without them costs due to misunderstanding, error and haggling can be high. Nevertheless, direct set-up costs are higher for greater levels of integration. Since exit barriers are higher under increased costs of organization or governance, higher levels of integration yield less flexibility of association. As noted before, there are well-known motivational advantages for the decentralization of ownership and control, with independent firms striving harder for efficiency and inno-vation (unless motivation is damped by monopoly or oligopoly and entry barriers). On the other hand, when close coordination and control is required, integration has advantages, as is well known from TCE. Decisions and conflict resolution do not have to be upheld in court, but can be based on administrative fiat and information needed for monitoring can be demanded far beyond that required from an outside firm. Control by integration is needed more to the extent that rivalry is greater, that is when partners are actual or potential direct competitors, i.e. have substitutive products or competencies rather than complementary ones.

The advantages of integration need some qualification. Inside a firm, administrative fiat and monitoring can have adverse effects on motivation; monitoring may be difficult, especially in professional work. It can lead to 'influence costs' (Milgrom and Roberts 1989): counterproductive meddling and jockeying for position to enhance careers. The transaction cost argu-ment has led to the claim that alliances with a dominant partner are more likely to be successful than alliances with a balance of power (Killing 1983 Anderson and Gatignon 1986). But the empirical evidence is not convincing and Geringer and Hebert (1989) offered the contrary argument that the dominated partner is ill-motivated to contribute, which has an adverse effect on performance. In their study of 49 cross-border alliances, Bleeke and Ernst found that of those with a majority holding, 31 per cent succeeded, and of those with an even stake, 60 per cent succeeded.

Williamson (1985) proposed that disintegration in the form of outsourcing yields advantages of scale (provided that production is not too specific), but the argument is not convincing. One can attain equal economy of scale by 'insourcing': producing for the entire relevant market oneself and selling off what is not needed for own production (Nooteboom 1993a). Williamson (1985: 92, footnote 8) recognized that this is logically possible, but argued that it will not occur because it is likely to mean that one sells to a competitor (since it is someone using the same input) and competitors are not willing to become dependent on rivals for their supplies. But this is the kind of argument that rejects problematic but interesting relations too easily. The problem can be circumvented, e.g. by symmetric, bilateral dependence, so that parties mutually hold each other hostage and thereby reduce risks of dependence. In any case, the argument is contradicted by the fact that in the aircraft industry rivals supply different parts of aircraft bodies to each other.

Concerning the number of partners, the spectrum of possibilities is indicated in Figure 3.1. There is a considerable variety of roles in franchising, consortia, associations, etc. There can be large similarity between participants, as in an association of similar firms that pool some common interest, or different roles, as in a consortium of firms with complementary competencies to produce a product for an outside party. There can be a supervisory agency with centralized decision rights for technical coordination or control of free riding, with distributed residual rights, as in franchising. There are roles for a third party to mediate between two protagonists. This will be analysed later, in Chapter 4. The number of partners is also important with a view to spillover problems (P11). Appendix 3.2 gives a simple game-theoretic model to determine the optimal number of partners, in view of the interest of all to maximize their own number of partners, in order to maximize sources of competence or support and minimize their partner's number of partners, to minimize risk of spillover. The result is perhaps not of much operational value, but it highlights the issues involved.

In the case of an association, for example for the purpose of political representation, joint advertising or the joint institution of a quality system, the number of participants can typically be large since there is no exchange of sensitive information and therefore no need to limit the numbers to control spillover.

The time perspective is important with a view to governance. As we know from game theory (Axelrod 1984), there is the phenomenon of the 'shadow of the future'. Relations with a future perspective elicit greater restraint of opportunism, in a trade-off between short-time gain from defection and the (present value of) a potential future stream of benefits from an ongoing relation (Heide and Miner 1992). Furthermore, as a relationship develops, habitualization may increase and trust may grow (Gulati 1995). The basic design principles indicated so far are summarized in Table 3.8.

Table 3.8 Basic design principles

D1	Control or governance is not a goal for its own sake: governance should be restricted and focused on where it is needed.
D2	Advantages of integration and disintegration.

Integration	*Disintegration*
Decision by fiat	Market incentive
Ease of monitoring	Flexibility of association
Ease of coordination	Variety of knowledge
Control of spillover	Lower costs and risks of set-up

D3	The number of partners requires a compromise between maximum number of sources and minimum risk of spillover.
D3	Shadow of the future: relations with a future perspective elicit greater restraint of opportunism.

Finally, the structure of a relation is characterized by the mode of governance employed: control, loyalty, value and binding. These are derived from a control model developed by Nooteboom (1996), which will be discussed in Chapter 4. From the basic principles one can derive more specific guidelines to steer the choice between a merger or acquisition (MA) versus other forms (JV, NEA) and to choose between a JV and a NEA. These are given in the next two sections.

MERGERS OR ACQUISITIONS?

Recently there has been a wave of MA in many sectors of both industry and services: banks among each other, banks and insurance companies, large accountant firms, pharmaceuticals. Reasons adduced for this are mostly economy of scale and scope (Ga1–4, Table 3.1), such as sharing fixed costs and risks in distribution channels, ICT networks or R&D.

In banking, an increase in efficiency can, for example, be achieved by eliminating one of two branch offices (or automatic teller machines) in locations where both banks are represented. Fixed costs in specialized knowledge of specific industries and in setting up ICT networks and databases can be shared. Reserves to cover risks of defaulting customers can be shared and spread. In an MA between banking and insurance there are economies of scope in the utilization of branch offices, ICT networks, advertising and customer relations. In MAs in banking, insurance and accounting an important motive also is the building of a worldwide network of offices from different companies pooling their offices in different continents, in order to yield global service to global customers.

But the question to be asked here is not whether there were reasons for the MA, but whether alternative forms of pooling resources might be better. Given the reasons that may arise for some form of pooling, as specified in Table 3.1, the question now is what form is best, given aims and conditions. Arguments for and against mergers/acquisitions are given in Table 3.9. In discussion of the table, attention is first given to the arguments for an MA and then to the arguments for the alternatives, an alliance in the form of a JV or NEA.

A consideration of efficiency that favours the MA is that the costs are avoided of setting up a new company, with its own offices, facilities, management and control, etc. Another consideration is that an MA may be needed to eliminate differences in ways of doing things and a culture that would obstruct cooperation between separate companies. However, the question is whether this will succeed. Several studies indicate that at best 50 per cent of MAs are

Table 3.9 Advantages of merger/acquisition or alliances

Aspect	Merger or acquisition (MA)	Joint venture (JV) or non-equity alliance (NEA)
Assets/efficiency	Save set-up costs of JV	Candidate for MA not available, too big, inseparable
	Integrate conflicting procedures	Prevent risks of cultural integration
		MA candidate difficult to evaluate
		Maintain existing brand name, access to sources
		Maintain autonomy for motivation
Competencies	Protect against 'spillover'	Maintain focus on core competencies
	More flexibility in other contacts	More diversity of sources for learning
Positional advantages Politics		Maintain local identity, legitimation
Strategic behaviour	Limit transaction costs in specific investments, by increased control	Maintain flexibility of combinations
	Prevent conflicting interests among direct competitors or the emergence of a new competitor	
	Prevent takeover of partner by a competitor, or of a competitor by a partner	
	Prevent free riding	
	Protect brand name, reputation	
Indication for choice	If competence of partner is part of own core competence and there is geographical overlap of markets	If competence of partner is complementary or there is geographical separation of markets

successful and that failure is mostly due to incompatibility of routines or culture (Ravenscraft and Scherer 1986; Scherer 1988; Mueller 1989).

The Dutch steel corporation ('Hoogovens') long ago undertook a merger with a German colleague. After ten years of struggle it was broken up again, because attempts to integrate the two companies remained unsuccessful. In 'Hoogovens' there are still two rival camps of those who supported the merger and are reproached that the failure is all their fault and the opponents who are blamed for having sabotaged the merger.

From the perspective of the resource–competence view, discussed in Chapter 1, this does not come as a surprise. Competencies are embedded in tacit knowledge of people and teams, in organizational structure, procedures, habits, routines and culture, which over the years have developed during interaction with the specific environment and conditions of the firm. It is very naive to think that these can be disentangled and turned into explicit, documented knowledge and reconfigured into a new, shared pattern of action. Organizations are not so easily composable. They are not made but are the outcome of an evolutionary process. One cannot make an instantaneous cross between a camel and racehorse.

Why do mergers and acquisitions occur so often in spite of their obvious frequency of failure? One reason is that in addition to the considerations of efficiency, governance and complementarity included in Table 3.9, there are also private interests of management: considerations of prestige, status, career, share value and managerial income (often connected to share value through share options). There also appears to be a 'prisoner's dilemma' mechanism: while everyone would be better off with fewer mergers and acquisitions, everyone considers the loss of position that would occur if they did not participate in the MA game while their competitors did. To prevent this happening there is a rush to be first. It is a game of taking over or being taken over. In other words MAs are often not supported by good arguments of efficiency, governance or complementarity (Schenk 1997).

Further anomalies occur for institutional reasons. National airlines cannot be taken over for reasons of national prestige which require the maintenance of a national airline, so other forms of cooperation have to be sought. By contrast, mergers and acquisitions in banking are sometimes due to the fact that for reasons of financial stability there are obstacles to banks entering bankruptcy, whereby the failure of inefficient firms to survive in the selection environment of the market is obstructed. Mergers or takeovers are often conducted to eliminate inefficiencies by shedding less productive assets and staff on the grounds that, due to the pooling of the two firms, they are now redundant. For reasons of economy of scale or scope that argument is plausible.

Arguments concerning the control of strategic behaviour reflect the importance of transaction cost considerations in the need to govern risks of dependence due to specific investments and problems of monitoring and control. This yields an argument, but not necessarily a conclusive one, for integration in a single firm and hence a preference for a merger or acquisition, in order to control strategic behaviour when interests are in conflict. This will be the case especially when products or activities are substitutive rather than complementary; when partners are engaged in the same activities in the same place. Another potential problem is that of free riding and the connected problem of protecting brand name and reputation.

In franchising the franchiser supplies goods, methods and brand name to franchisees who operate at their own profit and risk. There is a potential problem of free riding. While it is in the collective interest of franchisees to make an effort to maintain the good name of the brand, individual franchisees may be tempted to free ride on the efforts of the others. It is one of the tasks of the franchiser to deal with this problem by the monitoring of effort. Another measure might be an entry fee that the franchisee pays which is not refunded if he exits before some contracted period. The entry fee then acts as an exit barrier, which disciplines the franchisee to make an effort and maintain his customer base. But this only works to the extent that customers are not footloose and their decision to buy is to a considerable extent based on local experience with a single franchisee.

The franchising case shows that free riding can be fought without full integration. But in some cases it cannot be, for example, when monitoring of effort is impossible. Full integration will be needed in R&D cooperation if partners can benefit from each other's efforts without putting in effort themselves. This cannot be observed without full integration to enable direct supervision. However, rather than fully integrating two or more companies, this purpose could be served by means of a JV or an R&D consortium with shared monitoring of efforts.

Another class of arguments for integration relates to spillover risks. As already discussed, integration may be needed to control spillover when the knowledge involved is documented (rather than tacit), speed of knowledge change is not 'radical' and spillover cannot be monitored without integration. But there is also an argument of maintaining access to other contacts. This derives from the spillover risk presented to one's partners: for fear of spillover they may object to cooperation with their competitors. It may be that the new contact is so important that it is necessary to overrule the existing partner by takeover if there is no concession. Note, however, that by the same logic there is also a potential problem with MA. With an MA it will be necessary to review existing network relations of both partners to see if it entails novel connections with competitors of partners that present spillover risks.

Now attention is turned to the arguments for the alternative of a JV or NEA. One set of arguments concerns efficiency and feasibility. While it would be preferable to engage in an MA, there may be no fitting partner available, or it is not affordable because it is too big, or one is interested only in part of another firm which cannot be pried loose. Another argument is that it is not possible to evaluate the true worth of a takeover candidate. This is related to Arrow's paradox of information, discussed before. An intermediate stage of alliance may be necessary in order to assess the value of the candidate before taking it over. An example would be the temporary JV in 'white goods' between the Philips company and Whirlpool. Other arguments of efficiency are that it is often better to evade the problems of integrating two different cultures and to maintain the motivation of independence by leaving existing competencies intact and independent as much as possible (taking into account whether the technology is systemic or standalone).

> One often sees large or medium-sized firms growing 'externally', by taking over successful small innovative firms. For several reasons new small firms often take the wilder risks of more fundamentally new combinations, while the larger bureaucratic firms hold back until success is proven and then take over (Nooteboom 1994). This is not necessarily bad from a societal perspective or even the perspective of the small firm. It can yield a solution to obstacles to growth in such successfully entrepreneurial firms. However, the danger is that, rather than the outside entrepreneurial spirit energizing the large host firm, the reverse happens: it gets bogged down in the bureaucracy of the host.

An argument from political and commercial considerations is that by taking over a company one may destroy its local identity or legitimation, which should be maintained for the sake of political or market acceptance.

Concerning strategic behaviour, an important and obvious consideration, discussed before, is that with looser connections one maintains more flexibility of connection. It is easier to stop and disentangle cooperation between different firms than to hive off part of an integrated firm. For institutional reasons the latter is more difficult in Europe, for example, than it is in the USA.

Concerning policy regarding competencies, the arguments have already been discussed extensively. An MA is often not attractive because it brings along competencies that are not relevant, i.e. do not contribute to strengthening of core competencies. As argued extensively in the discussion of the theory of learning used in this book (Chapter 1), cooperation with a variety of sources, while maintaining weak rather than strong ties, enhances especially radical innovation. It maintains a wider range of components from which to create novel combinations. By integration and strong ties competencies converge and information becomes redundant. A final argument in favour of a JV or NEA is that it allows for the maintenance of an independent brand name and product identity or, in other words, prevents the dilution of a brand name or an incompatibility between brand names that might arise under an MA. It is possible to maintain separate brand names in an MA, but dilution, mutual contagion or conflict may be difficult to prevent. A final consideration in favour of a JV or NEA, indicated in Table 3.9, is the maintenance of access to other sources. It evades possible conflicts of interest concerning spillover in the networks of the partners that might arise under a MA.

Summing up, one can say that, generally speaking, an MA is preferred when partners have the same core competencies and use them for the same activities at the same locations. Then potential conflict is highest, requiring more centralized monitoring and control. Also, since activities are the same, the argument against an MA in order to stick to core competencies and to maintain flexibility of combinations with other complementary activities is weakest. As competitors they are also likely to have the same shared competitors, so the argument against an MA in view of possible network conflicts (creation of novel spillover problems) is also weakest. Problems of integration are also least since the similarity between the partners is greatest (having similar core competencies). Since the takeover candidate is similar, its value is also relatively easy to assess. Conversely, alliances other than MA are difficult when they involve the same products in the same markets.

> The argumentation is supported by an empirical investigation of 49 alliances by Bleeke and Ernst (1991: 131). Of alliances (i.e. non-MA) in different markets, 75 per cent were a success, versus 43 per cent of alliances in the same market. Also, Hagedoorn and Schakenraad (1994) found that 75 per cent of unrelated MAs failed.

What should be done if, on the basis of these considerations an alliance is favoured but it entails such high transaction costs that it is difficult? In extreme cases this can imply that one needs to opt for MA anyway, but the first priority will be to see if the problems can be solved without full integration. Thus we return to the core of this book: how can alliances be governed, while maintaining maximum independence, in spite of high transaction costs? This is the subject of Chapter 4.

In view of the analysis, do the MAs indicated at the beginning of this section, in banking, accounting and pharmaceuticals, stand up to scrutiny? To the extent that the firms involved were offering the same product to the same market segment at the same place, they are direct rivals and the logic set out before indicates that a merger or acquisition may indeed be the preferred form. But do these conditions apply so strictly? Could the accountant firms have pooled their complementary office networks in different continents, without an MA, in some NEA where they share methods and information jointly to provide the global service required for global customers? Or would that entail too great a risk of spillover of core competence in locations where they compete? Was full integration in an MA necessary to align procedures?

This would seem necessary only if the knowledge involved was highly tacit, but accounting procedures are sufficiently documented to be turned into computer software. In fact, because of this situation accountants are losing their professional core competence and are moving more into consulting. Does that, then, require integration for alignment of competence and protection of spillover? Regarding the pharmaceutical companies, could they not achieve their aim of pooling risk by joint R&D, in R&D consortia or joint ventures, combined with cross-licensing? Or has the choice of an MA been determined or influenced by less rational considerations such as blind imitation with lack of consideration of alternatives, or the prisoner's dilemma game of taking over to prevent being taken over, perhaps with personal career motives of CEOs to protect their jobs and expand their power?

JV OR NEA?

If the choice is an alliance rather than an MA, how is the choice made between a JV and an NEA? To a considerable extent, a JV can be considered as an intermediate form between an MA and an NEA, as is illustrated in Figure 3.1 which indicates that the choice lies along the lines indicated in the previous section. The arguments are summarized in Table 3.10.

Table 3.10 Arguments for JV or NEA

Aspect	Joint venture	Non-equity alliance
Assets		
Efficiency	More identity of a separate firm	Save costs of setting up and running a separate firm
Competencies/positional advantages	Control spillover	More diversity for learning
Strategic behaviour	Control of conflict of interest	Flexibility in change and extension
	Shielding from other activities	
	Block takeover of partner by competitor	

Concerning efficiency, an NEA is the most attractive: a JV brings high costs of the set-up of a separate firm. Also, although to a lesser extent than in the case of an MA, in a JV problems will be encountered in the integration of different ways of doing things, institutions and culture.

Well-known problems occur in personnel matters. For example, does one give staff allotted to the JV a guarantee of return to the mother company? If not, one may not be able to find staff willing to take the step. If one does, then this may detract from their motivation and commitment to the JV. They may act more as guardians of the interests of the mother company than those of the JV. There are also often problems of differences in pay scales and other benefits and promotion policy for similar jobs which can create dissent.

On the other hand, when the integration of staff from the parent is successful, a JV offers a stronger sense of identity, which may enhance motivation of staff and recognition in the market.

Also, a higher degree of integration from a JV is indicated when it is necessary to control conflicts of interest, as a result of actual or potential competition, dependence due to specific investments, or to control spillover. Less integration in an NEA is indicated especially when flexibility and learning are crucial due to turbulence of markets and/or technology.

However, a JV can better shield the new joint activity from spillover to other departments of the parents, or participants in their networks that are actual or potential competitors. Network partners can be better reassured that the cooperation will not lead to spillover because of the JV shield.

If there exists a sufficient share of ownership then takeover of the activity by a competitor can be blocked. But one cannot, as in the case of an MA, prevent the partner from taking over a competitor.

The risk of a partner being taken over in an NEA is illustrated in the case of two producers of garden equipment in Sweden and Norway ('Norpartner and Swedpartner'), discussed by Lorange and Roos (1992). A third party that competed with them both in Sweden and Norway, took over the owner of Swedpartner and ended its alliance with Norpartner, which in the meantime had become so dependent on the alliance that it went bankrupt. In this way the third party eliminated two competitors at one stroke.

Of course, there are many forms of NEA, as Figure 3.1 demonstrates: there are many intermediate forms of more or less integration. So, beyond the relatively simple choice between MA, JV and NEA, there are further choices between alternative forms of NEA. For this, a further, more detailed and sophisticated analysis is required.

MORE DETAILED ANALYSIS

Some examples of a more detailed analysis are now supplied, for specific combinations of goals (strategy; G) and conditions (context; C) to yield solutions (S) of problems (P). Even those still constitute generic cases. Intermediate cases require even more detailed evaluation. The purpose is not to give solutions for all conceivable situations, but rather the contrary: to show that often generic rules are too simplistic and more specific solutions should be made to measure, given specific goals and conditions.

Case 1

Goals: The goal is to utilize complementary resources (Ga5, Gc2, Gc3) or to achieve market entry (Gp1–7), with partners that are not competitors (so that there is no need to integrate in order to control competition).

Conditions: Technology is systemic (C7) and innovation is absent or cumulative (not radical, C6), so that coordination is crucial (P8). There is no problem of spillover (either because the goal is not to innovate, or because appropriability is secure, C7). There are no significant problems of dependence due to exit barriers from specific investments. Knowledge is not so tacit as to exclude specification of required products (C7). There is no uncertainty or excessive complexity or variability and outputs of effort or inputs and preferences are measurable (C4), so that contingent contracting is feasible. There are no other obstacles to contracting (P12, P13, P14). Then:

S1:   Choose a disintegrated structure with contingent contracts (Grandori 1997). Example: a building consortium.

But: When complexity and stochasticity become excessive and complete contracts become infeasible, then:

S2:   Some centralization of decisions and monitoring becomes necessary (Grandori 1997). Example: consortium for building a refinery, with project management by one of the participants.

But: If there are no competent partners and/or contingent contracts cannot be specified (uncertainty or unmeasurability of outputs and inputs and preferences of contributors P3; tacit knowledge P2; problems of legal infrastructure and contractual attitudes P12–15), then:

S3:   Engage in full integration. For example: in Russia at the moment sometimes outside collaboration cannot reliably be set up.

Note, however, that even when the conditions of S1 are satisfied, contracts will never be complete since some elements will always remain tacit, if only because one cannot keep on defining the terms of definitions. At some point this has to stop in the hope that sufficient common understanding has been reached. One can stop earlier to the extent that common understanding is greater. Furthermore, any cooperation entails a greater or lesser degree of socialization in a 'community of practice' (Brown and Duguid 1991), constituting a relation-specific investment which yields an exit barrier to some extent. Thus, when collaboration is successful, a preference will arise for continued collaboration.

Next, the problem of spillover is analysed more systematically and in more detail.

Case 2

Goals: Learning (Gc3), utilize complementary resources (Gc2).
Conditions: Knowledge is documented (rather than tacit, C7) and the speed of development is not radical (C5), then:
S4:   More integration yields better control of spillover, but:
S5:   Under conditions of radical speed of change, outside partners are needed to yield the requisite variety of knowledge. This entails no problem of spillover to the extent that the knowledge involved is either tacit or subject to radical change.

Case 3

Goals: Learning (Gc3), utilize complementary resources for novel combinations (Gc2).
Conditions: Incipient, radical innovation and radical speed (C5, C6), uncertainty (C4).
S6:   Industrial districts, virtual firms.

The argument is as follows. In radical innovation, systemic connections between component technologies break down, so that coordination across interfaces is not relevant, either for production, incremental innovation or diffusion. Varied sources of learning and variability of association are crucial. Under conditions of radical speed of change, outside partners are needed to yield the requisite variety of knowledge. This entails no problem of spillover to the extent that the knowledge involved is either tacit or subject to radical speed of change.

Case 4

Goals: Differentiated products (Gc1), learning (Gc3), utilize complementary resources (Gc2), market entry (Gp1–7),
Conditions: Exit barriers due to specific assets (C7), as a result of the goals, in production or development; contractual problems (P12–15), then:

S7: More integration to the extent that exit barriers are higher (P2). Monitoring requires close supervision (P3). Conditions for contracts are difficult (P12–15). Knowledge is tacit (P2). Risk of creating a new competitor is higher (P9). Threat to existing partners (P11) and behavioural uncertainty (P5) are higher.

S8: When in a vertical buyer–supplier, non-equity alliance the supplier unilaterally has to incur specific assets for the benefit of the buyer, the buyer should participate in their ownership.

MANAGEMENT OF ALLIANCES

In the previous sections it was shown that less integrated forms yield advantages of lower costs of set-up, organization and management, more flexibility and learning potential, but create problems to the extent that there is a threat of conflict of interest due to (potential) competition or dependence due to specific investments. The latter may require integration, with a JV as an intermediate step between an NEA and an MA. But one can try, for the sake of flexibility and learning, to solve the problems of cooperation between firms under separate ownership. This is analysed in detail in Chapter 4. It will be shown that the basic variables in the analysis of the management of alliances are:

- value of the partner relative to existing alternatives;
- costs of switching to an alternative;
- room for opportunism by the partner, left by incomplete contractual agreements and limitations in the monitoring of partner's activities ('information asymmetry');
- inclinations to use such opportunities, depending on incentives of self-interest (one's own dependence on the relation, protection of reputation or hostages) and inclinations towards opportunism (trustworthiness), depending on ethics, norms, values, habits, bonds, feelings of loyalty, friendship, kinship.

The analysis will yield four basic forms of management of alliances, summarized in Table 3.11.

Problems can be prevented by *opening*: not binding oneself and keeping options open towards equivalent partners. Here problems are solved by avoidance, but at a sacrifice in value. If ownership in specific investments is avoided, to prevent dependence, and all options are kept open, then the partner is not likely to commit himself and make specific investments and the added value of the relationship will remain limited. There will be lack of quality in the sense of conformance to specific demands, because these would require specific investments.

One can engage the risk of dependence by *binding*: go for symmetry in dependence by symmetry of ownership of specific assets or hostages, or some

Table 3.11 Forms of management

Form	Description
Opening	Keep options open; evade dependence
Binding	Commit the partner by increasing his share in specific investments, take hostages
Control	Limit room for opportunism by (partial) integration or contracts
Incentives	Limit incentives to opportunism by increasing partner's dependence or by a reputation mechanism
Loyalty	limit inclination to opportunism through norms, values, habits, bonds of friendship or kinship

combination of them. Incomplete distribution of ownership of specific assets can be complemented by exchange of hostages.

Figure 3.1 indicates the option of a minority participation. In Japan, for example, exchange takes place of small packages of shares (cross-participation). What is the use of this if share ownership is not large enough to achieve significant control? Perhaps this can be interpreted as exchange of hostages, as admitted by the Japanese 'Agency for Economic Planning', in a 1992 document (Scher 1996: 17).

Binding does not solve problems of potential competition, with partners having the same core competencies and the same products in the same markets. These problems require more integration, in a strategy of control: integration, hierarchy and contractual arrangements. The disadvantages of this approach include the following:

- it costs money for reorganization or contracts;
- integration tends to reduce motivation;
- contracts reduce flexibility of activities in the relationship and can produce a straightjacket that constrains innovation;
- it reduces flexibility of relational patterns;
- it yields a smaller variety of ideas and insights as sources of learning;
- it can lead to a vicious circle of distrust and regulation.

Risk of dependence can be limited by incentives of self-interest: reputation, the partner's own dependence on the relation. The latter is based on the fact that one offers high relative value to the partner, which yields an alternative to the strategy of binding by switching costs, as a means to commit the partner.

Finally, opportunities for opportunistic behaviour do not necessarily lead to opportunistic conduct: this depends on loyalty, as a function of ethics, norms, values, habits, bonding by friendship or kinship. But loyalty is seldom absolute and is vulnerable to the temptation of a golden opportunity and needs of survival under fierce competition or disaster. Loyalty is not an instrument in the sense that it can be installed like some machine. If not already present, it must grow and it is as much the outcome as the basis of a relationship. One can take this into account in the choice of partner; e.g. by entering business with a friend or relative. But such a choice can blind one to the risks of opportunism. Not everyone is able to resist opportunities or pressures if they become large enough.

The different forms of management can be combined, but the consistency of the mix should be carefully considered. If there is asymmetry in relative value, the least dependent partner may afford a greater share of ownership in specific assets, thus achieving symmetry in overall dependence. But tight control may obstruct the growth of trust. It is quite possible that, even in the presence of highly transaction-specific investments and potential competition, cooperation can be achieved without integration by some combination of mutual dependence, binding and loyalty. A more detailed analysis is given in the next chapter.

A much debated issue in the literature on alliances is whether a clear dominance of one side over the other is or is not better than balance of ownership or authority. The argument against symmetry is that it yields uncertainty about who makes the quick decisions needed in emergencies and too much effort is dissipated in squabbles concerning authority (Killing 1983; Anderson and Gatignon 1986). The argument against dominance by one side is that the dominated party will be insufficiently motivated and committed and less inclined to engage in specific investments (Geringer and Hebert 1989). On the basis of the preceding analysis, I am inclined to the latter view: in general, a balanced interest, with symmetric dependence, is the best.

This view appears to be supported by the survey of 49 international alliances by Bleeke and Ernst (1991), which indicated that of alliances with majority decision rights 31 per cent were successful, against 60 per cent of cases with balanced control.

But a more detailed analysis is required. A distinction should be made between decision rights and ownership rights that give a share in profit, which also lies at the basis of Figure 3.1. One can concentrate decision rights for the sake of efficiency of decision-making, while spreading profit for the sake of motivation. Thus, in a building consortium there will often be the need for a clear coordinator, but all participants maintain their motivation by a share in revenues. To this one can add the notion of redistributing the ownership of specific assets as a measure to stabilize a relation, as discussed previously. Much depends also on whether efforts and achievements are observable and measurable. The general principle applies that if someone's performance is not observable, he should have a share in the profits. An example is share options for management in large companies.

> Another example is the durability of a taxi. The vehicle is sensitive to the driver's handling, which is difficult to monitor by a central owner. So it makes sense for the driver to be the owner and therefore motivated to treat the taxi with care.

In this section some main lines were indicated for the management of alliances. A much more detailed analysis is given in the next chapter.

APPENDIX 3.1 POSITIONING OF ALLIANCE FORMS

The assumptions and calculations underlying Figure 3.1 are summarized in Table A3.1.1. H indicates the Herfindahl index of concentration.

Table A3.1.1 Positioning of forms

Alliance form	Number of part.	Asset range	Asset distr.	Horizont. H	Horizont. score	Activity range	Activity distr.	Vertical H	Vertical score
Association	100	1%	Equal	0.01	0.001	5%	80% central	0.64	0.032
Licensing	2	1%	80% licensee	0.68	0.007	5%	80% licensee	0.64	0.032
Ind. district	10	70%	Equal	0.1	0.07	100%	Equal	0.1	0.1
Virtual firm	10	70%	50% central	0.3	0.3	100%	Equal	0.1	0.1
Keiretsu	30	100%	50% owned by three	0.19	0.19	100%	50% by three	0.19	0.19
Co-makership	2	40%	Equal	0.5	0.2	50%	Equal	0.5	0.25
OEM production	2	40%	80–20	0.68	0.27	50%	80–20	0.68	0.34
Franchise	100	10%	Central	1.0	0.1	50%	80% Central	0.64	0.32
Retail chain	100	100%	Central	1.0	1.0	80%	Central	0.64	0.64
Build. consortium	5	90%	Equal	0.2	0.18	90%	50% Central	0.375	0.34
Purchase coop.	50	20%	Equal	0.02	0.004	50%	60% Central	0.64	0.38
Traditional supply	30	10%	Central	1.0	0.1	50%	Central	1.0	0.5
Balanced JV	2	100%	50–50	0.5	0.5	100%	50–50	0.5	0.5
Dominated JV	2	100%	80–20	0.68	0.68	100%	80–20	0.68	0.68
Minority part.	2	100%	90–10	0.82	0.82	100%	90–10	0.82	0.82
Centralized single Owner firm	1	100%	Central	1.0	1.0	100%	central	1.0	1.0
divisionalized	10	100%	Central	1.0	1.0	100%	40%	0.23	0.23
Holding cy.	10	100%	Central	1.0	1.0	100%	10% Central	0.11	0.11
Central. firm with with large bank holding	2	100%	30–70	0.58	0.58	100%	10–90	0.92	0.92
Central. firm with dispersed owners	1000	100%	equal	0	0	100%	90% central	0.81	0.81

APPENDIX 3.2 FREE RIDING

As discussed in the main text, a potential problem in cooperation in development or learning is 'free riding' or 'shirking'. Players may be tempted to free ride on the efforts of partners by benefiting from their efforts without making a full contribution. This problem arises when others' efforts are difficult to monitor. This tends to be the case in joint R&D between different firms. The reason to cooperate is that the partner has something to contribute which one cannot contribute oneself. It is therefore difficult to assess whether the partner is contributing to the full extent of his competence. The problem turns into a prisoner's dilemma when one-sided cooperation has a worse pay-off than mutual non-cooperation. This may well be the case as a result of spillover: if I transfer results from my R&D to a partner, it may carry the price of spilling over via the partner to a direct competitor.

Several solutions are conceivable. One is that absorption capacity is required in order to utilize knowledge or know-how from a partner. In order to build and maintain that capacity, one needs to fulfil one's own contribution to the joint R&D. A second but logically equivalent solution is that collaboration takes the form of joint production of new knowledge or competence: if one withholds one's contribution, no result will be obtained. Joint production and the need to contribute in order to achieve requisite absorption capacity occur especially when the knowledge produced is tacit. The production of new knowledge or competence entails intensive interaction, in learning by doing together.

Another solution is the redistribution of pay-offs by side payments: players pay for what they receive. A complication here is this: if the partner is supposed to repay part of the benefit that he receives, how is this determined in order to monitor compliance?

There is also the well-known solution from repeated games: when cooperation is ongoing and one's lack of cooperation becomes manifest with some delay, non-cooperation may jeopardize the returns from future cooperation.

All these elements can be combined in one game-theoretic model, as follows. The pay-off function is:

$$RET_i = -c_i.TRAN_i + s_{ij}.r_{ji}.TRAN_i + (1-s_{ji}).r_{ij}.TRAN_j + p_i.TRAN_i.TRAN_j \qquad \text{(A3.2.1)}$$

where: i and j index transaction partners

RET_i = utility/return of the exchange to i.

$TRAN_i$ = contribution (transfer of competence) from i.

c_i = unit cost to i of his contribution (mainly due to risk of spillover).

r_{ij} = stand-alone utility per unit to i of the contribution from j (and vice versa for r_{ji}).

s_{ij} = share of utility of i's contribution to j (r_{ji}) that j repays to i (and vice versa for s_{ji}).

pi = utility per unit to i of joint production of knowledge; teamwork. The multiplicative specification expresses the notion of both joint production and the need to contribute in order to be able to absorb the partner's contribution. In either case the return is zero if one's own contribution is zero.

Now, for simplicity, suppose that the partners have the choice of contributing (cooperation; $TRANi = 1$) or not (defection; $TRANi = 0$). The pay-off matrix of that game, in strategic form, is specified in Table A3.2.1. Utility of knowledge from partners (r) is high to the extent that advanced competence is important for survival and the field of requisite competence is complex and changing. Risk of spillover (c) is determined by several factors. When knowledge is more tacit, the risk is lower than when it is codified. The risk is lower to the extent that knowledge is embodied in teams, procedures, organizational structure or culture. Then one may be able to observe what a firm is doing, but fail to grasp the underlying logic and causality ('causal ambiguity', Lippman and Rumelt 1982). Typically the two go together: tacit knowledge is often embodied in elements of organization. Typically competence is embodied in the heads or hands of people, or in practices and routines developed by teams rather than in the form of blueprints or other documents. In that case exchange takes the form of employees from one company being stationed temporarily at the partner. Spillover would result from either buy-outs of such people or teams, or imitation, which accrues only after time and may be hampered by causal ambiguity.

Risk of spillover also depends on the presence of direct or indirect linkages to competitors. Thus the risk is higher, ceteris paribus, in horizontal rather than vertical relations. It depends on the number of partners, because then the chance is higher that there will be competitors among those partners. Spillover can be limited by 'technologies of monitoring'. If one can trace what happens to the competence supplied to the partner, in any subsequent diffusion in the partner's network one can demand control of diffusion by the partner and monitor his compliance. For example, if with the input of

Table A3.2.1 Cooperation in learning

		PARTNER 1	
		$TRAN1 = 1$; cooperate	$TRAN1 = 0$; defect
P A R T N E R 2	$TRAN2 = 1$ cooperate	$1{:}{-}c1 + s12.r21 + (1{-}s21).r12 + p1$ $2{:}{-}c2 + s21.r12 + (1{-}s12).r21 + p2$	$1{:}(1{-}s21).r12$ $2{:}{-}c2 + s21.r12$
	$TRAN2 = 0$ defect	$1{:}{-}c1 + s12.r21$ $2{:}(1{-}s12).r21$	0 0

competence that forms part of one's competitive advantage, one develops a specific component in collaboration with a supplier on the condition that it may not be used for other customers, if that component shows up in a competitor's product, one can blame the supplier for not complying. It is then important to design a technology of monitoring with sharp focus that sorts out what really belongs to the core of one's distinctive competence. If it is too coarse, the ban on diffusion will detract too much from the value of competence transfer to the partner.

Joint production (p) may take the form of more informal joint projects of development or more formal joint ventures. There will be a greater degree of formality and integration to the extent that cooperation does not follow directly from self-interest, and monitoring and control are necessary.

First, let us assume that there is no joint production ($p = 0$), so that cooperation takes the form of mere exchange of knowledge or competence. Suppose further that:

$$s_{ij}.r_{ji} > c_i \qquad\qquad (A3.2.2)$$

In other words: if partners repay each other a share (s_{ij}) of the benefit of information received (r_{ji}), sufficient to offset risk of spillover (c_i), then cooperation dominates defection. Note that there are two ways to approach this: repay a high share (high s_{ij}) or give guarantees against spillover (low c_i). If the condition is not satisfied, then if i cooperates, defection by j will yield less revenue than if i defects. Note also that this mechanism may solve the monitoring problem that it is difficult to judge the value of transfer to the partner. To get collaboration going it is in the partner's interest to offset my risk of spillover by a sufficient side payment from the benefit that he receives.

In case of joint production of knowledge, the partner will not be tempted to defect, so that mutual cooperation constitutes a Nash equilibrium, if:

$$s_{ij}.r_{ji} + p_i > c_i \qquad\qquad (A3.2.3)$$

To the extent that joint development is more formalized, it may also help to close off avenues of spillover, so that two means are merged: jointness of production ($p > 0$) and control of spillover (low c). This may explain the fact that joint ventures are increasingly popular, in spite of the fact that they consume additional resources in setting up and monitoring management of the joint venture. It may be preferred to the alternatives of, in one direction, merger/acquisition and, in another direction, informal collaboration, as follows:

1   More maintenance of dissimilarity of competence, compared with mergers and acquisitions.
2   More control of spillover than in more informal forms of collaboration.

If there is no utility of joint production of new knowledge ($pi = 0$), then (A3.2.3) is identical to (A3.2.2). Then there will be a prisoner's dilemma of non-cooperation if (A3.2.2) is not satisfied. It is advantageous to defect and this will yield the partner a worse outcome than non-cooperation. So, in case of no joint production, repayment of benefit received and/or reduction of risk of spillover are crucial for cooperation to emerge in a one-shot game.

There are two ways to escape from prisoner's dilemma's of non-cooperation. One is to alter the pay-offs. This is the approach indicated above: repay sufficient shares of informational benefits received, give guarantees against spillovers, engage in joint production of information. An alternative is to rely on the beneficial effect of an indefinitely ongoing relation, where the perspective of benefits of continued cooperation in the future may dominate the short-time benefit of defection. Cooperation may emerge in an open-ended repeated game, even if there is no joint production ($pi = 0$) and no repayments are made ($sij = 0$), if defection can be credibly punished by lasting non-cooperation (Axelrod 1984). This will happen if the present value of lasting cooperation exceeds the one-shot benefit of defection, which occurs if:

$$rij > (1 + d).ci, \text{ where } d \text{ is the discount rate} \qquad \text{(A3.2.4)}$$

in other words, if the benefit of information from the partner (rij) exceeds the appreciated cost associated with the risk of spillover of information given ($(1 + d).ci$). However, this solution has attendant problems. How credible is it that a single defection will forever block future cooperation (Gilbert, 1989)? Credibility depends, among other things, on reputation for retaliation in case of defection by the partner. In the absence of joint production of new knowledge, the value of information from the partner is likely to decline in time, possibly at a faster rate than the value of money.

Much more can be said about the governance of protracted cooperation, by means of formal contractual means and informal means for the generation of loyalty and trust ('relational contracting'), including the use of means for monitoring, mutual guarantees, posting of hostages, etc. but this is the subject of Chapter 4. One point, however, should be made here. The investment to be made on a basis for common understanding between firms with diverse competence, based on experience in diverse conditions, is transaction specific. Thus it creates dependence, with attendant risks of 'hold-up'. But it may also serve to create symmetry of mutual dependence, to provide the perspective of a reasonably stable ongoing relationship.

Now consider the effect of joint production of new knowledge: $pi > 0$. If (A3.2.3) is satisfied, mutual cooperation yields a Nash equilibrium even in a one-shot game. If the return of joint production already exceeds the risk of spillover ($pi > ci$), then (A3.2.3) is satisfied even without any repayment of utility from information supplied ($sij = 0$). Furthermore, in case of teamwork, the opportunities for monitoring and hence for controlling spillover of information to competitors increase, resulting in a lower value of c_i.

The analysis yields the following hypotheses:

H31   H311   Cooperation in the form of exchange of knowledge (or more generally competence) occurs relatively often when the worth of exchange is high (high r) and risk of spillover is low (low c). The first (high r) occurs when advanced technology is required for survival, is complex and is changing at a rapid pace. The second (low c) is the case when knowledge is more tacit, the relation is vertical rather than horizontal, there is a small number of partners in the case of vertical relations, or a technology of focused monitoring of spillovers is available.

H312   When risk of spillover is high (high c), exchange is accompanied either by longer term, open-ended relations (see A3.2.4), or repayment for exchange ($s > 0$), or joint production (see A3.2.3).

H313   When risk of spillover is high (e.g. in horizontal relations or vertical relations with many partners' partners, in the absence of an independent, sharply focused technology of monitoring), collaboration in the form of joint ventures prevails to better monitor spillover and shirking.

H314   To the extent that small firms are more characterized by tacit knowledge and tend to have lower numbers of partners, they are more likely to seek partners (less risk of spillover to competitors) and to be sought as partners (less risk of spillover for the partner). This is probably part of the mechanism of industrial districts.

The last hypothesis (H314) is perhaps the most uncertain and may require some further comment. Arguments for more tacit knowledge in smaller firms were given in Chapter 1. Concerning the number of relations of smaller firms: external relations are in principle more important to small rather than large firms (Johannisson 1986; Johnson and Kuehn 1987), in view of a lack of internal specialized competence, and for the same reason there is not enough management and staff capacity to set up and manage a great number of relations. One reason for the uncertainty of the hypothesis is that there is evidence of a countervailing effect. Independent entrepreneurs are often wary of cooperation with others, partly because their independence is part of their objective in being an independent entrepreneur (Kets de Vries 1977).

Hypothesis 31 is confirmed by empirical surveys: for new product/process development vertical relations predominate over horizontal ones. Our present explanation would be: vertical relations on the whole yield higher r and lower c.

APPENDIX 3.3 OPTIMAL NUMBER OF PARTNERS

Appendix 3.2 examined a game of cooperation in development between two partners, but the question arises as to how many partners one should have. Should one go for an exclusive relationship with one partner or for promiscuity? Also, we should perhaps take into account that, from the perspective of learning, a partner with multiple partners may not only carry the penalty of a risk of spillover, but also the benefit of a greater variety of sources of knowledge and competence. Suppose, therefore, that the pay-off function is as follows:

$$RET_i = r_i.TRAN_j + p_i.TRAN_i.TRAN_j + m_i.MUL_i$$
$$+ v_i.TRAN_j.MUL_j - c_i.TRAN_i.MUL_j \qquad (A3.3.1)$$

where: MUL = a dichotomous variable indicating exclusiveness ($MUL = 0$) or multiplicity of partners ($MUL = 1$).

as before: r_i = the benefit of transfer from the partner; p_i = the benefit of joint production; c_i = the risk of spillover (which occurs only if the partner has multiple partners).

m = benefit of having multiple partners, due to improvement of bargaining position, a spread of risk of partners dropping out or defecting, or due to having multiple sources of learning.

v = the added benefit in learning from a partner with multiple partners (sources).

Then the pay-off matrix is as specified in Table A3.3.1.

There is a Nash equilibrium at mutual transfer and promiscuity ($MUL = TRAN = 1$) if $p > c$ and as we found before there is a prisoner's dilemma equilibrium at mutual shirking ($TRAN = 0$). Mutual exclusive transfer ($MUL = 0$, $TRAN = 1$) is not an equilibrium and in that sense is not viable. Here we find the following hypotheses:

H32   H321   When there is an unconditional advantage of having multiple partners, promiscuity always dominates exclusiveness: it is always tempting to seek additional advantage from multiple partners.

      H322   In particular, mutual exclusive transfer, while optimal if spillover risk exceeds the advantages of multiple partners plus varied sources of learning ($c > m + v$), is not viable.

      H323   As we found before, we have a prisoner's dilemma of shirking ($TRAN = 0$) if spillover risk exceeds the benefit of joint production ($c > p$)

      H324   If spillover risk is less than the benefit of joint production ($p > c$) we have a viable cooperative outcome of transfer and promiscuity ($MUL = TRAN = 1$). This will tend to be the case when

Table A3.3.1 The attractions of promiscuity

	PARTNER 1			
	$MUL1 = 1$ $TRAN1 = 1$	$MUL1 = 0$ $TRAN1 = 1$	$MUL1 = 1$ $TRAN1 = 0$	$MUL1 = 0$ $TRAN1 = 0$
$MUL2 = 1$ $TRAN2 = 1$	$RET1 = RET2 =$ $r + p + m + v-c$	$RET1 = r + p + v-c$ $RET2 = r + p + m$	$RET1 = r + m + v$ $RET2 = m-c$	$RET1 = r + v$ $RET2 = m$
$MUL2 = 0$ $TRAN2 = 1$	$RET1 = r+p+m$ $RET2 = r + p + v-c$	$RET1 = RET2 =$ $r + p$	$RET1 = r+m$ $RET2 = -c$	$RET1 = r$ $RET2 = 0$
PARTNER 2 $MUL2 = 1$ $TRAN2 = 0$	$RET1 = m-c$ $RET2 = r + m + v$	$RET1 = -c$ $RET2 = r + m$	$RET1 = RET2 =$ m	$RET1 = 0$ $RET2 = m$
$MUL2 = 0$ $TRAN2 = 0$	$RET1 = m$ $RET2 = r + v$	$RET1 = 0$ $RET2 = r$	$RET1 = m$ $RET2 = 0$	$RET1 = RET2 =$ 0

the knowledge involved is tacit: then spillover risk is small while close interaction in the joint production of novelty is necessary.

If promiscuity is advantageous, how many partners should one have? In view of the advantages and risks of multiple partners, how many partners would one like to have and how many would those partners go along with? The advantages and disadvantages of having more partners are as follows:

Advantages:
1   the variety of sources of competence is increased;
2   one diversifies risk due to partners dropping out, either because of business failure or because of defection on their part to more profitable partners;
3   having alternatives improves bargaining position.

All three effects are likely to have decreasing returns.

Disadvantages:
4   resources are dissipated over multiple partners, requiring multiple set-up costs and relation specific investments;
5   having more partners increases risk of spillover.

For any given partner, the risk of spillover increases with the number of partners.

Thus the following conflict of interest arises: one would like to have multiple partners which each have few partners, but this also applies for each of those partners. In view of this, what is the outcome concerning numbers of partners? This can be analysed by game theoretic means. A simple representation of the problem is as follows:

The marginal utility of the nth partner, in view of points 1 to 5 is as follows:

$$du_i(n_i) = y - b.(n_i - 1) - a.n_j \qquad \text{(A3.3.2)}$$

where: $du_i(n_i)$ = marginal utility to i of his nth partner
   $y - b.(n_i - 1)$ reflects the net effect of points 1 to 4, including decreasing returns: the marginal utility of partners declines with the number of partners one already has $(n_i - 1)$.
   n_j = number of partners that partner j has.
   $- a.n_j$ reflects the effect of the second disadvantage.

Summation of utility over n partners yields:

$$u_i(n_i) = n_i(y - a.n_j) - b.n_i^2/2 \qquad \text{(A3.3.3)}$$

where: $u_i(n_i)$ = utility to i of n_i partners

Setting the first derivative with respect to the number of partners to zero, in order to maximize utility, yields:

$$n_i^* = (y - a.n_j)/b \qquad\qquad\qquad\qquad (A3.3.4)$$

where: n_i^* = optimal number of partners.

The formula constitutes a 'reaction curve' of i's optimal choice given the number of partner's partners. The same formula, with indices i and j exchanged, applies to partner j. The formula thus yields reaction curves between partners, whose intersection constitutes a Nash equilibrium, as follows:

$$n_i^* = n_j^* = y/(a + b) \qquad\qquad\qquad\qquad (A3.3.5)$$

This is illustrated in Figure A3.3.1.

At the Nash equilibrium, there is a balance of conflicting interests: the tug that results from wanting many partners who themselves have few partners. The analysis yields the following hypothesis:

H33   The number of partners increases with the utility of employing partners (y), which depends on the importance of technology for survival and decreases with a higher rate of decline of marginal utility of partners (b), which depends on the complexity and specialization of required competence, and decreases with a higher risk of spill-over per partner's partner (a), which depends on the nature of the competence involved (more or less tacit) and available 'technology of monitoring'.

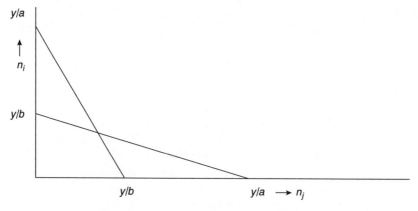

Figure A3.1.1 Nash equilibrium in number of partners.

4 Governance

On the basis of the extended theory of transactions set out in Chapter 1, a general scheme is set up for the design and control of governance, aimed at maximizing joint value and controlling risk due to dependence. Relational risk has two dimensions: the size of loss one may incur due to accidents or opportunism by the partner and the probability that this loss will occur. Size of loss is determined by the value of the partner (relative to the next best alternative) plus the costs of switching to that alternative, which together determine one's dependence or 'captiveness'. This dependence may tempt the partner into opportunistic behaviour, but this temptation is modified by the extent that the partner is dependent on the alliance. The probability of loss depends on incentives for the partner, the room that the partner has for opportunistic behaviour (in view of contractual restrictions and the monitoring that takes place to enforce them) and on trustworthiness: 'propensity towards opportunism', which depends on character, institutions, habits and bonding between the partners (friendship or kinship). This scheme provides the basis for a thorough and systematic analysis of possible mixes of instruments of governance.

INTRODUCTION

As noted before, the notion of 'governance' includes the notion of control, but is a wider concept. The notion of 'control' sometimes has a connotation of rational design, mastery and one-sided influence of one actor on another. Uncertainty is generally too great to achieve that. Unforeseen contingencies and effects of the control mechanism are bound to occur. Relations enter into a dynamic of interaction that is difficult to predict. Often one must shift from the 'substantive' rationality of choosing the best of foreseeable outcomes to the 'procedural rationality' of following heuristics that are likely to take one in roughly the right direction; of setting conditions in which relations are likely to work. Rather than trying to impose conditions on the alliance partners that will force them in the desired direction, it may be better to step into their shoes and see what would make it attractive for them to move in that direction. If one takes control in a wide sense, to allow for all of this, the notion of governance is synonymous with the notion of control.

Of course, relations are entertained for the added value that they produce. As in any investment, value and risk should be traded off against each other. Especially relevant here is the resource–competence view taken in this book, as discussed in Chapter 1. It entails firms seeking and achieving more or less firm-specific resources that enable them to differentiate their products from those of competitors, thereby achieving a higher profit than under pure price competition between perfect substitutes. To achieve profits, such resources should remain firm-specific for a while. This raises the issue of spillover: the risk that through partners in the alliance core competence leaks to competitors. This risk depends on the extent to which the knowledge is documented rather than tacit, the extent to which knowledge flow can be monitored, the speed of spillover relative to the speed of knowledge change and the number of competitors with whom the partner has relations. The resource–competence view and the theory of knowledge and learning set out in Chapter 1 also highlight the need for external partners. To the extent that knowledge and competence are firm-specific and path-dependent, there are things that others can perceive, understand, evaluate and perform that one could not do oneself. Firms need to focus on their core competencies, in order to have any chance at winning races to the market, but this carries the risk of missing threats and opportunities. To compensate, firms need to utilize complementary competencies from other firms, which also makes them dependent on them. The more unique the value that a partner offers, the more dependency is involved.

The purpose of alliances is to generate mutual benefit from complementary resources, but in this chapter the focus is on the governance of relational risk due to the possibility of opportunism, because this is the most difficult issue. But in addition to this risk and that of spillover there are other risks: lack of competence rather than opportunistic intentions and outside events, such as a partner going broke, accidents or novel potential partners appearing on the scene. Unpredictability of outside events increases risks of opportunism, because they may present more 'opportunities for opportunism' that could not be foreseen in any contract.

For the analysis of risks of opportunism and the diagnosis and design of alliances to cope with this risk, use will be made of transaction cost economics, extended with the resource–competence view and considerations of innovation and learning and with allowance for trust next to opportunism, as discussed in Chapter 1.

The scheme to be developed here is as general as possible so that it can be applied to many different kinds of relation: vertical relations between suppliers and buyers; horizontal alliances between (potential) competitors, relations between managers and owners of firms; even personal relations such as friendship and marriage.

VALUE, DEPENDENCE AND RISK

A general scheme for the analysis of relational risk is proposed in Figure 4.1, and is discussed below.

In the appendix to this chapter the scheme is applied, by way of experiment, to marriage. An analysis of causes and instruments of dependence in marriage can be enlightening, because we have more experience with marriages than with alliances in business. Instruments to guide successful marriage could perhaps be transformed into logical equivalents for alliances: for example, an engagement period, wedding rings, children, alimony, dowry, marriage settlement, godfather/mother.

In the management of relations it is crucial to take into account the effects of one's actions on the position of the partner, his reactions and their effects on one's own position. This is why in the consideration of *X* one should also include the position of her partner *Y*. The causality is symmetrical for

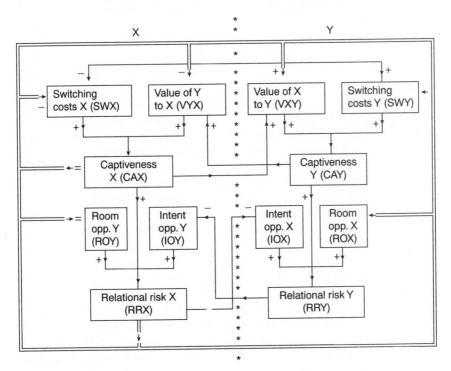

Figure 4.1 Relational risk of *X* and *Y*.

X and Y, but here the analysis is conducted from the perspective of X. The scheme in Figure 4.1 is explained in two rounds: first the variables will be defined and then the lines connecting them.

The reason for X to engage in a relation with Y lies in the relative value that Y offers, i.e. the contribution to the joint surplus or added value that the relation generates, in comparison with the next best alternative for X (VYX). There are two ways in which relative value can become negative. One is that the value itself, regardless of alternatives, becomes negative: the partner detracts value rather than adding value. This covers the problems of competition and spillover in a relationship: that is when the partner takes away value rather than adding it. The second possibility is that the value of the partner is positive (he adds value), but the value of an alternative partner would be greater. Then X would prefer another relationship. Neither possibility alone implies that X will break up and switch to another relationship. That depends on switching costs and on the room he has, in view of contractual obligations. X might also decide to improve the relation so that he no longer wants to exit: for example, by getting a competing partner to cooperate rather than compete, or to help a partner whose value is deteriorating compared to alternatives to get back to scratch. Relative value is maximal when there is no alternative; when Y is the only source for some resource that X needs. Usually there will be some more or less close and imperfect substitute.

As discussed in Chapter 1, investment in relations entails risks to the extent that it is 'specific', i.e. entails costs of switching to an alternative. But switching costs can be more than the need to engage in specific new investments for a novel partner. They could also include the value of hostages supplied to the partner which can be appropriated by him. The 'captiveness' of X (CAX) is defined as the sum of switching costs (SWX) and the relative value of Y (VYX): $CAX = SWX + VYX$. With a greater relative value of the partner, one has more to lose when the relation breaks. It will be more difficult to find a partner of equal value and meanwhile one incurs a loss of sales, quality or high costs due to high replacement costs. The sum of relative value and switching costs determines the inclination of X to continue the relation and his dependence on it, or 'captiveness' as it is called here. If it is positive, but the relative value of the partner is negative, one is continuing the relation only because of switching costs. Then one can try to increase the value of the partner to make the relation worthwhile or reduce switching costs to get out. If an alternative comes along that is so much better than Y that captiveness becomes negative, this means that the alternative is so much more attractive that switching is worth the costs.

When X's captiveness is high, partner Y may be tempted to 'holdup': to exert pressure for an increase of his share in the surplus or added value of the relation. Whether he tries this depends on two things: the room that he has for opportunistic conduct (ROY) and his intent to utilize opportunities for opportunism (IOY).

Room for opportunism is determined by the tightness of contractual regulations and the monitoring of their compliance. Contracts are tight – i.e. yield little room for opportunism – to the extent that relevant contingencies can be specified, there is effective monitoring of compliance and the detail with which conditions have been specified in the contract. There are obstacles to all of these. When uncertainty of external conditions is large, all contingencies cannot be foreseen. Monitoring of compliance may be difficult to the extent that neither outputs nor inputs of efforts can be reliably observed, taking into account that information is 'asymmetric' between X and Y to the extent that they are different organizations, shielded from each other. Detailed specifications in contracts are costly in time and money and even legal language cannot yield semantic closure.

Y's intent towards utilizing chances for opportunism depends on material incentives, including his own dependence on the relationship. In other words, intent depends on bargaining position; on the uniqueness of values that partners offer each other and switching costs. It also depends on inclination towards opportunism, beyond self-interest. This is the dimension of 'real' trustworthiness, in the strong sense discussed in Chapter 1. Finally, relational risk is defined as that which results from the partner's possible opportunistic behaviour, which can take two forms:

1   The partner wants to break up the relationship, against the letter or intent of agreements and X pays a price in the form of costs of switching to a different partner (or doing without).
2   The partner wants to misuse the dependence of X to extract a greater share of the surplus or added value generated by the relation (better price, better quality, etc.).

This risk has two dimensions: the penalty for X if it occurs (PEX), i.e. the price that X pays and the probability that it will occur (PRX). If relational risk (RRX) is defined as expected loss, then we have: $RRX = PEX \times PRX$. The maximum penalty equals captiveness, i.e. the sum of the partner's relative value and switching costs: $PEX = CAX = VYX + SWX$. That is the maximum to which X can be held up: if it were larger, it would be better for X to exit than to give in to the hold-up. The probability of loss is determined by the room for opportunism and the intent to utilize it and, more specifically, by their product: $PRX = ROY \times IOY$. Thus we obtain:

$$RRX = PEX \times PRX = (VYX + SWX) \times ROY \times IOY \qquad (4.1)$$

In Figure 4.1, causality is indicated by single lines. Most of them are clear from the above discussion, but some require comment. There is a line running between the switching costs of the two partners, with the minus sign of a negative relation. This is intended to indicate that ownership of transaction specific assets can be shifted, increasing switching costs for one partner and decreasing them for the other, so that higher switching costs for one entail lower switching costs for the other. Note also that there are lines running from the captiveness of a player to the value he offers to his partner. This reflects the fact that a more captive partner offers a better perspective for returns not only now but also in the future.

Double lines in Figure 4.1 indicate a control loop to change the relation by changing the values of its variables. The origin of a double line indicates what triggers control.

> This is associated with Hirschman's (1970) distinction between 'exit' and 'voice'. If one is dissatisfied with something one can walk out (exit), but one can also try to improve the relation by deliberation (voice).

Control action is triggered mainly by relational risk; when it is considered to be too high, taking into account the risk incurred by the partner. But control action may also be triggered when captiveness by itself is considered to be too high. On the basis of the scheme one can analyse systematically what can be done to control the relationship. One can try to influence the basic variables, as follows:

V: Change the relative value of the partner (VP), or the value that one offers to the partner oneself (VS).

S: Change own switching costs (SS) or those for the partner (SP).

R: Change own room for opportunistic conduct (RS) or that of the partner (RP).

I: Change own intent towards opportunistic behaviour (IS) or the partner's (IP).

This demonstrates the difference between classical transaction cost economics (TCE), as developed by Williamson and the extended theory used here. While TCE limits itself to S, R and the self-interested part of I, this book includes trust beyond self-interest and also pays more attention to the values that partners offer each other. Control actions can be taken in an aggressive, adversarial or more cooperative fashion, depending on whether the interest of the partner is taken into account. Control can be aimed at strengthening or weakening the relation. This taxonomy of control actions will be developed in more detail later.

Note that each of the variables can in principle be affected on the side of the partner (P) or on the side of oneself (S). A crucial issue of governance is the ability not only to focus on the variables that determine one's own risks of dependence, but also to step into the shoes of the partner and consider the situation from that perspective. Thus one's own risk of opportunism can be reduced by raising the partner's dependence by increasing one's unique value to him. This is a particularly constructive mode of governance because it reduces risk by increasing value. This is more constructive than refraining from specific investments, which decreases value, in order to reduce risk of dependence by lowering switching costs. It is also more productive than safeguarding risks by means of detailed contracts, which limit flexibility and innovation and tend to create mistrust. Another example is that one's alternative option can be deliberately limited by allotting exclusiveness to a given partner. Thus, one's own dependence is increased, as compensation for the partner being bound to the relationship by engaging in specific investments, thereby encouraging him to do so (see Bakos and Brynjolfsson 1993). Yet, as will be detailed later (Chapter 5), practice shows that firms do not see such options simply because they are not used to looking at the relation from their partner's perspective. It can be very fruitful to protect oneself by helping the partner, and to help oneself by protecting the partner.

Next, the basic variables from Figure 4.1 are analysed in their underlying determinants.

VALUE

The purpose of a relationship is the value of the partner. This is especially important from the resource–competence perspective taken in this book: the firm-specific, path-dependent competencies or other resources that one needs in order to complement one's own. As indicated, the concern here is with value relative to the next best alternative, including the possibility of doing without any partner and doing it oneself. In other words, 'opportunity costs' of not using alternatives are taken into account. The dimensions of value are specified in Figure 4.2, with the now familiar grouping of resources into assets, competencies and positional advantages.

Most of the components of value can take on a negative value, which signifies that rather than complementing one's own resources the partner detracts from them. For example, the partner's contribution to technological

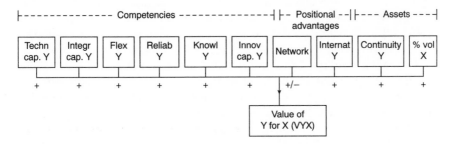

Figure 4.2 Value of *Y* for *X*.

capability may have a net negative value because more knowledge belonging to one's core competence value spills over to the partner than is received from him. It may spill over to a competitor through the partner, or the partner may use it to engage in competing activities. Internationalization ('internat') is negative when the partner detracts from one's international presence by competing abroad. One may accept negative values in some components if these are amply compensated by positive value elsewhere.

An illustration is given by the account of the long lasting and successful Japanese JV between Xerox and Fuji given by Lorange and Roos (1992). It started out as a classic product–market entry alliance, with Xerox providing the product and Fuji providing entry in the difficult Japanese market. After a while, technology spilled over to Fuji and it developed a capability for its own design and production of copiers. At Xerox this was seen as a loss; as negative value due to spillover of technology, the building of a new competitor and a threat to home country employment. But this was amply compensated for by the fact that Fuji developed a low-end product that was complementary to Xerox's range and helped to stop competitive entry to the market by IBM.

Each of the different components of value is now discussed. Value of course depends on the extent of the partner's involvement: the percentage of one's activities in which the partner is involved, indicated by the variable 'per cent vol X'. This can refer to several things. The relevant measure may be the share of transactions with this partner in the total value added in X's activity under consideration. For example: if X is a supplier to Y, it is the percentage of sales in the product going to this customer; if X is a customer of Y, it is the share of Y's supply in the total purchase expense of the input under consideration; if X and Y engage in a joint venture it might be the percentage of one's share in added value or profit of the joint venture in the firm's total added value or profit; if the alliance is an R&D consortium it is the share of one's contribution in total R&D commitment in the area under consideration. The percentage is related to the number of other partners with whom one cooperates in the same activity.

Under the conditions concerning technology and markets, as discussed in Chapter 2, the value of the partner depends on a range of competencies: his technological capability, which includes the level of quality, speed of contribution and costs. It also includes the reliability of quality, time and costs. It may also involve the partner's integrative ability: the ability to integrate contributions from others. For example, a 'main supplier' is expected to integrate the products from lower level suppliers in the hierarchy or 'pyramid' of different 'tiers' of suppliers, including logistics, quality assessment and control, supplier rating and selection. Flexibility also is important, in production volume, personnel, time, organization, specification of activities performed, goals of cooperation. Of increasing importance is the value of the partner as a source of knowledge, concerning technology, markets and innovative capability.

Positional advantages are international presence and network position, i.e. connections with other players or sources outside the relationship. Network position has a number of aspects. One is indirect access, through the partner, to resources beyond, which may include materials, components, apparatus (machinery, instruments), labour, reputation, legitimation, permits, licences, distribution channels. An apparently risky or even loss-generating alliance may be warranted if it yields access to an otherwise inaccessible resource, e.g. a market.

> This covers alliances where one side offers the other entry into a market. It explains the fact that sometimes suppliers accept unfavourable conditions to become a 'preferred' supplier to a prestigious customer, in order to gain access to other customers on the basis of prestige derived from it. It also explains why buyers sometimes prefer foreign suppliers for their willingness to accept unfavourable conditions in order to gain a foothold in the country of the new customer.

The consequences of breaking a relationship are greater to the extent that it cuts one off from access to important resources. A well-known example is that of a 'main supplier' who provides access to various sources which he coordinates. This saves costs for his customer but also makes him more dependent.

However, the partner's network position can also entail a threat. A customer A can yield indirect access, through him, to another customer B, to whom one also supplies directly. If one gets into problems with B, he may exert pressure on his supplier A also to withdraw his custom, so that one loses not only the sales to B but also the sales to A (Berger *et al.* 1995). Another problem can be the risk of spillover to competitors, through the partner, as discussed before, particularly if the knowledge involved is not tacit but documented. One may try to prevent that through patents, but often such protection is not cost-efficient or even undesirable on the grounds that the public information on the patent is enough to yield an undesirable spillover, because it gives sufficient information to set competitors on the track of substitution or imitation by some 'work-around' that dodges patent restrictions. A problem for especially small firms is that the application for a patent entails fixed set-up costs which make it relatively expensive and because the threat of litigation to protect the patent may not be credible. An important question is whether spillover can be monitored, so that partners who leak information to a competitor can be punished.

> In the car industry and many other industries knowledge is embodied in a publicly available product, and then spillover can be traced. The use of knowledge is 'published' as it were (Lamming 1993: 197). One can disassemble a competitor's product to see whether use has been made of firm-specific competence supplied to a partner. One can then blame the partner for not keeping to agreements of secrecy or exclusiveness.

Internationalization of the partner is closely related to network position, but merits separate attention. It can be extremely important that the partner supplies his services for markets at different locations. Local presence may be crucial to enable 'just-in-time' supply or to yield the same service to different locations or subsidiaries of a customer.

> The latter is the case for accountancy firms: efficiency and controllability increase if the same accountant can perform his services in all locations of some multinational customer. Together with economies of scale in setting up and widely utilizing information networks, this has been an important reason for the merger of accountancy firms with offices in different parts of the world.

Finally, value as well as costs of governance depend on how long the relationship is expected to last. For value this was already indicated: a longer duration increases the present value of future benefits in relation to the specific investments needed for the relation. The effect on costs of governance is based on the notion of the 'shadow of the future' (Telser 1980; Axelrod 1984; Heide and Miner 1992). One is less inclined towards opportunism to the extent that the relationship and its benefits are expected to last indefinitely, because then the benefits of opportunism, which would be followed by a breakdown of the relationship, become less in relation to the aggregate value of the relationship over years to come.

Recall that the risk of breakdown of a relationship is not only due to opportunism. It can arise from accidental failure of the partner, other calamities or the fact that the partner is taken over by someone who has no interest in continuing the relationship, e.g. because he is a competitor. An illustration of this is the case of a non-equity alliance between two producers of garden equipment in Sweden and Norway ('Norpartner and Swedpartner', Lorange and Roos 1992), mentioned in Chapter 3. A third party, which competed with both sides in the NEA, took over the owner of one of them and thereby created serious problems for the other side.

An example of vulnerability to disaster is given by Reitman (1997). A supplier to Toyota was hit by a fire. Toyota had only a few hours' supply in stock. Toyota's local companies and suppliers pooled resources and together rebuilt the plant in a few days.

To a greater or lesser extent, firm size has an effect on these dimensions of value. Small firms usually have fewer products in fewer markets and therefore often less international presence, for example. For reasons discussed in Chapter 1, there are effects of scale in transaction costs. Small firms often cannot afford the infrastructure for quality assurance systems, R&D, electronic data interchange (EDI) or distribution. Integrative capability is often limited in smaller firms. On the other hand, small firms can often be more flexible and more innovative. For a further discussion of strengths and weaknesses of small firms see Nooteboom (1994).

Due to a lesser spread of risks, small firms are also more vulnerable to bankruptcy and can be taken over more easily, thus presenting a risk of discontinuity of the relationship. However, the division of a large firm with whom one has a relationship can also be sold off. The threat of takeover depends on more than just firm size, but also on the structure of ownership, such as constructions to block takeovers.

On the European continent there are generally more obstacles to takeover than in the UK and USA. This is connected with the phenomenon that, in general, Anglo-American countries are more oriented towards the market mechanism, while continental European countries are more oriented towards government involvement or lasting network relations between firms (Nooteboom 1997b, 1998d). Several justifications of obstacles to takeover are conceivable. One such justification derives from the above discussion: obstacles may serve to safeguard alliance or network partners from nasty surprises of discontinuity of relations due to takeovers. This fits with the greater orientation, on the European continent, towards cooperation in networks.

Summing up, the value of the partner consists of resources in the form of assets, competencies and positional advantages, in other words, economic, social and cultural capital. In terms of the multiple causality discussed in Chapter 1: material and formal causes (economic capital), efficient causes (human resources, as part of both economic and cultural capital), final and exemplary causes (cultural capital) and conditional causes (social capital).

SWITCHING COSTS

The factors that determine the extent of switching costs are specified in Figure 4.3.

Switching costs due to specific investments are determined by the total of such investments in the relation, multiplied by one's share in their ownership. Note that if specific investments are one-sided, their ownership can be redistributed. The partner can participate in ownership and thereby participate in the risks carried, which tends to lessen the intent towards opportunism. This is a well-known part of 'private ordering': governance by the mobilization of self-interest (Williamson 1985).

In a study of suppliers in the car industry, Semlinger (1991) found conditions which in his view contradicted TCE. Suppliers of car parts had to invest in the highly transaction specific dies for stamping the parts into shape. According to Semlinger's interpretation of TCE, the prescription would be that the buyer should either give guarantees of custom for as much or as long as needed to recoup the investments, or take full ownership of the dies. Neither occurred. The buyers did offer to take ownership of the dies, but the suppliers refused. Does

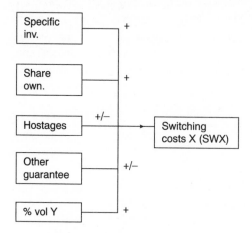

Figure 4.3 Switching costs for *X*.

this contradict TCE? The suppliers refused because they did not want to relinquish decision rights on the dies, which would eliminate their value for the customer and hence all dependence of the customer. The customer could then transfer the die to a different supplier at any time. But this still leaves the possibility of shared ownership, with the supplier retaining sufficient decision rights to prevent that.

Recall that specific investments by X can cause switching costs for Y, even if ownership is not shared. If the relation breaks, the partner will at least temporarily suffer a loss before he finds an alternative partner who is able to engage in similar investments and before such investments are in place. Note, however, that this is already included in the relative value that is offered to the partner, as part of total 'captiveness'. Note also that this does not automatically imply that dependence is symmetrical. In general, loss due to loss of specific investments made is greater than loss due to discontinuity for the partner.

Other switching costs, which are also part of private ordering, are the provision of hostages and the supply of other guarantees.

A true hostage satisfies the condition that it has value for the giver but not for the keeper, to ensure that when the time has come that the giver has honoured his commitments, the keeper will not be tempted to retain the hostage and will not hesitate to return it.

In this context there is the following riddle. When in the past a king had to supply a hostage to guarantee a treaty with another king and had the choice between giving an attractive or an unattractive daughter, whom he loves equally, which one should he give? The standard answer is the unattractive one, because that better satisfies the condition of a asymmetric value. The attractive daughter could more easily assume value for the hostage keeper, who might then be tempted never to return her. But what if the first king did not really intend to honour the treaty? Then he can better give the more attractive daughter, because she would be less likely to be harmed. But the second king might see through this and become suspicious when the attractive daughter is offered, unless the first king can create the false impression, without being found out, that he does not love his unattractive daughter. Then the second king might demand the attractive daughter, for fear that the unattractive one would not keep the first king from betrayal. Then the second king would fall into the first king's trap.

In relations between firms people can play the role of hostage, for example, intermarriage between family businesses or the exchange of staff between the partners. But information, knowledge or technology can also play the role. Earlier the problem of 'spillover' was discussed, but here we see that sensitive information, with the threat of spillover, can be put at risk on purpose, as a device for establishing commitment to a relation. Cross-participation between firms can also be interpreted as an exchange of hostages. In the Japanese system, for example, cross-participation by exchange of shares is not motivated by the value or diversification of profits, but by the stabilization of relations; by the prevention of adversarial action. This use of cross-participation was admitted in a document in 1992 from the Japanese Agency for Economic Planning (Scher 1996: 17).

> When some years ago the Dutch minster of economic affairs accompanied the cooperation between Volvo and Mitsubishi in a new joint venture NEDCAR (the former Dutch car producer DAF), he kept in his care what he called a 'shoe box' with the design of a new model of the Volvo to be produced in Holland (which is now on the roads). This served as a hostage, to make sure that Volvo would not shift the higher value-added activity of design and development to Sweden.

Such measures are not needed if one's value in competence is so high, possibly due to specific investments, that the other side becomes so dependent that they would not want to act opportunistically.

> In the case of NEDCAR: if the Dutch subsidiary had such unique competencies in the design and development of new cars, which are so embedded in local workers, teams, organization, culture and suppliers, the competence could not be taken away without destroying it.

If X and Y exchange hostages and the mechanism works well, then if X reneges on agreements he will lose his hostage and Y will not lose his. In that sense the height of switching costs is conditional on who reneges. Guarantees can take several forms. One is a minimum duration or a minimum volume of transactions, so that specific investments may be recouped. Or the buyer can guarantee that in case of premature exit he will refund whole or part of what is left of the specific asset after depreciation. Another form of guarantee is price indexing so that the risk of price increases of materials, components or labour is shared, or benchmarking as a guarantee that increases of quality or productivity will be in line with average or best practice in the relevant industry. The supply of guarantees often requires counter-guarantees against misuse. This may entail, for example, agreements to monitoring, by the giver of the guarantee or some third party who supplies arbitration, to verify that the conditions for effecting the guarantee are satisfied: for example, to check whether the investment is indeed so specific that it cannot and is not used for other partners. Note that there is a special effect of hostages. Both hostages and guarantees can be given and received and net switching costs depend on the balance: hence the +/– sign attached to them in Figure 4.3.

A special form of guarantee is the possibility that if withdrawal by one side jeopardizes the continuity and hence the employment of the partner, one will be held up on that by being made responsible for the loss of employment. One is pressed to compromise by social obligation. That would add to switching costs. This cost of switching would depend on the percentage of the partner's total production that the partnership covers. Hence the box in Figure 4.3: share in volume Y.

This yields a reason especially for big firms in alliances with small firms to demand that the small firm does not become too dependent. It has been given as a reason for the oil industry not to contract small firms in, for example, supply to the offshore industry. The reason that in Japan large firms are less hesitant to contract small firms for 100 per cent of their sales may be that they are not in this way held responsible for employment in the small firm, the burden of responsibility is shared in a larger group of firms (*keiretsu*), or they have a greater commitment and better means to prevent the small firm's failure, on the basis of a greater involvement in its operation, development and sharing of resources.

Switching costs due to specific investments can be lowered by reducing the transaction specificity of the investments, i.e. by making technology more flexible, so that a single general purpose installation can at low cost be adjusted to produce a variety of specific products for different customers (see the appendix to Chapter 1 for a formal analysis of specificity).

Thus a programmable machine, e.g. for metal working (such as a computer numerically controlled workbench) can yield more opportunities for different product forms, handled by a single operator, than when for different forms different skills are needed, to be supplied by different craftsmen. Lamming (1993: 129) mentions another interesting example. As discussed before, the die in which forms of metal or plastic are pressed or stamped into shape is a classic example of a specific asset. An innovation is that the 'male' part is replaced by water under high pressure, to press the material into the 'female' part. This reduces specificity by about 50 per cent. Another possibility is to shift the de-coupling point in production, where a generic flow of production is split into separate flows for specific products further downstream in the production process. In the extreme case, different products consist of different assemblages of standard components. Yet another example is the following: thermo-hardened material for the pressing of plastic shapes can increasingly be replaced by thermoplastic materials. One advantage is that the material can be re-used for new pressings. Another is that thermoplasts require less pressure, allowing for less robust and therefore cheaper dies. Both contribute to a lower degree of specific investments.

Finally, it should be noted that investments made to reduce the probability of opportunistic action, to be discussed in the next section, are in themselves specific investments and can thus further add to switching costs. Thus such investment has opposing effects on relational risk. The question is whether the positive effect on probability of opportunistic action exceeds the negative effect on switching costs.

ROOM FOR OPPORTUNISM

The factors that determine the room for opportunism are indicated in Figure 4.4. This comes straight from TCE.

According to TCE, chances for opportunism depend on ability to monitor compliance with agreements, which depends on asymmetry of information and the legal tightness of agreements, which depends on the predictability

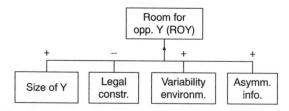

Figure 4.4 Room for oppportunism *Y*.

of contingencies, in view of the uncertainty or variability of the environment and contractual detail of legal constraints. The reliability and cost of such 'legal governance' depend on institutions in the form of 'legal infrastructure': the quality of laws and their administration. This includes incorruptibility of the legislature and police.

TCE does not take into account that a formal legal approach can ruin 'atmosphere' and enhance perceptions of and inclinations towards opportunism, goading partners into a vicious circle of regulation which can stifle the relationship. This connection between room for opportunism and intent towards opportunism is not indicated in Figure 4.1, but should be kept in mind.

Firm size affects room for opportunism, as a result of the effects of scale in transaction costs discussed in Chapter 1. A larger firm tends to have a wider reach, with a wider market, more customers and suppliers, more specialists inside and around the firm, a higher level of training and more political influence. Thus one can expect a large firm to have more room for opportunism and less vulnerability to opportunism in a single relation. On the other hand, a large firm is more visible and may have to be more careful in protecting its reputation. Firm size also has effects on the availability of information. Because in small firms there is less need for formal information, operations can be supervised by direct inspection and there is less specialization of work and hence less need for coordination and its cost is higher due to set-up costs of information systems, small firms tend to have less documented information, which makes them less accessible to evaluation and monitoring. This also makes it more difficult to give them guarantees to cover risks of specific investments, because of the difficulty of monitoring counter-guarantees to ensure proper conformance to the conditions for those guarantees.

INTENT TOWARDS OPPORTUNISM

Opportunism entails that someone dodges the letter or intent of agreements to his advantage and at the expense of the partner. This can take the form of breaking the relation or exploiting the partner's dependence on the relation ('hold-up'), with the maximum of the partners captiveness, i.e. sum of relative value offered to him and his switching costs. The probability of opportunism is determined by room for opportunism and intent towards opportunism. In TCE, intent is based only on self-interest, including the degree to which the partner is dependent on the relation and considerations of reputation. In the extension of the theory with trust next to opportunism, it also depends on what is here called 'inclination towards opportunism' which consists of trustworthiness 'in the strong sense', as discussed in Chapter 1. This may be based on ethics, bonds of friendship or kinship, as summarized in Figure 4.5.

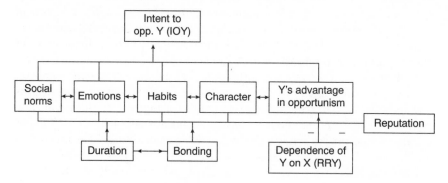

Figure 4.5 Intent towards opportunism *Y*.

Y's self-interest depends on the benefit he might acquire by opportunism, in the form of a greater share in joint surplus, added value or the switch to a more attractive partner. This depends on his own dependence, or more precisely relational risk (*RRY*). As illustrated also in Figure 4.1 his intent is affected not just by captiveness (*CAY*), which is the price to be paid if the relation breaks, but also by the probability of opportunistic conduct by the partner. That indicates the possibility of retaliatory action by the partner. Opportunistic conduct can be penalized by contractual sanctions, loss of hostages or counter-actions by the partner to appropriate added value. It also depends on the possible effects of reputation mechanisms. But intent is also dependent on trustworthiness, along the lines discussed in Chapter 1. This may be based on ethics, habits or routines and bonds of friendship, kinship or empathy. The effects of these are mediated by emotions and character. They depend on the duration of the relation and the bonds, shared ethic or habits based upon it ('process-based trust').

Figure 4.5 aims to illustrate that trustworthiness and self-interest are not separate, but influence each other. The weight of self-interest depends on strength of character to resist 'weakness of the will' in short-term temptation, for the sake of long-term interest. As discussed before, trustworthiness is limited by lack of resistance to 'golden opportunities' and pressures of survival. The latter also depend on the degree of competitive pressure in the industry.

Since *X*'s relational risk depends on *Y*'s advantage in opportunism, which depends on *Y*'s relational risk, the causality of the system becomes recursive. Thus, an iterative process of mutual adjustment arises, until the relationship falls apart or some equilibrium is reached, perhaps like a 'Nash equilibrium' in game theory. Given the current actions of partners, the other partner sees no need to change its action. But there may be different possible equilibria, which may or may not be reached, depending on where one starts and what strategic orientations are chosen. If an equilibrium is reached, this takes time and it may be that no equilibrium is reached due to unending cycles of adjustment or because meanwhile conditions and pay-offs have changed. If an equilibrium is reached, it may be upset by external conditions, such as the appearance on stage of a more attractive partner for one of the players so that the process of adjustment starts again. This process of adjustment will be analysed in more detail later. It makes governance complex, often unpredictable and imperfectly manageable. This is one of the reasons why ambitions to 'control' a relationship should be modest and preference given to the term 'governance'.

The argumentation strongly seems aimed at individual behaviour, especially where there is talk of character and emotions, while here we are dealing with alliances between organizations. On the individual level they do play a role for the people engaged in contacts between the organizations. On the organizational level, the culture includes ethical and social norms of conduct that constrain and guide individual conduct (it is an institution), with the use of exemplars in the form of role models. This 'multi-level issue' was discussed in Chapter 1.

CONTROL OF RELATIONAL RISK

The results are now be combined in a more detailed scheme for the analysis, diagnosis and design of alliances, in Figure 4.6.

Earlier, four avenues were identified for control of relational risk, corresponding with the basic scheme in Figure 4.1: influence on value (V), switching costs (S), room for opportunism (R) and intent towards opportunism (I). These can be influenced on one's own side (S) or on the partner's side (P). This can now be refined and made more concrete on the basis of the detailed scheme of Figure 4.6. Not all logically possible options are specified, but only salient and frequently manifested ones, in Table 4.1.

In Table 4.1 not all factors from Figure 4.6 have been assigned instruments. Not all determinants of room for opportunism can be influenced, for example, legal institutions. This may require political action on the basis of coalitions (such as employers' associations). Norms and values of conduct also cannot easily be changed in the short term. Limitation of uncertainty and the variability of conditions are also difficult and when possible would require collective action. One has little direct control of the partner's size. It is, however, possible to achieve joint power by pooling resources with others, as in consortia or associations.

Note that the different instruments of strategy are not independent and can reinforce or neutralize each other. Formal legal measures can have a negative effect on 'atmosphere'. A vicious circle of distrust can develop, in which partners engage in an accumulation of constraints on actions. Adversarial action can invite retaliation. The cooperative strategy of increasing the partner's dependence by means of more transaction specific

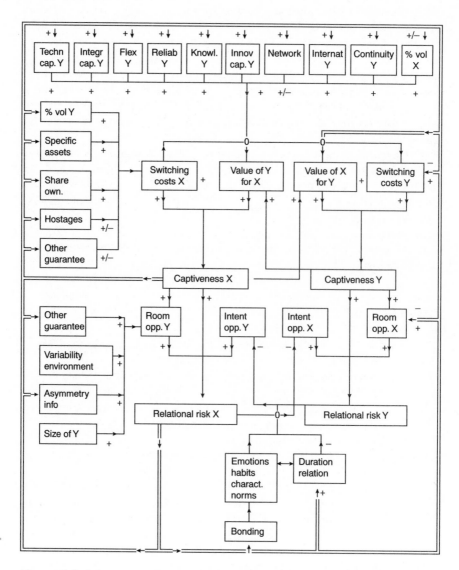

Figure 4.6 Relation management by *X.*

investments can increase the price of dependence. But an investment in a reputation of reliability can also benefit alternative relations and thereby reduce switching costs.

Thus, when choosing a package of measures their consistency should be considered, not to undo in one area what one tries to do in another. The complication is that the optimal package depends on conditions and on partner responses.

Table 4.1 Instruments

Influence on value

VPH   Increase the (relative) value of the partner. In case value is low due to competition, try and turn competition into cooperation. In case relative value is low due to more attractive alternatives, increase value by investing in partner's resources. This may entail specific investments, which also increase switching costs. The purpose may be to revitalize a relationship that needs to be continued because of high switching costs.

VPL   Lower partner value by destroying his resources, or by shifting volume to alternative partners.

VPSL Reduce both the partner's value and one's own value to the partner by expropriating his resources.

VSH   Increase own relative value for the partner. Generally this will entail specific investments, which also increase switching costs. The goal may be to make the partner more dependent and thereby ensure his loyalty and reduce relational risk.

VSL   Lower own value by stopping to invest in it or by creating or finding alternatives for the partner.

Influence on switching costs

SSL   Lower own switching costs by stopping specific investments.

SSLPH   Lower own switching costs and simultaneously increase those of the partner by selling part of one's share in specific investments, or by demanding more guarantees for continued partnership or refunds for specific investments when the relation is broken prematurely.

SSHPL   The reverse: accept higher share of specific investments, or give more guarantees.

SPH   Increase the partner's switching costs by demanding a hostage.

SSH   Increase own switching costs by posting a hostage.

SSPL   Lower switching costs for both sides by switching to a more flexible technology or by developing common standards for contracts, procedures and techniques.

Influence on room for opportunism

RPL1   Restrict room for the partner, by tighter legal or other formal constraints, with corresponding sanctions.

RPL2   The same, by closer monitoring of the partner's activities and performance.

RSL1   Accept constraints on one's own room for action.

RSL2   The same, by accepting closer monitoring.

RSH1   Increase one's own room by loosening constraints.

RSH2   The same, by shielding off monitoring.

Influence on intent towards opportunism

IPSL   Bonding: investments in the relation to enable or enhance the development of institutional ties such as norms or values of conduct, or emotional ties, or habituation. In other words: invest in 'atmosphere'.

ISH   Signal greater inclination towards opportunism by a show of indifference, lack of interest, antipathy or loss of norms, so that the partner perceives a heightened risk of opportunism.

Table 4.2 Effects of instruments

Action effects on variables in Table 4.1 by X

	VYX	SWX	CAX	ROX	IOX	RRX	VXY	SWY	CAY	ROY	IOY	RRY
VPH	+		+		+							
VSH						+		+				+
VPL	−		−		−							
VSL						−		−				−
VPSL	−		−		−	−		−				−
SPH							+	+				+
SSL		−	−		−	−		−				
SSPL		−	−		−			−	−			
SSLPH		−	−		−		+	+				+
SSHPL	+	+		+			−	−				
RPH						+				+		
RSPL			−	−						−		−
RSL1		−										−
RSL2		−										−
RPL1				−						−		
RPL2				−						−		
RSH1		+										+
RSH2		+										+
IPSL				−	−					−	−	
ISH					+							+

One step further in the analysis is to trace the effects of the actions on the basic variables in Figure 4.1: value, switching costs, room and intent towards opportunism for X and Y, and the implications for their inclination to continue or discontinue the relation and their relational risk. The results are specified in Table 4.2, by means of pluses and minuses to indicate the directions of change. The table only indicates first order effects. Of course, due to the recursiveness of the scheme, there are secondary and further effects related to the reactions of the partner, one's own reactions, etc.

STRATEGIC ORIENTATIONS

The previous sections have created a rich inventory of phenomena and instruments of governance. Now complexity is reduced by means of a typology of strategic orientations: adversarial versus cooperative; binding versus loosening, which increase viz. reduce ties between the partners. This is illustrated in Table 4.3

In the strategy of 'tying down' one binds the partner aggressively by limiting his room for conduct, increasing the closeness of monitoring, taking more hostages. In 'prettying up' one binds a partner cooperatively by increasing mutual value, reinforcing bonds of emotions, norms, values and

Table 4.3 Typology of strategy[1]

	Binding	*Loosening*
Adversarial	RPL1, RPL2, SPH	RSH1, RSH2, VPL, VPSL SSLPH, SSL
	Tie down	Devolve
Cooperative	IPSL, VPH, VSH RSL1, RSL2	SSL, SSPL VSL
	Pretty up	Set free

Note: A cooperative strategy is also: yield, i.e. accept an aggressive strategy of the partner (tie down, devolve); i.e: RSL1, RSL2, SSH, VSL, SSHPL1, SSHPL2.

habits, limiting one's own room for opportunism. In 'devolution' one aggressively increases one's own freedom at the expense of the partner, by increasing room for action, withdrawing from monitoring, expropriating value from the partner, developing alternative relations and shifting responsibility for the relationship to the partner by increasing the burden of transaction specific investments, guarantees and penalties for lack of performance and disloyalty. In 'setting free', one's options are opened up in a way that allows the same for the partner, by helping him to engage in other relations, or preparing such alternatives and facilitating switches. In 'yielding' one submits to an aggressive action by the partner.

The question now is which strategic orientations are preferable under what conditions. Game theory yields an approach to investigate this. The crux of the analysis is that when considering an action one should take into account the response of the partner. Three positions will be investigated which are interesting because they occur often.

Case A: Both sides wish to continue the relation because for both the (relative) value of the partner is positive (the partner is more attractive than the next best alternative). How do they deal with the temptation to profit from the partner's dependence?

Case B: Both sides have found more attractive partners elsewhere and continue the relationship only because of switching costs. How do they arrive at disentanglement? Or will they try to infuse the relation with new life?

Case C: One side (*X*) has a more attractive alternative and continues only in view of switching costs. But his relative value for the partner (*Y*) is still positive. How will *X* try to free himself and how will *Y* respond? Or will someone try to revitalize the relation?

Our intuition tells us that with an equal degree of dependence (A, B) cooperative actions will prevail and in case of unequal dependence (C) the least dependent side may act aggressively. A detailed account of a simple game-theoretic analysis is given in Appendix 4.1. It confirms the intuition. The verbal account of cases A to C is given below.

Case A

The game (in the so-called 'extensive form' of a tree of successive choices) for case A is given in Figure 4.7.

For both sides X and Y relative value of the partner is positive: $VXY > 0$ and $VYX > 0$, so that they are in a strategically equivalent situation. This already excludes the strategy of 'yielding': there is no reason to submit to an aggressive action of the partner. For the four remaining orientations for X, from Table 4.3, we consider the most probable reaction by the partner Y. Only those actions are specified for Y. The two most probable options for X are printed in italics and the most likely of these is also printed in bold type. If cooperative loosening is not attractive for either side, both are likely to opt for 'prettying up'.

Since X has a positive interest in the relation (compared with alternatives), there is no reason to consider a loosening action, unless it is intended as a bluff to manoeuvre for a better bargaining position. But here we assume that there is sufficient information for Y to know that it would be bluffing. X might be tempted to 'devolution': a demand for one-sided guarantees or ownership of specific assets by Y and one-sided room for opportunism and limited monitoring to X's advantage. There is no reason for Y to accept that, since by assumption he knows his value to X. Y is likely to view such a move by X as a trial that must immediately be put down. Y would probably respond with an equal action of devolution, which would probably deter X. X might consider 'setting free', if he wants to diversify his sources of learning across multiple relations and is willing to allow the same for Y. How attractive this is depends on risks of spillover and the value of a greater diversification of learning. Problems arise when this is asymmetric for the partners. If it is attractive for X but threatening for Y, then Y will probably

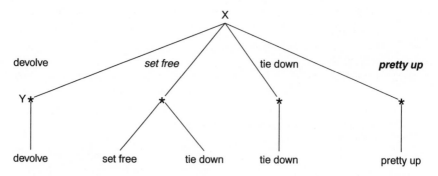

Figure 4.7 Case A: $VYX > 0$; $VXY > 0$.

respond by 'tying down', to prevent X from promiscuity. If X wanted to tie Y down, Y would probably respond in kind. A tug of war arises where both sides limit each other's room for action with formal contractual means and monitoring and demand reciprocal hostages. The option that remains for X is to 'pretty up' and Y would probably reciprocate such constructive, trust generating action. Both sides have an interest in the relationship and are willing to make further investments in it. Y might interpret X's move as a sign of weakness and test this by opting for 'devolution', but X would probably retaliate quickly to deter such action. The conclusion is that one of the cooperative actions is the most attractive to X, and the most attractive response for Y is to respond in kind. If for either side cooperative 'setting free', to achieve multiple partnerships, is not attractive, X and Y will probably both engage in 'prettying up'.

Case B

The game tree for case B is given in Figure 4.8.

Here also the two sides are in a strategically equivalent position, which again excludes the strategy of 'yielding'. Since X would derive greater benefit from an alternative relation ($VYX < 0$), a loosening strategy is the most obvious candidate. The other side has the same perspective. If X took an aggressive loosening strategy of devolution, Y would respond in kind. Mutual 'setting free' is the most likely outcome, to move out with the least hassle and haggle for the more attractive alternatives. Tying down is not attractive and becomes even less so in view of the likelihood that Y would not accept such an action and would either retaliate in kind or by 'devolution' to get X to change course. A real alternative for X is 'prettying up': try to revitalize the relation, if Y were to reciprocate such action. This might occur if both sides feel that renewed investment in one's own and the partner's value will render relative value positive again. This can be more attractive than the disentanglement of 'setting free'.

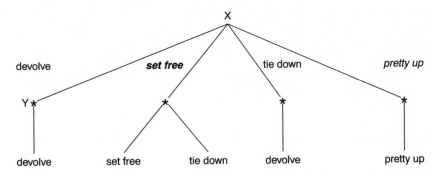

Figure 4.8 Case B: $VXY < 0$; $VYX < 0$; $COX > 0$; $COY > 0$.

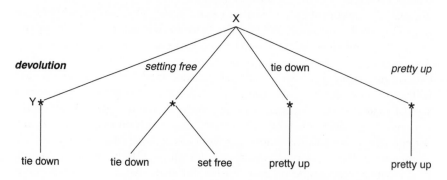

Figure 4.9 Case C: $VYX < 0$; $COX > 0$; $VXY > 0$.

Case C

The game tree for case C is given in Figure 4.9.

In case C there are unequal strategic positions: for one side relative value is positive and for the other negative. X has more attractive alternative partners, but switching costs prevent the switch. The least likely action for X is tying down. If this was chosen, Y is likely to respond with 'prettying up', in an attempt to eliminate X's desire to switch. But X will first consider a loosening orientation. How would Y react if X opted for an aggressive strategy of loosening? Y is not in a good position to react aggressively, but may be desperate. He may react with 'prettying up', but he then runs the risk of further increasing the damage, in the form of higher switching costs, if X does decide to move out. If Y has no effective ways of 'tying down' X, he may have no option but to 'yield'. But if he does have opportunities for tying X down, he will probably resort to this, which would yield problems for X. This may make it attractive for X to opt for 'setting free'. Then Y also might react by 'tying down', but X can then threaten to revert to 'devolution' and Y would probably prefer to go along with 'setting free'. X also has the option of 'prettying up'. Y would no doubt welcome such an attempt at revitalization and respond in kind. But this outcome is likely only when Y has such good opportunities for tying down that X has no opportunity to get away without serious damage. If Y has limited opportunities for tying X down, there is little obstacle for X to devolve and Y can only yield to that. If Y cannot tie down X effectively, but can create a great deal of trouble for him, the mutual strategy of 'setting free' is the most likely.

RELATIONAL DYNAMICS

Alliances need to be set up and are subject to development in time. They often have only limited duration. This may be intended because the relation is aimed only at performing a specific project, for example, in a building consortium, or in achieving some other well-defined, specific goal such as setting a technical standard, as in the Philips–Sony collaboration over the introduction of the audio compact disc. It may also be unintended, as when a relation runs out of steam, stumbles on a change of conditions or shifts from cooperation to competition. This may be because: a novel, better alternative appears on the scene for one or both partners; the value of one or both partners is exhausted; one partner expropriates resources from the other; a partner is taken over by a third party or falls into bankruptcy; a partner takes over a firm which is a competitor of its partner; goals, technical or market conditions change.

An alliance has a path of development or 'life cycle' with stages of emergence, performance, adaptation or decline. A comparison can be made with a marriage relationship, with its stages of engagement, marriage, children, divorce or death. Thus, it is crucial that one see the relationship as, on the one hand, needing a certain continuity and, on the other, as something that needs to adapt and is likely to end at some point. Continuity is needed to recoup specific investments, build up mutual understanding and trust for a deepening of the relation and for cheaper and more effective governance. Adaptation is needed to take into account changed goals and shifting conditions of markets and technology.

In their study of 49 alliances Bleeke and Ernst (1991: 131) found that of the alliances that were able to adapt their perspective 79 per cent was successful, against 33 per cent for alliances whose aim and scope remained the same.

The question now is how a relation can be governed in its different stages. How to start one, but certainly not less important: how to end one and how and when should one prepare for that?

An example is discussed by Faulkner (1995): the alliance between Honda and Rover for the development and production of cars in the UK. This was a non-equity alliance. For Rover it yielded access to efficient Japanese production methods and for Honda a bypass of European import restrictions and access to experience with European tastes of styling. A threat arose for Honda when Rover was taken over by BMW.

The lesson to be learned from such cases is that in the design and governance of an alliance one should not only consider one's partner's interests, but also possibilities that the partner may be taken over and the interests of potential novel owners. This might yield an argument for substantial equity participation (as already indicated in Table 3.9).

An example of an alliance getting into trouble because one side takes over a company that forms a competitive threat to the other is discussed by Lorange and Roos (1992). This is the case of the joint venture for production and distribution of sanitary products in the UK between Swedish Mölnlycke and British Scott. Scott's sales network provided entry to the British market for Mölnlycke, which yielded complementary products, thus increasing the utilization of the network (economy of scope) and also offering Scott access to advanced technology. All went well for eleven years, until Mölnlycke acquired French Peaudouce in order to expand its market to other countries. But Peadouce also had a sales organization in the UK, thus creating a potential problem for Scott. It weakened Scott's relative value in the alliance and thereby raised the risk of opportunism by Mölnlycke.

The lesson to be learned from this case is that even though the partner is not a competitor, it may have an interest in taking over a company which is a competitor.

The beginning of a relationship is not simple insofar as one does not know what it will yield and yet relation-specific investments are needed to build mutual value and get it going. In marriage, the blindness of infatuation helps, which is oblivious to risk and yields only rosy visions of the unique value of the partner. In business relations, blind friendship or kinship does help to get relations going, but this is not generally advisable: they often yield the most vociferous problems. In business relations it is wise to gather information on the partner and his reputation. In view of the previous analyses of strategic manoeuvring, at the beginning of a relationship there will be plans to 'pretty up', as a cooperative strategy of binding. This would entail: investment in good atmosphere, shared norms and values (*IPSL*), the value of the partner (*VPH*), the value offered to the partner (*VSH*) and voluntary constraints on the room for opportunism (*RSL*).

An adversarial approach of binding by 'tying down' the partner would hardly encourage him to contribute to the building of the relationship. Such a strategy might include: legal or other formal contractual constraints (*RPL1*), monitoring (*RPL2*), demand of hostages (*SPH*). These actions are likely to scare off the partner because they entail the incurrence of switching costs and loss of flexibility before the worth of the relationship has been proven. They are likely to produce an atmosphere of distrust and reciprocative formal constraints, which threaten to lock up the relation in formalities that inhibit development. This is inadvisable at the beginning of a relationship when the boundaries of usefulness are difficult to indicate and room for development is needed. Yet such action can be required to restrict one's own switching costs and risk of hold-up. They can be warranted when it is clear to the partner that these costs and risks are one-sided and the sharing of cost and risk is needed to get the relationship started. The problem may be mitigated by starting small. The extent of costs and risks is therefore limited with only limited contractual constraints and guarantees. By aiming at quick results, proof is offered that the relationship is indeed worth further investments and risk taking, and trust is allowed to develop.

It is sometimes said that right from the beginning one should specify the precise limits of the alliance, in aims and time. In general, this seems bad advice. Thereby one limits both the perspective and flexibility of the relationship and the willingness to make sacrifices. As the theory of repeated games (and commonsense) teaches us, if one knows beforehand when a relation will end, then the opportunistic search for short-term advantage will prevail. It is precisely the open-endedness of the relationship that sets off the potential for long-term cooperation against the short-term advantage of opportunistic action that will end the relation.

A next stage in the cooperative strategy is to continue, step by step, to increase mutual value with incremental specific investments. This may require the provision of guarantees or redistribution of ownership of specific assets. Then the party receiving the guarantees should yield sufficient openness to monitoring to ensure that conditions of the guarantees are satisfied.

If, for example, a supplier X requires a guarantee from customer Y (long-term contract, minimal frequency or total volume of sales, or payback of the residual value of the asset in case of a premature stop), to ensure that a specific investment is recouped, then Y may want counter-guarantees that the asset is indeed specific and is not used for production for another customer, particularly a competitor of Y, perhaps by the right to monitor X's order book or sales.

Typical of this stage of development is also the development of mutual understanding and a mutual language, technical standards, procedures, norms, culture. These provide the basis for a further deepening of cooperation, a basis for trust to grow. It also constitutes a mutual specific investment which contributes to balanced dependence.

In the marriage relationship analysed in the appendix at the end of this chapter, this is the 'courtship', which used to develop into an engagement. This is symbolically confirmed by the exchange of rings. In business the label of 'official dealer' might be the analogue to such a ring.

As the relationship develops and bears fruit, the basis arises for further specific investments to increase mutual value ('pretty up') and offer mutual guarantees ('yield'). We are in the situation described by case A. Continuation of the mutual strategy of 'prettying up' is plausible. Bonds increase, with habituation and trust, in the double sense of trust in competence and trust in loyalty, founded also on an assessment of mutual advantage in continuation. Mutual commitment may be confirmed by exchange of hostages, in the form of knowledge of each other's technology, licences, exchange of staff, minority participation. But this may also have happened, in one form or other, at an earlier stage of development. Thus, in general, a step-by-step development is wise, unless market pressures for speed overrule such an option. It is important, whenever possible, not to take too large steps and to let each step produce visible results.

As the relationship proceeds, its limits become more visible. There is an increasing risk that its potential is running out of steam and new, more attractive options may present themselves. If this applies more or less equally for both sides, we obtain the situation of case B and the partners are most likely to 'set each other free'. It may be desirable at this stage to define the limits of cooperation and fine-tune guarantees. The basis for this is better available than at the beginning: the value of the relationship has proved itself, restrictive measures are less likely to form undesirable constraints, since the limits of the relation can now be defined. Provided it is done openly, it is less of a trigger of mistrust, since on the basis of experience a fair assessment can be made of the partner's reliability and competence. It can be made clear that up to certain limits it is mutually profitable to reinforce and support each other, even when a (moderately) more attractive novel partner comes along. Agreements can be made on what is and is not expected from each other and where each allows the other freedom.

The situation may also arise that both sides want to continue the relation (case A), but with a certain diversification to other relations. In that case also they may easily arrive at mutual 'setting free'. Relations often run this course as a matter of routine: after a while specialties often become commodities. A product that was specific for a given user becomes more current, so that the market widens. A dedicated investment receives a wider range of use, possibly because after a period of innovation it turns into a 'dominant design' (Abernathy and Utterback 1978). User-specific standards, e.g. in EDI, evolve into industry standards, thus eliminating transaction specificity.

A more problematic situation arises if value decreases only for one side, no longer needing the partner's resources, either because they have become exhausted without renewal, have spilled over to the partner, or some novel alternative has entered the stage. Then we arrive at the situation of case C.

A typical example is where *X* is engaged in an alliance to learn from the special competencies of *Y*, and *X* has acquired those competencies without *Y* developing new ones. In other words, *X* has learned all there is to learn from *Y* while *Y* has not developed new knowledge. There is a whole range of examples of alliances between European or American firms and Japanese firms, where the Japanese provided entry to the otherwise inaccessible Japanese market and the western companies provided technology, which was in due course copied and improved upon by the Japanese, with the Japanese market remaining closed to foreigners. But the reverse also happens: the side that first needed a partner to gain access to a market has now found its own access, while maintaining technological superiority.

One must remain alert to this possibility and either choose, design or adapt the relation for ongoing symmetry of value, or take timely measures when irremediable asymmetry of value becomes apparent.

Take the case where a company *X* from country *A* adds a product to the product mix of partner *Y* in country *B*, by which *X* obtains entry for his product in country *B* and *Y* improves the utilization of his distribution channels. The danger for *Y* is that when *X* has become familiar with the distribution system in country *B* he no longer needs *Y*. The relation can be stabilized by symmetry: *Y* also adds his product to the product mix of *X* in country *A*. Thus there is a threat of retaliation: what *X* can do to *Y*, *Y* can do to *X*.

In the situation of asymmetric value (case C) there is a great temptation to hide loss of interest and to make secret preparations for break-out. The reason for this, as illustrated by the game-theoretic analysis in the previous section, is that one will be less inclined to ongoing investments in the relationship.

There is a temptation to try and sneak into an undetected strategy of 'devolution': to reduce own switching costs by looking for alternative partners, in preparation for defection and to let the other side continue its investment for as long as he remains unsuspicious. Reconnaissance and development of novel alternatives are kept secret.

This can yield 'white lies': deeper objections are hidden by haggling over trivialities. In business relations, objections against lowered quality, flexibility or ability to innovate, which are relatively difficult to redress, are shrouded in haggling over the price. This can perhaps explain the puzzle that industrial buyers maintain that price is of secondary importance to quality, flexibility and innovativeness, while in the experience of suppliers price appears to prevail in the buyer's interest. This is illustrated in Table 4.4. While buyers say that price comes only in fifth place, suppliers claim that in fact it stands in first place.

If intentions to break out are announced, the partner might make trouble with attempts to 'tie down' before measures have been taken to counter it. This is in line with the observation that when relations break they do so suddenly (Casson 1991). But with sneak devolution the risk is run that when the other side detects it, the first response will certainly be to attempt to 'tie down' the partner. This may trigger the first partner to intensify 'devolution' more openly now: maximal reduction of the volume of activities in the relation, insofar as possible within contractual constraints, reduction of those constraints, obstruction of monitoring, breaking down partner's value, decreasing one's own value to the partner, among other things by

Table 4.4 Perceptions of suppliers and buyers concerning demands, in order of priority

Demand	Buyers	Suppliers
Quality	1	3
Supply reliability	2	4
Flexibility	3	2
Delivery time	4	5
Price	5	1
Codesign/comakership	6	6
Production technology	7	7
Scale	8	8
Dependence	9	9
Physical proximity	10	10

Source: Coopers and Lybrand (1989).

pestering him. A bitter fight may arise of aggressive devolution versus vociferous attempts to tie down. This can be very disruptive and may have negative effects on the reputation of the partner that is trying to escape.

A more cooperative approach may be better, in an attempt to achieve mutual 'setting free'. This requires resisting the temptation to keep the wish of escape secret and announcing the intention to disentangle the relation, helping the partner to get off without too much damage. This entails helping the partner to reduce switching costs, by stopping transaction-specific investments and finding or developing alternative relations to fill the impending gap. This may prevent the mutually destructive process of disentangling, in the vicious circle of 'devolution' versus 'tying down' already described.

ROLES OF A GO-BETWEEN

In studies of alliances there is a tendency to look only at dyads of firms and to consider networks as aggregates of such dyads. But there are several roles for a third party, which can play a central role as a go-between in the development of relations. I propose that this yields a perspective for looking at the roles of banks, technology transfer centres and trade and industry associations in European business systems and of banks and trading houses in Japanese enterprise groups (*kigyo shudan*). The role of the go-between is particularly important in alliances that are aimed at innovation; at the development of products, processes and competencies.

Already in classical TCE the possibility was indicated of using a third party, in 'trilateral governance', as an alternative to integration of the activity within the firm or bilateral governance between firms, for solving the hold-up problem that arises in the case of dedicated investments. This is recommended when the transactions involved are infrequent, so that the volume of transactions does not warrant the cost of setting up bilateral governance, while there are significant advantages of not integrating the activity within the user firm. Thus the argument for trilateral governance is one of efficiency: it is cheaper. Only limited explicit agreements between the partners are made and the most important one is procedural. If disagreement arises, the third party will be called on to arbitrate. An important part of this role is to help the partners to set realistic goals with balanced advantages and risks. A classic example is the role of an architect as third party in transactions between a builder and a supplier of building materials.

Clearly, a condition is that the third party must be trusted by both partners regarding both competence and intent. He must be knowledgeable on the technologies, markets and strategies involved and fair in judgement and adjudication. The basis for this trust may be self-interest: the third party has an interest in ongoing relations with both partners and therefore an interest in doing his best and being fair, in order to maintain his reputation. The basis may also be more intrinsic, stemming from desire, self-esteem, moral or social obligation. The question then arises: if there is such a basis for trust in the go-between, why does it not also arise between the partners themselves, so that the go-between is superfluous? The answer is that between the partners there is the temptation to defect, because it yields advantage, while for the go-between there is no such temptation. But note that the go-between is not needed if between the partners the advantage of defection does not exceed their resistance to temptation.

Another instrument of governance recognized by TCE is the exchange of hostages, in order to guarantee that agreements are kept. The characteristic of a hostage is its asymmetry in value: it has value for the giver but not for the taker. This condition serves to keep the taker from the temptation of keeping the hostage permanently, even if the other side has kept their end of the bargain.

In relations between firms, people could be hostages: in intermarriage between family businesses or the detachment to each other of key executives. It can also take the form of cross-participation between firms, pieces of technology or knowledge that are sensitive to competition.

A previous section discussed the problems in holding hostages. The hostage keeper may be tempted to hold on to the hostage, in spite of the fact that the hostage giver has upheld his side of the agreement. This problem can be reduced by having a third party keep the hostages. This solution is ancient and was used in treaties between medieval rulers (de Laat 1996). It works only if the third party is less tempted to retain the hostages after completion of the agreement than the party in whose interest the hostage is taken. But note that the third party would jeopardize the relationship with both partners by not keeping the agreement and is thus likely to be disciplined by this double jeopardy. There would no longer be the temptation to play the game of deceit discussed before. If the hostage giver supplied his attractive daughter with the aim of breaking the treaty, on the gamble that the hostage keeper would not damage such an attractive lady, and then did break the treaty, his partner in the treaty would demand from the go-between to sacrifice her. The ploy would no longer work.

Particularly when firms cooperate for innovation, the knowledge they are pooling will tend to be tacit. In order to exchange tacit knowledge an intensive interaction must be set up in which mutual understanding is created. Note also that the setting up of such interaction and mutual understanding constitutes a dedicated investment. How do you judge whether such investment is worthwhile before you commit it? This is the revelation problem: how can the value of knowledge or competence be revealed before it is transmitted? Here we are dealing with Arrow's paradox: if you give information that is sufficient to judge the value of the information, then little may be left to trade or hold back. Here lies a third role for the go-between. Having ongoing relations with both partners, it has already made investments in ability to understand and judge competence. Thus it can act as the judge of value and relevance for both partners before they invest in their relationship. Having the trust of both partners and knowing them well enough to assess both on the value and relevance to each other, it can inform them without actually supplying the underlying information.

Closely related to this is the role of the go-between in spillover control. Partners do not only want to have an indication of value before they commit dedicated investments. They also face the problem that by giving information about their knowledge they reveal at least part of it, which may then spill over to competitors. The fourth role of the go-between is to serve as a screening device: the go-between does not make the knowledge available to the partner, but assesses it for him. Next, when the partners proceed to pool and exchange knowledge, the go-between can perform or monitor spillover control. Spillover control might otherwise require mutual in-house monitoring of streams of information by the partners themselves, to check that it does not leak to competitors. But such mutual monitoring may increase rather than control information exchange and hence aggravate rather than relieve the spillover problem. Especially at the beginning of the relationship, such in-house monitoring is likely to be unacceptable to the partners. Both the risk of spillover and the unwillingness to grant monitoring to guard against it will be greater to the extent that the partners are actual or potential competitors, or have intimate linkages with competitors.

Recall that the whole issue of spillover is relevant only under certain conditions. The first is that the nature of the knowledge involved indeed enables spillover. This is not the case to the extent that the knowledge is tacit or embedded in the organization. When knowledge is tacit, its transfer requires intensive mutual interaction, or a buy-out of the people in whom the knowledge is embodied. Even this may not be effective, to the extent that their performance is contingent upon supporting the knowledge, procedures or organization that remains behind. The second condition for the problem of spillover is that the partner is a potential competitor, or has connections with competitors. The third is that development is not so fast that spillover no longer matters.

Related to the previous roles, there is a fifth role in the building of trust. This was also recognized by Uzzi (1997), who described the role of a go-between in creating the embeddedness of partnerships. It was also discussed by Deutsch (1973) regarding mechanisms in the transmission of trust. One aspect of this is the transitivity of trust: if X trusts Y and Y trusts Z, then X can be disposed to trust Z. Here Y is the go-between. Relationships are often initiated with partners that are trusted partners of one's own trusted partners. If X and Z both trust Y, then they may be disposed also to trust each other. Here again Y is the go-between. Such bringing together of partners in a disposition towards trust is only a beginning. Next, intermediation may help to set up initial small steps of cooperation and to ensure that they are successful and do not raise misunderstanding which might antagonize or raise suspicion. This is important in the building of both competence trust and intentional trust. It was noted before that breach of competence trust calls for very different action from breach of intentional trust. In the first case, one might help to improve competence, but that would not help in the second case, where it might be more appropriate to signal a warning or even retaliate. But it can be difficult to tell which of the two is the case. The third party can act as an independent observer, with access to inside information. He can eliminate misunderstandings that might otherwise destabilize the relationship. This role is particularly important where trust is not pre-existent as part of a group culture or set of norms and values and has to be built up in the relationship.

The beginning of relationships tends to get most attention but, as noted above, the ending of relationships is at least as important and often more difficult. When in an existing relationship one partner runs into a more attractive alternative, there is substantial risk of fierce antagonism, whereby the other partner tries to evade loss by keeping the first partner from cutting loose and the first partner retaliates with nasty behaviour to badger the second partner to let go. In expectation of this, the first partner may keep her wish to exit secret and prepare her defection in silence. But this makes the problem worse for the second partner, because she has less time to adapt and may react all the more fiercely in trying to tie the first partner down. One can observe this in both firm relationships and marriages. The better road may be for the first partner to announce her intentions at an early stage, but stay on for the time being to help the second partner to find an acceptable way out. But such an announcement breaks trust and the destructive spiral of mutual antagonism is difficult to prevent. Careful counselling by a trusted third party may be needed to guide and control this process.

An alternative is for the first partner to give the relationship another chance and help the second partner to increase its attractiveness. But this entails that the second partner further increases the relation-specific investments, while a threat has appeared that the relation may break. Here also, trusted counselling may be needed.

An argument against embedded, voice-based network systems is that the relations between firms, oriented towards the longer term and based on relation-specific investments and trust, create exit barriers and entry barriers and thereby limit the efficiency, flexibility and adaptiveness of the system. Uzzi (1997) called this the 'paradox of embeddedness'. This leads to a sixth role for the go-between: to act as a boundary spanner between an existing network and potential outside sources of innovation. It may be threatening for partners who are active in ongoing exchange relations to maintain outside exploratory relations for scanning novel opportunities. In fact, one of the most threatening and potentially destabilizing events in a trust relationship is the appearance on the stage of a new player who might present a more attractive substitute for one of the partners involved. The fear of this may create a taboo of outside scanning in order to maintain the integrity of the network and this can be disastrous for innovation on the basis of outside sources. The problem of losing positional advantage to an outsider and being left with idle dedicated assets is aggravated by spillover risk: one may also lose part of one's core competence. A go-between who does not participate in exchange can perform outside scanning under less suspicion, since it is not in her own direct interest to defect to more promising outsiders, while it is in her interest to maintain her reputation for confidentiality and fair dealing. Summing up: outside scanning is less threatening when done by a go-between without a direct stake in exchange and this opens the network up to potential novelty from outside.

In fact, this role is related to some of the previous ones: the role of revelation, spillover control and the management of trust. One can bring in judgements of the potential of outside novelty while maintaining confidentiality of its content and source, without which that information would not have been obtained. Conversely, one can give an assessment of the value of what the network could offer to outsiders without giving it away or specifying the precise source in the network (which may tempt the outsider to pry that loose from the network). When novel opportunities for redesigning the network have thus been identified and assessed, the go-between can next help in the phasing out of the 'losers' in the old network, by providing ways out, in exit to another network, or helping them to break up and redistribute their resources. The go-between might even administer some insurance developed by the network to deal with such contingencies.

There is evidence that in the Netherlands the recently instituted 'innovation centres' play such roles, not entirely consciously and largely by trial and error. This evidence comes from my own experience in giving lectures along the lines of this chapter to the centres and informally testing to what extent they play the roles indicated, by asking them to give specific instances. The role of trilateral governance was recognized clearly: the coaching of partners in lieu of contracts; particularly the setting of realistic goals, monitoring their achievement, eliminating misunderstandings and making adjustments along the way. This role was clearly integrated within the role of building and managing trust, as one might expect. The role of revelation was also clearly recognized: here lies the central mission of the centres. Hostage keeping and spillover control were not recognized directly, but part of the experience was that the care and confidentiality with which information was treated was enhanced by the fact that the centre acted as a go-between. This could be interpreted as a hostage mechanism: players were careful with information received from their partner because sensitive information from themselves was held by the go-between. It could also be interpreted as a reputation mechanism: they want to maintain a good reputation with the centre, not jeopardize future dealings and potential future partnerships. The role of the boundary spanner was not relevant here because the networks in which the centres operated had not yet reached the degree of consolidation in which such a role becomes relevant.

More specific evidence comes from a longitudinal case study by Klein Woolthuis (1997) of cooperation between eleven firms, in various configurations, in the development of medical products, based on an initiative by an Innovation Centre and a Regional Development Centre (RDC) in the province of Overijsel. Development projects were submitted for subsidy in the EU EFRO programme (when awarded, it yields a 50 per cent subsidy of product development costs). The Centre and the RDC were particularly important in the start-up stage. An important factor for the firms was that they trusted the initiators and hence also the partner firms which they brought together. Yet, 'parties were reluctant to reveal information and were hesitant to engage in any relationship before it was completely clear what the others' motives were and what role they would fulfil ... This made the start difficult and time consuming ... Therefore it was important that the Centre and the RDC took on a guiding role ... they could ease the negotiations ... this included chairmanship at meetings, encouraging and guiding the first contacts.' This gives evidence of the roles of the go-between in trilateral governance and the building of trust. An external committee was instituted, with one member from the Ministry of Economic Affairs and two managers from local hospitals, to help in the assessment of project proposals and to watch over fair distribution of work and subsidies from EFRO. It is noted that, 'It is very important that the committee should make fair evaluations. Parties should be able to trust the board ... The perception of equal treatment is therefore of crucial importance.' The task of the 'umbrella' of the go-betweens, consisting of the Centre, the RDC and the advisory council, was summarized as follows: 'In the first stage the umbrella performed an important role because it provided firms with a platform to get to know the others. The umbrella became of decreasing importance when direct links between firms evolved ... firms started to know each other and envisage future potential for more dense relationships.' This again indicates the role of trust building and also suggests the role of revelation. There is no mention of the roles of hostage keeping and spillover control. They may have been present but unnoticed by the researchers reporting the case.

It is interesting that the go-betweens who were the initiators (the Centre and the RDC) instituted a separate advisory council to guide the development of projects. This makes sense, for two reasons. First, it was noted that the go-between requires expertise to generate competence trust and it may be too much to expect relevant and sufficiently deep expertise of a single agency in a wide variety of relations. With a separate council the go-between can seek specialized support that is tailored to the situation. That is why in this case hospitals were included. Second, by creating a special council the go-between insulates itself to some extent from the risk of losing reputation when something goes wrong in the judgement and guidance of cooperation. Then the advisory council takes the direct blame and, since it is unique to the situation, its loss of reputation is less serious.

CONCLUSIONS

Organizations need an instrument to analyse and assess a relation; to deal with the paradoxes of cooperation. They need to assess their position concerning opportunities and threats, to arrive at an evaluation and diagnosis of the relation and actions to improve or re-design it. This chapter developed such an instrument (Figure 4.1). The simplest use of the scheme is as a checklist of factors that influence relational value and risk. The causal relations between the factors can be used to identify possible actions one could undertake and to analyse possible reactions from the partner, to see where it might end. The instrument becomes stronger if one can also quantify the effects of actions. Empirical studies to be discussed in Chapter 5 demonstrate that such quantification is possible. Then one can simulate effects of actions and counter-actions, to produce possible paths of development of a relationship and to test alternative modes of governance under different conditions of technology, competition and institutional environment. The building of such simulation models is in hand.

Such steps are important in practice, but also for scientific progress, to arrive at a closer investigation and experimentation of types of strategies and relations, 'life cycles' of relations, further to deepen the analysis given.

APPENDIX 4.1 MARRIAGE

By way of illustration and experiment, the general scheme for the governance of relations in Figure 4.1 is applied to marriage relationships. This
may be enlightening: perhaps actions from these contexts can be transposed
to instruments in the governance of alliances. Previously some similarities
were mentioned in passing. Here a more systematic analysis of similarities
and differences is given. For ease of reference Figure 4.1 is repeated here.

The reader may object to an analysis of marriage in terms of opportunism. But note that a view of marriage as an arrangement of reason is
neither new nor exceptional and is still pervasive in some cultures.
Furthermore, as in standard TCE, the assumption is not that everyone is
equally opportunistic all the time, but that, for one person more than another,
opportunism can appear, depending on the situation, and its emergence is
difficult to foresee, even for the perpetrator. Opportunism can rest on hidden
motives or inclinations. Agendas can be partly hidden, even to the owner.
Opportunism can be a viper under the fresh green grass. Furthermore, note
that in contrast with classical TCE, here trust and loyalty are taken into
account, next to opportunism.

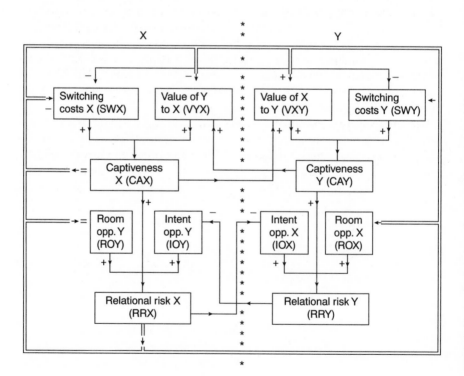

Figure A4.1.1 Relational risk of *X* and *Y*.

In a love relation, value consists of a number of highly personal dimensions such as, in arbitrary order: humour, beauty, charm, strength, wealth, imagination, liveliness, perceptiveness, sensitivity, intelligence, etc. Relation-specific investments arise in the form of time, emotion and money spent on the partner, the relation, a home. Investment in decorations or alterations to a rented house are more sunk, i.e. are lost to a greater extent and thereby more relation specific than in an owned house. Investment in an owned house is more sunk to the extent that the house is more special, appealing to rare tastes. Next to these specific investments there are switching costs due to alimony. Venereal disease and AIDS are risks of promiscuity.

An important difference is that people in a marriage get older, whereby the switching costs increase: it becomes more and more difficult to make a switch. And the scope for alternative relations dwindles, thus increasing relative value of the partners to each other. There is great wisdom in this arrangement, since at least at a greater age it helps to prevent the problematic situation where the emergence of a more attractive alternative for one partner destabilizes the relation (case C in the foregoing game-theoretic analysis). Firms, by contrast, can rejuvenate and maintain their attractiveness to others.

In marriage, children function as 'two-sided hostages' (if that is not a contradiction in terms). For both partners they are of irreplaceable, personal value, can be damaged by both partners and cannot with preservation of value be 'sold off'. In contrast with business alliances, such hostages can be forced by the female through a sneak pregnancy.

Formal contractual binding and control are available in divorce law, including regulations for alimony and sharing of assets and pension benefits. There are further institutional constraints on the room for opportunism: in norms and habits concerning marital faith, absence, childcare, etc. One cannot easily change such norms, but one can select an environment with more or with less strict constraints. Wedding rings serve as symbolic commitment devices and to signal that one is already 'taken', to mitigate the risk of promiscuity. Ability to monitor compliance to agreements depends on extent and type of absence, associated with the professions the partners have. Figure A4.1.1 gives the substitution from the inventory of instruments in Table A4.1.1.

It was already mentioned that infatuation helps partners across the threshold of commitment at the beginning of a relationship. It yields a solution to the problem that one has to invest in something with uncertain expectations. Without infatuation the human species might not have survived: too few people would have embarked on reasonably faithful marriage relations.

When in a marriage the limits of value become clearer and more attractive alternatives appear, promiscuity is less accepted than in business relations, although in some cultures men have several wives. In general, due to a greater emotional content, switching costs are high in marriage, particularly when there are children. Due to a process of habituation and bonding and the erosion of alternatives, marriages may also last when the children leave home.

Table A4.1.1 Instruments in a marriage relation

Influence on value

VPH	Increase attractiveness of partner by investing time and money in clothing, adornment, health, education, etc.
VSH	Same for oneself, to increase value for partner.
VPL	Lower attractiveness of partner, search for alternative partners.
VSL	Make oneself less attractive, offer alternative partners.

Influence on switching costs

SSL	Make less effort specific to the relation, careful use of contraceptives to limit risks of promiscuity.
SSLPH1	Lower own switching costs and simultaneously increase the partner's, by having community of property if one is the poorest partner, or anti-nuptial agreement if one is the richest; leave care for the children to the partner, let the other party share costs of home decoration, etc.
SSLPH2	Same, by obtaining additional guarantees from the partner, e.g. in the form of a savings account that is allotted when the other breaks the relation.
SSPH	Take children.

Influence room for opportunism

RPL1	Constrain partner's room, by narrower legal and other formal constraints, with corresponding sanctions, move to a community with tighter norms and social control.
RPL2	Same, by more monitoring of his/her activities, if necessary by means of a private detective.
RSH1	Increase one's own room by furthering looser formal constraints and norms of fidelity.
RSH2	Same, by hiding from monitoring; choosing a profession or job with much travel or other absence in unobservable activity.

Influence inclination to opportunism

IPSL	Bonding: create emotional bonding, habituation.
ISH	Signal greater inclination towards opportunism with indifference, antipathy, animosity.

The analysis shows that in marriages men usually have the best position. He has, or had, lower switching costs, more room for promiscuity and a greater inclination towards it because:

- he is/was master of the purse;
- he encounters more alternative partners through his work, depending on his job;
- he benefits from greater information asymmetry, making him more difficult to monitor;
- he encounters less erosion of attractiveness to alternative partners as he ages;
- he is/was less emotionally bound to the children, which lowered his switching costs.

In view of the weaker position of the wife regarding these instruments of private ordering, a legalistic ordering was necessary to compensate, in the form of divorce law and an institutional ordering, in the form of religious and social rules. During emancipation, women have gained more access to instruments of private ordering, whereby legal and social regulation becomes less necessary. The most important instrument was a job, facilitated by child-care provision, and greater mobility yielding more access to alternative relations, more absence from home, yielding information asymmetry, hence less controllability, plus own income to allow for easier switching. Also there has been a tendency for fathers to become more involved with their children, both emotionally and in the amount of time spent with them. This does not yet, however, yield a level playing field for the battle of the sexes.

What can be learned from this for business alliances? Perhaps the analogue of wedding or engagement rings is useful: some widely visible and understood emblem which indicates that one is already engaged in a relationship, in some area and intends to be loyal, thus discouraging distractions and temptations by alternative partners on the prowl.

Perhaps joint ventures can be seen as children (we already talk of 'parent' companies). In that case we might need to add another reason for a JV, in addition to the ones listed in Chapter 3 (Table 3.10): a JV as an instrument of bonding, or bilateral hostages, between parent companies who cooperate in a much wider range of activities with limited formal legal ordering. The JV acts as a device to ensure loyalty and constructive cooperation.

In a relationship with asymmetric power (dependence), the equivalent of alimony might serve as a guarantee for settlement for the partner who is the most dependent, with the highest switching costs, to ensure that in case of break-up some compensation for one-sided switching costs can be counted on, without reliance on the benevolence of the partner.

In such an asymmetric relationship, a dowry might help to entice the most powerful party to enter into a commitment, with guarantees (such as alimony), to the weaker party.

The analogue of godparents might serve as a special case of the go-between discussed in a previous section. In particular, perhaps they can be seen as guardians of hostages (as real godparents do in respect to children). If JVs can be seen as analogues to children, the analogue of godparents may be seen as go-betweens to help stabilize and govern such joint ventures, as a cheaper and more flexible instrument than detailed legal regulation.

The analogues of divorce and custody laws might be considered to facilitate alliances in general and JVs in particular, by instituting baseline rules for the equivalents of alimony and governance of the break-up of alliances in general and JVs in particular.

5 Buyer–supplier alliances

Vertical relations between buyers and suppliers form an important area of inter-firm relations. They are called 'vertical' because it is customary to represent the supply chain vertically, from 'upstream' to 'downstream' activities. Horizontal relations obtain between firms in the same stage of a supply chain and tend to involve potential or actual competitors. In contrast with horizontal relations, in vertical relations the risks of competition are relatively small: complementarity of resources prevails. But there may still be conflict of interest, for example, in the division of the proceeds from the added value created in the relation. As discussed in previous chapters, the mutual adjustment needed to provide high quality, product differentiation and innovation generally entails specific investments, which yields dependence, with ensuing risks of 'hold-up'. This chapter considers the following questions. What kind of buyer–supplier relations (BSR) require special attention? What issues appear in practice? What problems are there and how can they be solved? The methods developed in Chapter 4 are applied for answering these questions. First, tests of the theory of Chapter 4 are reported: to what extent do we find the issues, problems and solutions in practice? The analysis is used to assess the effects to be expected from developments in information and communication technology (ICT). Next, an assessment is given of how the theory and methods can be applied for an 'audit' and (re)design of buyer–supplier relations. Also, the outcomes are reported of a more formal analysis of different 'generic types' of BSR: which performs best under which conditions? This analysis is inspired by the contrast between Japanese practice and past practices in Europe and the USA. The more formal analysis is provided in an appendix. Finally, an assessment is given of implications for public policy.

INTRODUCTION

The subject here is not operational matters of BSR, such as procedures for the assessment and selection of suppliers, organization of the buying process, negotiation, logistics, etc. The subject is: strategic issues of cooperation and dependence. The context here is the need to concentrate on core competencies, as discussed in Chapter 2. This entails that, more than in the past, one should purchase and outsource goods and services, even if they are 'sensitive' in the sense that:

- They must satisfy specific demands concerning design, specification, quality, reliability.
- There are risks of dependence due to specific investments.
- There are risks of spillover of proprietary knowledge to competitors.

Suppliers have to satisfy more stringent and more specific demands. An important question is how they can satisfy them without becoming too dependent. These are the issues studied here and are primarily related to business management, but to some extent also to government, since the support infrastructure of supplier industries is one of the determinants of national competitive advantage (Porter 1990).

The focus is on outsourcing rather than simple purchasing. One difference between the two is that for outsourcing there is the alternative of own in-house production, while for purchasing there is no such alternative. The second difference is that purchasing refers to standardized products produced on stock, to be sold to a multiplicity of buyers. In contrast, in outsourcing the function, specification, design, prototyping and testing, production, quality control and logistics of the product to be supplied are to a greater or lesser extent subject to control by the buyer. The two aspects of outsourcing often go together: if there exists sufficient competence to specify the product, one might be close to the competence of producing it. But this is not necessarily the case and, in fact, often is not. An important question concerning outsourcing is in what proportion and in what kind of interaction do buyer and supplier contribute to specification, design, trial, prototyping and testing, production, quality control and logistics. Who takes the initiative? Who has the leading competence in what area? Who makes the decisions? Who carries the risks?

These questions are analysed from the resource perspective: outsourcing should be seen as a means of utilizing supplier resources to complement one's own. A comparison will be made between Japanese, European and US practices. Learning from Japanese practices, but not necessarily copying them, EU and US practice is shifting towards more initiative and responsibility for the supplier, in 'lean supply' (Lamming 1993).

There are two kinds of outsourcing: capacity sourcing, where temporary use is made of outside capacity, and specialty outsourcing, where use is made of resources that form a specialty of the supplier. The first serves for flexibility in the volume of production, e.g. to absorb peaks in demand without generating excess capacity outside them. The latter includes many forms. Outsourcing occurs for the buyer's process of production, logistics and management and can involve manufacturing, materials, components and services. Services can be distinguished in services to support primary production processes, which are called 'strategic' and services for secondary activities. The first includes R&D, design, prototyping and testing, software, logistics, specialist support, installation, maintenance, repair, etc. The second includes non-specialist maintenance, cleaning, catering, etc.

Outsourcing takes place in the building industry, process industry (oil, chemicals, foods), wood and metal industry, production of machines, apparatus, instruments, means of transport. Supply takes place in the wood and metal industries, rubber and plastics, machines, apparatus, instruments, building and installation, maintenance and repair, catering, transport and storage, finance and insurance, rental and leasing, accountancy and consultancy, information and communication, training, medical services, recreation.

Suppliers are often small firms, which determines the image that many people have, but suppliers can also be large and supply to small firms.

> Small buyers are found, for example, in the plastics industry, where small producers of plastic goods are supplied materials by large chemical firms. But here the supply mostly concerns bulk commodity goods, so that it is more a matter of purchasing than outsourcing as defined above. Supply of materials becomes more in the nature of outsourcing when it concerns chemical specialties, special metal alloys, or components. Producers of plastic goods in turn supply often to large firms (such as Norplast's supply of plastic components to Philips's electrical/electronic goods). There is also supply from large firms to large firms, such as the supply of electronic components from Bosch, Siemens and Philips to the car industry.

The definition of outsourcing implies that a greater or lesser amount of adaptation is necessary between buyer and supplier. These are accompanied by more or less specific investments. As discussed before, these yield dependence, which entails risks of discontinuity and 'hold-up'. Previous chapters developed instruments for the analysis of these issues. In this chapter they are applied in more detail to BSRs, to answer questions that are specific to these types of alliances.

QUESTIONS

The following questions arise in BSRs:

- What precisely are the advantages and drawbacks of outsourcing?
- When should one buy rather than make?

- What forms of outsourcing are best?
- How should they be organized?
- How can buyers and suppliers govern their relations to maximize advantages and minimize risks?
- To what outcomes can this lead?
- What role, if any, is there for governments?

Answers to the first two questions are given in Table 5.1. The remaining questions often arise from attempts to learn from 'Japanese success'. During the 1960s Europe was confronted with the 'American challenge' (*Défi Americain*, after a book from that time by Servan-Schreiber) from the large, diversified, international corporations. During the 1980s Europe encountered the Japanese challenge from methods and organization of production, in

Table 5.1 Reasons to outsource or not

Reasons to outsource

Assets
- Volume flexibility: absorb peaks through capacity outsourcing.
- Fixed costs of assets are transformed into variable costs of purchase.
- Life cycle production: keep production going without new investment for a product that serves as a 'cash cow' at the end of the product's life cycle.
- Lower wages: sometimes wages are lower and labour is more flexible, in small supplier firms.

Competencies
- Specialization: through specialization and scale a supplier can produce more cheaply.
- Stronger incentives: supply through the market yields greater incentives for effort.
- Technical competence: the supplier has competencies which the buyer has not.
- Innovative competence: the supplier has greater innovative competence.

Positional advantages
- Strategic flexibility: outsource to keep options open concerning production technology.

Reasons not to outsource

Assets
- One can produce more cheaply oneself (due to scale, scope, experience).

Competencies
- Technical competence: no competent supplier available.
- Risk of spillover.

Positional advantages
- Dependence/risk: vulnerability to interruptions of production, quality, availability; risk of 'hold-up'.
- Desire to maintain competencies to preserve possibilities for entry into novel markets.

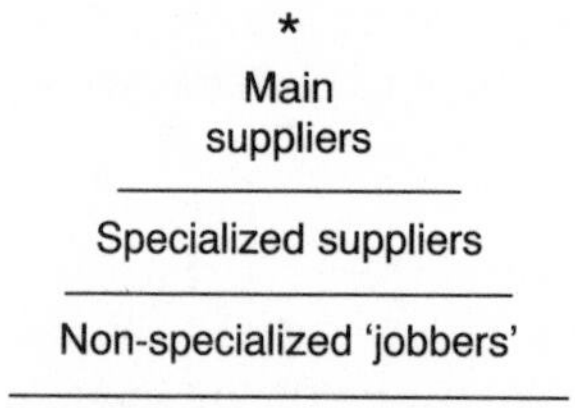

*

Main
suppliers
_____

Specialized suppliers
_____

Non-specialized 'jobbers'
_____

Figure 5.1 Pyramid of supply.

which BSR formed an important part (Dore 1989; Womack *et al.* 1990; Cusumano and Fujimoto 1991; Helper 1991; Helper and Levine 1992; Dyer and Ouchi 1993; Lamming 1993). One aspect of this is the phenomenon of several 'tiers' of supply in the 'supply pyramid', as illustrated in Figure 5.1.

The principle shown in Figure 5.1 is that the buyer concentrates on direct relations with the highest echelon of a limited number of 'main suppliers', which have to satisfy special demands. These concern the supply of entire subsystems, in which elements from lower tiers are integrated, with the addition of services of coordination, vendor selection, monitoring of quality, development. On the second tier are firms which offer special products and technical competencies. On the lowest tier are suppliers without special competencies, which are often used for capacity sourcing, or to supply standardized goods, materials or services. Fluctuations in demand are often devolved to the lowest tier. Volume flexibility on that level is often based on less job security for workers.

Special demands are made on main suppliers, entailing specific investments, but in return they are awarded a longer term contract, technology transfer and other support from the buyer. This is entirely in line with the analyses in previous chapters, but will be examined in more detail later. The focus of attention to main suppliers in the course of the past decade has shifted from mere price and quality of the supplied product to additional demands on technological capability, flexibility and innovative capacity. Especially striking, in contrast with BSR in western countries, was that buyers had only one main supplier (for each type of activity), at least for the duration of the life cycle of the particular product model involved (Kamath and Liker 1994). While in Europe and the USA buyers were used to dictating design and price, regardless of whether the supplier could achieve a sufficient profit, in Japan this was reversed, in the practice of 'price minus costing': the buyer takes as his point of departure a sufficient profit margin for the supplier and then sees it as a shared responsibility, with a pooling of resources, to design and develop the product so that an acceptable cost to the buyer is achieved. This will be subjected to detailed scrutiny later.

Lower in the pyramid, firms will tend to have multiple customers. This makes sense in the analysis from preceding chapters. If there is a single customer, with dedicated investments, there must exist compensatory power in the relation on the basis of unique products or competencies. If one supplies undifferentiated staple goods, one should have multiple customers.

In practice the pyramid principle is not adhered to rigidly, but serves to indicate that there are levels with different functions, demands and conditions. There are firms that supply directly, on the first tier, but also indirectly through other main suppliers. Indirect supply through main suppliers is not a feature only of small firms and need not be tied to lack of influence or power. Second tier specialists can be especially powerful due to scarce competencies.

> In the car industry there are 'main suppliers' that offer system supply for the interior, e.g. seats. They in turn outsource the material for the upholstery to specialized producers. The supply of electronic instruments for the dashboard (by large firms such as Bosch, Siemens, Philips) illustrates how a firm can supply indirectly through a main supplier and yet be involved in joint development with the ultimate buyer.

In more detail the following characteristics determine the position that a firm can take in the pyramid:

1 Competence to integrate component technologies, including the logistics involved.
2 Competence to coordinate several participants.
3 Direct supply.
4 Specialization in some (technological) area.
5 International presence, to supply 'just in time' at different locations.
6 Flexibility, in volume, availability of people, competencies.
7 Competence in teamwork inside the firm, with the customer and with lower level suppliers.
8 Innovative competence.
9 Multiple customers, as a source of learning.
10 Support in service: design, training, maintenance, repair.

For a typical main supplier, on the first tier, the desired characteristics are, in particular: 1, 2, 3, 6, 7, 8, 10 and perhaps also 5. A technical specialist, on the second tier, will typically need: 4, 5, 8, 9, 10. But other combinations may occur. These dimensions of value have been built into the analysis, in the dimensions of value that partners can have for each other, in Chapter 4 (Table 4.2).

DEVELOPMENTS

In Europe and the USA there has been a certain development towards 'Japanese practice', with attention not only to price and quality but also technological and innovative competence. There is also concentration on fewer main suppliers and some semblance of pyramids emerges.

For example, in the car industry the number of direct suppliers is systematically reduced. Table 5.2 gives some figures for the US car industry. But Table 5.3 shows that in Europe and the USA the reduction of first-tier suppliers has not yet progressed as far as in Japan.

Table 5.2 Reduction of numbers of direct suppliers in the American car industry

Manufacturer	1980	1985	1990
Ford	3,200	2,600	1,300
General Motors	4,000	3,500	1,800
Chrysler	1,600	1,300–1,400	700–800

Source: Hoffman and Kaplinsky *Driving Force: Auto Components and Global Restructuring*, 1990, quoted in Ministry of Economic Affairs (1991).

Table 5.3 Direct suppliers in the car industry in Japan, USA/Canada and Europe

Producer	Number of direct suppliers (domestic)	Number of cars produced (domestic, millions)
Japan		
Toyota	340	4.0
Nissan	310	2.2
Honda	310	1.3
USA/Canada		
GM	2,500	5.9
Ford	1,800	4.0
Chrysler	2,000	2.2
Europe		
Fiat	900	1.9
Renault	1,050	1.7
PSA	900	2.0
VW/Audi	1,580	1.9
D Benz	1,650	0.7
Rover	850	0.52
BMW	1,420	0.44
Volvo	590	0.33
Saab	485	0.15
Jaguar	540	0.05
Porsche	600	0.03

All figures apply to 1988, except 1987 for BMW.
Source: Lamming (1993: 172).

The reduction of the number of direct suppliers, on the first tier, is a general phenomenon: the pyramid is getting 'steeper'. The reason is simple: often the '20–80 rule' applies: 80 per cent of volume is supplied by 20 per cent of the suppliers. The remaining 20 per cent of volume is supplied by 80 per cent of the suppliers and one would rather shift the relatively costly task of managing these relations. If the end product is based on diverse, non-related 'families' of technology (Lamming 1993: 185), as in the case of cars, then it is also impossible for the buyer to have sufficiently deep competence to be able to judge supply to its lowest level of detail in all families. This also specifies a limit to the reduction of the number of direct suppliers: for each technology family at least one supplier.

Lamming (1993: 185) reports that in the middle of the 1980s Peugeot identified 257 families, Fiat 250 and Renault 150. On the basis of two suppliers for each, one arrives at the numbers of direct suppliers indicated for the Japanese industry in Table 5.3.

The orientation towards vertical cooperation in BSR, not only for efficiency, but also and increasingly primarily for improvement and innovation of products, is exhibited in a survey by McKinsey (1988), as summarized in Table 5.4.[1] It provides a self-report from firms which is not necessarily a reliable picture of actual activities. It is likely that since 1988 the focus on product improvement and innovation has increased.

Table 5.4 indicates that improvement and innovation of products and processes are considered more important than control of costs. For this

Table 5.4 Sources of improvement

Main activities	How does one intend to realize improvement (percentages)						
Percentage of firms that judge activity as one of the two most important	Alone	In cooperation			With support		
		Horizontal	Vertical	Both	External	(semi) gvt	Research institute
Development of new products or processes: 85%	13	13	49	7	11	4	31
Improvement of present products or processes: 79%	25	14	45	5	9	1	16
Better control of costs of products/processes: 23%	39	9	12	3	21	0	12
Better control of costs of product-process development: 10%	25	25	13	0	33	0	4

Source: McKinsey (1988)

purpose one considers especially vertical cooperation, while for cost control one needs others less. These results are in full agreement with the analyses in previous chapters: the learning theory in Chapter 1, goals of alliances in Chapter 3 (Table 3.1), dimensions of partner value in Chapter 4 (Table 4.2). It was noted that cooperation is needed especially in innovation and learning, particularly under conditions of rapid change of technology and markets. Vertical cooperation is easier to control than horizontal alliances between competitors and there is less risk of spillover.

However, in outsourcing general practice does not go as far as Japan's model. In particular, there is more preservation of the independence of both buyer and supplier. The buyer usually does not want any supplier to be dependent for more than 30–50 per cent of total sales (Ministry of Economic Affairs 1991). Also, the commitment to contribute to the development of the partner's competence is less. These points are probably related. The question is: what approach is the best? Or is the difference to be ascribed to national culture or to other institutions in the business environment?

On the whole, there appears to be a somewhat paradoxical development: on the one hand more outsourcing and less integration, but on the other stronger linkages between firms, in forms of governance 'between market and hierarchy', which themselves are forms of organization or 'quasi firms' (Lamming 1993). A central question relates to what structures this will ultimately lead. As long as liberalization of world markets prevails, outcomes will be determined most of all by what has the best chance of survival in international competition. A central problem for firms is how to govern relations of mutual dependence for the sake of cooperation. What factors play a role in relations of dependence and power? How can one assess cooperative relations? What instruments does one have for governing them? In what strategies do they fit? What strategies should one pursue? Here one arrives at the application of the instruments for analysis and design developed in previous chapters. First, some results are discussed of studies aimed at testing the theory.

EMPIRICAL TESTS

The practical value of the tools for analysis, diagnosis and design of alliances should be tested in practice. Does one then find the causalities postulated in the theory? And when the method is sufficiently tested, it might be applied. Are any opportunities for better design and governance being missed?

An often heard complaint of TCE is that it is difficult to operationalize and test in empirical research. Variables such as asset specificity, transaction costs and, in the extensions of TCE proposed in this book, innovation and trust are difficult or perhaps impossible to measure, or so the complaint goes. But there are methods to treat such variables as 'latent' ones, which can be seen as being 'spanned' or 'indicated' by 'indicators' that can be measured, if necessary as judgement by people, e.g. on a five- or seven-point scale. The methodology is derived in part from psychographics. The indicators can then be combined into a joint variable. As Erin Andersen, a researcher who applied TCE in marketing, graphically put it: 'with many small, weak sticks one can build a strong bridge'. In this way one can subject hypotheses to 'hard', quantitative empirical tests on the basis of 'soft', qualitative indicators.

In the empirical studies described below, most 'indicators' were five-point Likert scales. They were chosen on the basis of their hypothesized relation to latent variables that resulted from the theoretical analysis. Confirmatory factor analysis was used to test the measurement hypotheses. Cronbach's alpha was used to determine overall construct reliability, with the cut-off point at the usual value of 0.7. Factor loadings were used to determine whether each item contributed significantly to the joint factor, with the cut-off point at the usual value of 0.3. When an item had a lower loading, it was dropped and the analysis was repeated for the remaining items until a scale with reliable loadings emerged. The items were then added to yield a measure of the latent variable.

In the first study, Berger *et al.* (1995) tested part of the basic causal scheme of governance of Figure 4.1 on the basis of a postal survey, prepared and later complemented with interviews, among 80 suppliers to Océ van der Grinten, a Dutch producer of copying machines (annual sales about $1.5 billion, about 12 thousand employees). The response was 84 per cent. The focus of the research was on the hypothesized effect of a number of variables on the perceived dependence of suppliers on the buyer. That perceived dependence was measured in two ways: independently from the perceived dependence of the buyer ('gross dependence') and the degree to which the supplier perceived himself to be more dependent on the buyer than vice versa ('net dependence').

Not all hypothesized effects could be tested in this way. For example: the effect of shared ownership of specific assets was so predominant that it applied to all suppliers to approximately the same extent and therefore did not exhibit the variation needed for testing effects. Yet this gives confirmation in showing that the problem of specific investments is indeed covered at least to some extent by shared ownership, as predicted.

The data allowed testing of the effects indicated in Table 5.5. The table also shows whether the predicted effect on perceived dependence was positive or negative and in how far the effect was statistically significant. The measurement of the variables and the results will be discussed below.

The variable 'specificity assets' is measured as the sum of different types of specificity, entirely in line with TCE: location specificity (measured by one indicator); physical asset specificity (two indicators); dedicated capacity (four indicators); knowledge specificity (two indicators). 'Extensiveness of contract' is measured as a sum of indicators regarding supply conditions, technical specifications and security stocks. Trust in loyalty (lack of opportunism) is construed on the basis of six indicators. The remaining variables

Table 5.5 Tests of effects on dependence perceived by suppliers

	Net perceived dependence	*Gross perceived dependence*
Dependence buyer		−
Length of supply	−	−
Trust in buyer's loyalty	−	− **
Competence trust in buyer		−
Specificity of assets	+ ***	+ ***
Extensiveness contract	−	−
Knowledge exchange	−	− **
Sales size supplier	− **	−
Supply to buyer as % total sales	+	+ ***
Indirect supply	+ **	+ *
Bundling of supply	−	−

Source: Berger *et al.* (1995).

are more easily measured and are all based on a single indicator (direct measurement). When the theoretical effect, hypothesized on the basis of the analyses of preceding chapters, is indeed found this is indicated with one asterisk (*) when the statistical reliability was more than 90 per cent, two asterisks (**) if it was more than 95 per cent and three asterisks (***) if it was more than 99 per cent.

The disconfirmation of hypotheses can be as interesting as confirmation, or even more so. It is interesting to find that the extensiveness of contracts had no significant effect on perceived dependence, which confirms earlier studies (Macauley 1963). This confirms the suspicion that extensive contracts in formal legal governance can have only limited value: a closed contract is impossible anyway. It can limit the flexibility of operations and can even have a negative effect, in confirming and stimulating mutual suspicion. Of course this does not imply that there should be no contracts at all, but only that they should not be too extensive.

The strongest result is the positive effect of the transaction-specificity of assets, which confirms a central thesis of TCE. Of great theoretical importance is the effect of trust on the partner's loyalty, because that is one of the two main extensions of TCE offered by this book. It does have the expected negative effect on gross perceived dependence, but not on net dependence. This could make sense: net dependence would depend on the balance of loyalty. If the partner's loyalty is reciprocated by own good faith, then the effect on net dependence (degree to which supplier is more dependent on buyer than vice versa) is not to be expected: partner's dependence is as equally reduced as one's own. The expected effects of the share of supply in total sales (positive) and of total sales as a measure of the effect of the size of the supplier (negative) were also confirmed. The confirmation of the negative effect of information transfer from the buyer to the supplier is interesting. The theory of this was that thereby the buyer makes herself more vulnerable, by weakening her bargaining position and by the risk of spillover to competitors (information as hostage), which reassures the supplier with respect to her own perceived dependence. Interesting also is the confirmation that supply to other suppliers of the same buyer ('indirect supply') increases supplier dependence. But the expected effect that a bundling of supply, as the main supplier, would decrease dependence is not confirmed.

Summing up: effects from both TCE and its extensions are confirmed. This indicates that the framework developed in previous chapters is indeed fruitful. One of the shortcomings of the study is that it concerns only one buyer, so that effects due to the buyer cannot be investigated. This is eliminated in the second study.

In the second study, Nooteboom *et al.* (1997) conducted a survey of ten companies supplying components and sub-assemblies to producers of electrical/electronic apparatus, with ten customer relations for each of the ten companies. The firms were visited by a member of the research team at the beginning of 1994. These visits took an average of three and half hours. During the visit, data pertaining to the relationships with ten of the firm's most important customers were collected. The questionnaire was based on one developed and tested in the previous study (Berger *et al.* 1995). Items that had proved to be of little value were omitted and some new items were added. The questionnaires were completed by the respondent who was either the general manager or the sales manager of the firm, with the researcher clarifying questions when necessary. This minimized the risk of misunderstanding the questions and also guaranteed that there was no non-response and hence no missing data. To maintain comparability between relationships, the questionnaires were completed horizontally, i.e. a question was answered for all ten relationships before moving on to the next question. In this way, data were obtained with regard to 97 relationships.

Two dimensions of trust were hypothesized: habitualization and institutionalization. By the latter was meant the emergence of common norms to regulate behaviour within a relationship. The indicator variables (five-point Likert scales) are specified below. Cronbach's alpha for the constructs is also given.

HAB: Habitualization ($\alpha = 0.75$)
- Because we have been doing business so long with this customer, all kinds of procedures have become self-evident.
- Because we have been doing business for so long with this customer, we can understand each other well and quickly.
- In our contacts with this customer we have never had the feeling of being misled.

INST: Institutionalization ($\alpha = 0.73$)
- In this relation, both sides are expected not to make demands that can seriously damage the interests of the other.
- In this relation the strongest side is expected not to pursue its interest at all costs.

HI: Habitualization/institutionalization ($\alpha = 0.77$) = Habitualization + institutionalization + item:
- In this relation informal agreements have the same significance as formal contracts.

The last item is kept apart from *HAB* and *INST* because it could, with equal theoretical and empirical justification, be added to either of them; in both cases Cronbach's alpha increases with ten percentage points. The resulting variables were included in an econometric model to explain perceived relational risk, with two dimensions: the probability that the relation goes wrong and the penalty involved if it does. These were operationalized as follows:

SLE: Size of loss ego ($\alpha = 0.90$)
- Actually, we cannot afford a break with this customer.
- If the relation with this customer breaks, it will take us much effort to fill the gap in turnover.

PLE: Probability of loss ego
- The risk in this relation is sufficiently covered by contractual and non-contractual means.

The trust variables competed for explanation next to other non-trust-related explanatory variables as illustrated in Figure 5.2, which is derived from the basic scheme of governance in Chapter 4 (Figure 4.1).

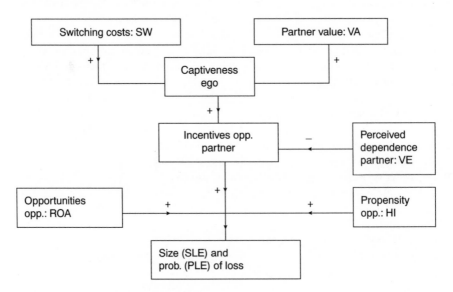

Figure 5.2 Determinants of size and probability of loss.

Factors that contribute to the (relative) value of the partner (competencies; *VA*) and to one's switching costs (*SW*) should determine the size of loss (*SLE*) (see Chapter 4, formula 4.1 and the surrounding text). Factors that limit the room for opportunism (such as contractual, legal governance and monitoring; *ROA*) and factors that limit incentives to the extent that the partner is dependent (shared ownership of specific assets, guarantees, own interest in the relation, due to the value of the focal partner; *VE* and propensity towards opportunism (on the basis of the trust-related variables habitualization and institutionalization; *HI*) should determine the probability of loss (*PLE*).

One of the explanatory variables was 'continuity' of the relation (*CON*), which was expected to have a positive effect on the value of the partner (in view of the perspective of cooperation in the future, see Chapter 4, Figure 4.1) and hence on *SLE*, as well as on loyalty (due to habit formation, growth of familiarity and trust) and hence on *PLE*.

Chapter 4 stressed the 'recursiveness' of the system: dependence of one side depends on dependence of the other side, because to the extent that someone is dependent he is less likely to exploit the partner's dependence. This is why the value that the supplier thinks it has for the buyer was also included, with the hypothesis that it would have a negative effect on the perceived probability that things go wrong due to the partner's opportunistic conduct.

Control variables were added to control for firm-specific attributes such as size (measured by annual sales; *SE*) and risk or uncertainty avoidance (*UA*). This was expected to have a positive effect on perceived probability of loss: risk-averse firms take a more serious view of risks of dependence. The operationalization and measurement of the variables (*ASE, VA, ROA, VE* and *UA*) are specified in Appendix 5.1.

The empirical results are specified in Table 5.6. It shows that trust has a significant effect on perceived probability of incurring a loss due to opportunism, next to the effects of other variables that one would expect from transaction cost economics. One disconfirmation of hypotheses was that instead of the expected positive effect of uncertainty avoidance on probability of loss there was a negative effect. But this can be interpreted very well: risk-averse suppliers make sure they have low-risk partners. The second disconfirmation was that a high perceived value offered to the partner did not have the expected negative effect on the perceived probability of loss. Our interpretation of this is that firms are not sophisticated enough in their assessment of the situation. They did not take into account the motivations of the partner, and did not question what they would do if they were in the same position.

Table 5.6 Results

	size of loss (SLE)	probability of loss (PLE)
Value partner (VA)		
% share turnover (%S)	☺ 0.52 (0.000)***	☺ 0.02 (0.78)
Remaining value (RVA)	☻ 0.07 (0.42)	☺ −0.05 (0.60)
Switching costs (SW)	☺ 0.17 (0.031)**	☺ 0.11 (0.21)
Restriction opp. partner (RO)	☺ 0.07 (0.36)	☺ −0.34 (0.003)***
Trust (HI)	☺ −0.03 (0.75)	☺ −0.22 (0.033)**
Own value for partner (VE)	☺ +0.01 (0.87)	☻ −0.05 (0.58)
Continuity (CON)	☺ 0.306 (0.000)***	☺ −0.249 (0.019)**
Uncertainty avoidance (UA)	☺ 0.05 (0.48)	☻ −0.201 (0.022)**
Firm size (SE)	☻ 0.01 (0.94)	☺ 0.08 (0.43)
Adjusted R square	0.52	0.32

Between brackets: significance level (T).
Confirmed hypotheses are indicated with ☺.
Lack of confirmation is indicated with ☻.
  * indicates a significance > 90%
 ** indicates a significance > 95%
*** indicates a significance > 99%

There is independent evidence of this lack of sophistication. It was also observed in a study of a European producer of telecommunication services. The firm (X) was one-sidedly dependent on a single American supplier (Y) of hardware and software for communication that was unique in its products, service and innovation. Out of fear of this, X considered employing a second source. But that would yield huge costs of duplication of systems, because the products from the different suppliers were not mutually compatible in the complex systemic coherence of apparatus and software. Nevertheless, X attached so much weight to the risk of dependence that it was at the point of accepting these costs. The question was not asked what interest Y would have in exploiting his opportunity of taking advantage of X's dependence. It turned out that X had so much value for Y, in offering privileged access to a large chunk of the fast-growing European market, that Y would be mad to jeopardize that. X's unique value to Y gave sufficient compensation for X's dependence.

EFFECTS OF ICT

In Chapter 2 the general tendency was noted of ICT to reduce transaction costs. Here, following Nooteboom (1992b), a more detailed analysis is given of the effects of ICT on costs of search and marketing, dependence and switching, the room for opportunism and the propensity towards opportunism.

One of the developments noted in Chapter 2 was that ICT offers fast and reliable systems for bookings and payment.

This sounds like a simple matter of efficiency, but it has strategic implications. In the investments needed for electronic trade in general and electronic payment in particular, there are effects of scale in the set-up costs of network hardware and software, training, organization of procedures and communication. For example, one needs to install systems for scanning bar codes and for control of customer's credit. A fixed, dedicated telephone line is cheaper than use of a shared line, provided that its utilization is sufficient, which for the volume of trade in a small shop is not the case. Thus, a novel effect of scale is introduced, which affects the strategic position of small shops. More important is the fact that information from scanning data provides a quantum jump in market information. The effects of price reductions, advertising or other promotional activities can be monitored virtually continuously, for one's own products and those of competitors, in relation to market segmentation down to the individual consumer. This is important to the retailer, but even more so to the producer, which further strengthens the strategic position of the large retailer.

In Chapter 2, computer aided design (CAD) was recognized as one of the means to reduce transaction costs. But note that insofar as that technology has not yet been standardized, with different buyers using different standards, it constitutes a specific investment for the supplier, who has to switch between systems for different customers, thereby increasing transaction costs.

ICT offers opportunities for more flexible design, by means of CAD, fast and cheap testing of virtual prototypes by computer simulation rather than physical testing of real prototypes and flexible production by means of programmable equipment. This increases efficiency, but also has strategic implications for the traditional division of work between large firms, which had an advantage in large volume production, and small firms, which specialized in low-volume, customized products. ICT yields opportunities for 'mass customization'.

For example, there are systems in place whereby a consumer at some remote location can configure the model he wants, including special functions and features (ABS, air bags, motor power, dashboard functions), colour, type and design of seat covers and push the button to order his customized car.

This constitutes a threat to small firms. But on their side, ICT offers opportunities to reduce disadvantages of small scale by employing efficient and flexible forms of cooperation in 'industrial districts'.

Generally speaking, firms need to see ICT no longer as a tool for the efficient execution of strategy based on other grounds, but as a basis for strategy (Cash *et al.* 1992). Applications started for operational reasons or cost reduction often turn out to have implications for strategic position, because they affect the function of products for users, competitive relations, organization, relation between production and provision of service, the make-or-buy decision; in short, the whole business.

One example is the case of OTIS elevators (adopted from Cash *et al.* 1992). The breakdown of an elevator is annoying and disruptive and it is crucial to detect the source and make the repair quickly. It is highly inefficient if the repairman arrives only to find that he does not have the right equipment or components with him. ICT offers the instruments to detect and diagnose a breakdown, which can be communicated to the service centre. This can be done day and night, with a computer not only establishing a diagnosis but working out a therapy, tracing a competent mechanic, adjusting his work schedule, taking into account priorities assigned to preferred customers and calculating an optimal route to get to the customer. With ICT support, the mechanic can efficiently make a report and bill the customer. At first sight this may seem a purely operational matter, but there are strategic repercussions. The mechanic obtains more room to act as a marketing agent, which changes his function. ICT further yields information to register and analyse breakdowns, as a function of type and conditions of use, type and age of the elevator, which provides input for product development. This has strategic implications. Earlier, one might have been inclined to outsource repairs, leaving them to a specialized firm that can better utilize a network of mechanics. But now such work may need to be kept in-house to avoid risk of the important product market information spilling over to competitors.

A generic example, as in the famous cases of 'American Hospital Supplies' and airline reservation systems, pertains to the location of computer linkages at customer or distributor sites (Cash *et al.* 1992). This was also initiated by considerations of efficiency: greater speed of transmission and processing, the fact that data need not be entered repeatedly, which is costly in manpower and errors. But when the computer link and corresponding software are specific to the relation, this creates switching costs and hence dependence, which can be exploited by the firm that is the first to move into the new way of doing things.

However, experience shows that such situations are temporary, as is often the case for monopolies. A market arises for intermediaries, offering conversions between the different standards, which reduces binding by switching costs. And there is increasing pressure from users to arrive at a uniform standard. Governments can exert pressure from considerations of competition policy. This happened in the case of airline reservations: airlines that achieved competitive advantage by placing terminals with proprietary linkages at travel agents were forced to open their systems for bookings on competing airlines. The US government also intervened in breaking IBM's coupling of application software to its proprietary operating system software. It is now at the point of intervening in the monopoly of Microsoft.

But there is another strategic snake in the grass. For reasons of efficiency in logistics or quality control ICT is used to gain insight into a partner's production process, but thereby its strategic position can be affected.

> A chain store in furniture or clothing (for instance) can then play suppliers off against each other on the basis of information on stocks and work in progress. In case of high inventories, indicating slack demand, pressure can be exerted to give special discounts to clear them.

Conversely, a producer can exert pressure on its distributors on the basis of calculations of profit contributions. In distribution often the 80–20 rule applies: 80 per cent of profit is made from 20 per cent of the distributors. The remaining 80 per cent of distributors cost much trouble to sell little. ICT helps to separate the more profitable distributors from the less profitable.

> Important problems in insurance are those of 'adverse selection' and 'moral hazard'. The first entails that people who most profit from insurance are the ones who offer the worst risk. The second problem entails that once someone is insured she will take less care in evading risks.

In both cases the insurer would want to charge a higher premium. ICT, with detailed information and refined analysis of the course of claims, in relation to characteristics of customers and insurance salesmen or distributors, can offer opportunities for such differentiation, which affects the strategic position of those middlemen.

In view of these developments it becomes problematic to maintain the traditional distinction, in the business strategy literature, between on the one hand strengths and weaknesses of a firm and on the other opportunities and threats in the competitive environment. Inter-firm linkages determine the one as well as the other. This view is consistent with the objection from the resource perspective to the 'positioning' view that opportunities and threats are dictated by the environment, apart from a firm's resources. Inter-firm linkages, yielding positional advantages, are based on relational competencies, which exploit other firm-specific resources.

Now a more systematic review is given of the effects of ICT on the central variables identified in the governance of inter-firm relations: the value that partners have for each other, relative to alternatives; switching costs, in particular specific investments; contracts and monitoring; opportunism.

ICT yields many effects on the dimensions of value that firms can offer each other, as specified in Chapter 4 (Figure 4.2). ICT can contribute to the integrative capacity of main suppliers: reliability (through better control of logistics by tracking and tracing; quality by CAD and monitoring of production); innovativeness and flexibility of firms; connections through firms in networks; international presence (through better opportunities of control and communication across large distances). The lowering of search costs, discussed in Chapter 2, helps to identify attractive novel partners, whereby the current partner's relative value can more easily become negative, so that relations are more easily destabilized. ICT can also help to monitor spillover: to see that sensitive information supplied to the partner does not leak to competitors.

Flexible production automation reduces the specificity of production equipment and thereby reduces switching costs. One programmable machine can enable the manufacture of components of many different shapes and functions. Guarantees to safeguard a partner's specific investments can more easily be supplied, since there are more possibilities to control their legitimacy and to protect against expropriation. The legitimacy of claims of specificity can be controlled ensuring that the investment is not used for the production of others.

As indicated in Chapter 2, ICT reduces the costs of contracts and improves opportunities of monitoring to control for contract compliance. This reduces chances for opportunism. Changes in the environment can be better monitored, whereby novel possibilities for opportunism can be anticipated.

Concerning the effects of ICT on incentives towards opportunism, it can be expected that with ICT the efficiency of reputation mechanisms is increased, which may help to constrain opportunism. The effects of ICT on the institutional environment of norms and values of conduct are difficult to predict.

What are the net effects of ICT on the make-or-buy decision? If ICT can be used to improve coordination both within and between firms, the temptation of switching increases and switching costs decrease, but on the other hand there are better opportunities for contracting and monitoring. ICT can also be used to improve coordination within firms, but since coordination problems are generally greater between firms, the effect is likely to be greatest on inter-firm coordination. According to the analysis of relational risk in Figure 5.2, the possible size of loss, determined by the sum of the partner's relative value and switching costs, tends to decrease and the probability of such loss, determined by the room and intent towards opportunism, also tends to decrease, both reducing relational risk. Added to this, ICT can help to reduce the probability of spillover. As a result one would expect that inter-firm relations will occur more often and will tend to last for a shorter period. The latter expectation follows not only from lower switching costs, but also from a perspective of learning. As argued in Chapter 1, learning and innovation require a diversity of sources of knowledge, which militate against exclusive and overlong relationships. The pressures of competition, which increase due to a lowering of transaction costs, will exert more pressure to innovate. As discussed in Chapter 2, it also yields opportunities (from consumer preferences) and pressure (in order to escape from pure price competition) to differentiate products, which also contributes to the need to concentrate on core competencies and cooperate with others.

The next question is what effect ICT will have on the number of outside partners. One factor is the set-up cost of ICT links in relation to the cost of their operation. If the set-up cost is relatively high and has to be repeated for each partner, this militates against a large number of partners. Generally the set-up cost of a network is still high relative to operating costs, but this will change if firms start to use some widely shared existing network such as the Internet. There are several other arguments in favour of a smaller number of partners, of more exclusiveness. The most important is that with multiple partners set-up costs of specific investments and bilateral governance are multiplied. However, this effect is less to the extent that ICT lowers asset specificity and set-up costs of governance are low because governance is based on trust, with savings on the set-up costs of contracts. Another argument is that insofar as there is a risk of spillover (when knowledge is documented and technology is not subject to radical change) and this risk cannot be controlled with the help of ICT, then it may be necessary to reduce spillover risk for one's partner by limiting relations with his potential competitors. It may also be necessary to reduce that number in order to make oneself more dependent, thereby making it acceptable to the partner also to increase his dependency by engaging in more specific investments, which may be needed to achieve desired quality and product differentiation.

But there is one important counter-argument. Innovation requires flexibility to make novel combinations and learning requires a diversity of sources, both being enhanced by a multiplicity of partners. In part, this is the reverse side of spillover. Learning can exist without spillover when technology changes so fast as to eliminate its risk. Such speed of change would also enhance the need to use outside sources for learning.

Summing up, developments in ICT will enhance the tendency towards inter-firm alliances as follows:

* an increased comparative advantage of more non-integrative forms over more integrative ones such as mergers and acquisitions;
* a preference for multiple relations, for the sake of sufficient diversity for learning and innovation, with the use of ICT to control the ensuing risk of spillover;
* a shorter duration of relations, but durable enough to recoup specific investments, adapt to each other's competencies sufficiently to exploit complementarities and to build trust as a cheap and flexible governance device.

GENERIC SYSTEMS OF SUPPLY

Many authors have reported fundamental differences in practices of outsourcing between firms in the West (USA, EU) and Japan, mostly on the basis of studies in the car industry. While in some respects European practice is somewhat closer to the Japanese, it remains more similar to the USA. The past success of Japanese industry appears to be due to some, perhaps considerable, extent to their supplier–user relations. (See e.g: Dore 1989; Womack *et al.* 1990; Cusumano and Fujimoto 1991; Helper 1991; Helper and Levine 1992; Dyer and Ouchi 1993; Lamming 1993.)

Traditional relations of supply in Europe (and more strongly in the USA) can be described as 'arm's-length' contracting in ad hoc transactions rather than ongoing relations. The evasion of long-term relations is inspired by reluctance towards dependence on a partner and a focus on maintenance of the bargaining position for low costs and maximal share of profits. Buyers focus on competitive tendering and suppliers withhold information on their costs, stocks and orders in the pipeline to maintain bargaining position. Given the short-term focus of transactions and the reluctance to engage in transaction specific investments, there is limited scope for product differentiation and joint innovation. When specific investments do occur with the need to prolong transactions, and in that sense a relation rather than isolated transactions arises, there is a tendency towards the use of adversarial strategies of 'devolution' as a loosening strategy and 'tying down' as a binding strategy. As indicated in Table 4.3, devolution entails: the shift of the burden of ownership of specific assets to the partner; exploitation of asymmetric information by giving little information and demanding much, thus shifting the balance of monitoring and spillover risks to one's advantage; reduction of the partner's relative value by developing alternatives; utilization of the resulting bargaining advantage for 'hold-up', i.e. for extorting a larger share in the proceeds of joint added value. Tying down entails detailed contracts and monitoring of compliance, the demand for partner's participation in the ownership of specific assets, demand for hostages.

Japanese supply relations are reported to be more cooperative. The most cited example is the auto industry.

> According to Lamming (1993) the (large) buyer sees the (small) supplier on the highest tier (main supplier) as a source of competence, for efficient production but also for product development and innovation. Thus he is included in development, including specification of parts to be supplied. This is illustrated in Table 5.7.

The Japanese relationship is more cooperative in the following sense: the buyer does not impose a cost price on the supplier without regard to his opportunity for profit. He acknowledges the supplier's need for profit and turns the issue around in 'price minus costing'. He takes into account a profit margin for the supplier, deducts that from a price that is acceptable to the buyer, to arrive at a cost price at which the supplier should perform. He then makes the commitment to a joint effort, with pooled resources, to achieve that target. Figure 5.3 suggests that this is not a myth: in contrast with the USA and EU, in the Japanese car industry profitability of buyers and suppliers is at the same level and is preserved in the adversity of falling profitability.

Table 5.7 Contribution to product development of suppliers of components in the car industry: Japan, USA and Europe

	Extent of involvement of supplier in engineering parts (%)		
	Japan	*USA*	*Europe*
Standard parts wholly developed by supplier	8	3	7
Specification by buyer; detailed engineering by supplier	62	16	39
Specification and engineering by buyer	30	81	54
	100	100	100

Source: Lamming (1993); quoted from Clark (1989).

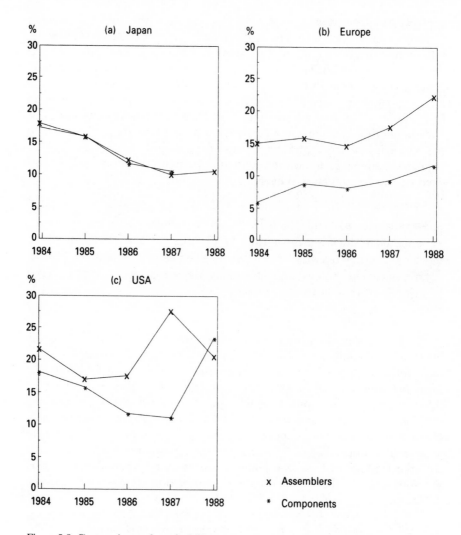

Figure 5.3 Comparison of profitability as a percentage of net assets: car manufacturers and their suppliers of components in Japan, USA and
Europe, 1984–8.

Note: ª Figures are weighted average returns for profit before interest and tax as a
percentage of net assets.
Source: Boston Consulting Group, *The Competitive Challenge Facing the European Automotive
Components Industry,* January 1991, Executive Summary, p. 22, quoted by Lamming (1993: 45).

For the buyer just in time (JIT) production does not entail, as it often
does in the USA and EU, that the burden of stocks is simply shifted to the
supplier, but that the buyer helps the supplier to produce at demand, with
few stocks. The result is a high turnover of stocks for both sides, as illustrated in Figure 5.4.

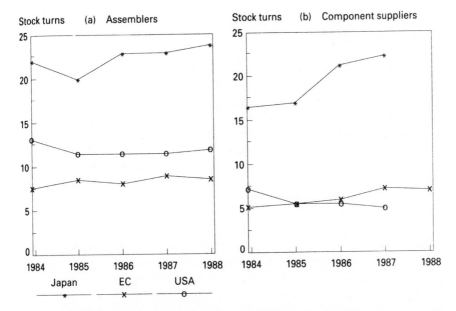

Figure 5.4 Comparison of stock turnover: car manufacturers and their suppliers of components in Japan, USA and Europe, 1984–8.

Source: Boston Consulting Group, *The Competitive Challenge Facing the European Automotive Components Industry,* January 1991, Executive Summary, p. 22, quoted by Lamming (1993: 45).

However, the buyer clearly has a leading role: he is often owner of part of the supplier's capital and has the initiative. The supplier has limited independence, 'not as a slave but as a younger brother'.

For the development of the policy of firms, nations and the EU, it is of some importance to answer the following questions:

• How can these differences in supply systems between Japan and the West be understood? Why do they arise? What is their rationale?
• Is 'Japanese practice' indeed better?
• Should US and EU firms emulate the Japanese, to what extent are they able to do so and, if not, what are the obstacles?
• Is there perhaps a 'third way', better than both 'Western' and 'Japanese' practice?
• What would be required to shift to the latter practice?

From these policy questions the following research questions are derived:

• Can we deduce generic forms ('cost based' and 'quality based') of outsourcing from theory?
• How do these forms relate to differences in market structure?

- Can we find new alternatives?
- What perspectives or obstacles are there for the transition to novel, better forms?

To answer these questions, a formal model was developed in Nooteboom (1998c), with the use of the notion of a 'Nash equilibrium' from game theory: what is the outcome of a relation in the sense that in the outcome a sequence of strategic actions and reactions stops; given the actions of the partner one cannot improve one's position by further strategic action. This yields a criterion of whether some constellation of strategic actions is realistic in the sense that it is viable. If it does not satisfy the Nash equilibrium condition, the interplay of actions and reactions will proceed to yield some other outcome. How viable, in this sense, are the 'Western way' and the 'Japanese way' and is there perhaps some 'third way'?

One should not expect any system of supply to be universally best. It is likely that under some conditions one system is the best and in other conditions another. Therefore, the analysis takes into account different formalized 'possible worlds'. The research question was as follows:

Can the stereotypes of Western and Japanese contracting be reconstructed as Nash equilibria in some plausible worlds, how efficient are they and is there an alternative that is better than both, in any plausible world?

'Plausible worlds' are realistic in the sense that they are internally consistent and capture the core characteristics of those that exist, have existed or may soon exist in some significant part of the world. One world is designed to give 'Western contracting' a chance of being an appropriate strategy. A second world is designed to give 'Japanese contracting' a chance. The third world is aimed to represent the future which is emerging now, in order to investigate what might be a viable system in the near future. The resulting worlds are as follows:

1   The world of the *clan* (W1): here there is no opportunism, due to actors being tied together in clans, with pervasive trust based on norms, values and rules, kinship relations, social control or the need to maintain reputation (see Ouchi 1980). This eliminates the central issue of hold-up risk and the world thereby becomes something of non-case.

2   The *'Fordist world'* (W2): standard products and stable markets and technology. In this world there is no global competition, little need for product differentiation, integrated firms and a focus on price, cost and economy of scale. There is advantage in the flexibility, bargaining position and varied contracting with multiple partners. Due to stability and

homogeneity of perceptions there is no great need for learning by knowledge transfer from other firms. This world is expected to favour 'Western contracting'.

3   The '*world of efficient quality*' (W3): high quality is required in terms of close fit to specifications of differentiated products. Due to differentiated products there is limited economy of scale, a premium on specific inputs and corresponding assets and close cooperation between supplier and user, for optimal use of complementary competencies. Turbulence, in terms of change of markets and technology, is limited so that learning from many outside partners is not essential.

4   The world of '*raplex: rapid change and complexity*' (W4): intense competition in global markets, differentiated products (in both input and output markets), fast technological development. In this world, like the previous one, there is a need for specific investments to produce differentiated products, but in addition all forms of learning from outside partners are important and the benefits from knowledge transfer exceed the risk of spillover. Within this world we recognize special cases, where the risk of spillover is small due to three different causes:

• '*radical speed*' (W4a): change is so fast, that the life cycle of products is shorter than the development time of new products. Here spillover does not matter. By the time sensitive information reaches a competitor, through linkages in the partner network, it is obsolete.

• '*monitoring against spill-over*' (W4b): there are technologies to monitor what happens to transferred competence so that their spillover can be controlled.

• '*radical differentiation*' (W4c): competing producers are so radically differentiated that they cannot greatly benefit from information that spills over from them.

This last world (W4) is designed to capture conditions that are presently emerging in the industrialized world. In this world we are curious to see what equilibria come out, as some 'third way' in contrast to the 'Western' and 'Japanese' forms of contracting and in what respects it differs from those two.

The formal model and its analysis are specified in Appendix 5.2. The outcomes are as follows:

• The stereotype of 'Western contracting' is found to be an efficient Nash equilibrium in the 'Fordist world'. It is efficient in the sense that it yields maximal benefits if returns from knowledge transfer, varied learning and joint development are zero, which is consistent with this world view.

• The stereotype of 'Japanese contracting' is found not to be an efficient equilibrium in the world of 'efficient quality', which was designed to give this form a maximal chance. Exclusive relations of mutual transfer and joint development in the production of differentiated products tend to fall back into the appropriation of the benefits by the user, with the user failing to guarantee a margin for the supplier. Alternative viable outcomes (Nash equilibria) are: monopoly on the part of the supplier, or shift to one-sided transfer from a leading and technologically independent supplier. Do these outcomes represent the reality of Japanese contracting more than the benevolent story of the buyer allowing a profit to the supplier? Is this story a myth after all, in spite of the evidence from Figure 5.3?

- In the 'raplex' world of rapid change and complexity, where product differentiation is more important than scale and learning is important, in all forms, both the Western and (modified) Japanese forms are surpassed in efficiency by the 'third way': mutual transfer of know-how with multiple partners and full learning. However, this requires that learning is so important that any risk of spillover is accepted; that speed of change is so fast as to eliminate spillover risk; or that firms develop a technology of monitoring against spillover. Of course, the condition of monitoring for spillover is more easily specified than fulfilled and would entail some 'flagging' of information transferred to the partner.

The 'third way' resembles Western contracting in its orientation to multiple partnerships and the absence of guarantees for supplier margin (price minus costing). It resembles Japanese contracting in its orientation towards specific investments with guarantees, open book contracting, mutual transfer of competence and cooperation in development.

A familiar question in game theory is how equilibria are attained: by anticipation and calculation, bargaining, trial and error, or evolution. Evolution seems most likely here and this seems to agree with history. In the West, the form of 'Western contracting' evolved in a 'Fordist world'. Once evolved, the form is difficult to change because it has become embedded as 'normal practice'. A generation of buyers has been trained to go for minimum price. It is difficult for them to adopt a practice where price becomes a boundary condition rather than the central objective, guarantees are given to cover specific assets, the focus is on optimal usage of joint expertise, specifications are not a dogma but are subject to comment, improvement and initiative from the supplier and gains from improvement are shared. They find it difficult to accept such a break in principles and are not trained to have sufficient competence to implement them. 'Japanese contracting' has evolved from a different perspective on markets and efficiency and in a different system of corporate control and other institutions (Groenewegen 1997). The Japanese may have become so used to exclusive contracting, in closed networks of relationships (*keiretsu*), that they find it difficult to widen their perspective to different partners and mutual monitoring for spillover. However, on the basis of empirical evidence, if not the present analysis, practitioners from both sides may be moved to change their ways, to adjust to the present 'raplex' world of global markets. Some conclusions for policy are the following:

- There is no single most efficient and strategically viable solution (in the sense that it constitutes a Nash equilibrium) in all possible worlds.
- The Western form was good in the Fordist world, but not in the present world of global markets, product differentiation and rapid change.
- The Japanese form appears to be less equitable than is described in the applied literature: it gravitates away from guarantees for supplier profit and towards expropriation of benefit by the buyer. Apart from this asymmetry in the distribution of surplus, joint efficiency is higher than in the Western form, when markets require a shift from a focus on scale to a focus on differentiated products and mutual use of competence between partners, but it offers insufficient learning in the present world of 'raplex' global markets.
- The raplex world of global markets requires a 'third way'. But this is viable only if speed of change (in markets and technology) is radical or a technology is developed to monitor spillovers. It resembles the Japanese way in its orientation to openness, specific assets covered by guarantees and mutual transfer of competence between partners. This requires a transformation of practice in the west. However, it is closer to the western perspective in its orientation to multiple partners. The Japanese would need to open up their more exclusive relations.

LEAN SUPPLY

Even if there may be doubt surrounding the 'Japanese way', this does not imply that nothing can be learned from it. The scheme of Figure 4.1 and Tables 4.1, 4.2 and 4.3 give a basis for the analysis for further exploration. From the analysis in the previous section one can draw the following lessons for business practice.

The interests of the supplier can be served to the point that he is willing to engage in specific investments and to open up to monitoring and exchange of know-how for joint development, on the basis of the following instruments:

- Buyer participation in the ownership of specific assets. This increases buyer switching costs.
- Ongoing relation, to allow the supplier to recoup his specific investment, with allowance for a profit margin.
- Contribute to the development of supplier's competence.
- Accept that thereby the supplier holds a hostage in the form of knowledge which could be taken to competing buyers.

The buyer is prepared to accept this dependence and the loss of some flexibility if it contributes to his goal of differentiated products, the utilization of the supplier's specific competencies, innovation and joint development

and learning. In other words, the interests of the buyer can be simultaneously served with the following instruments:

- Utilization of outside complementary competencies that are not available inside the firm and could not be easily developed.
- Maintain the motivation of an independent supplier, which is perhaps
  less sharp than in a fully free relation, but is still higher than it would
  be for an in-firm supplier. The supplier must keep on earning the
  commitment and custom of the buyer.
- Maintenance of flexibility which is less than in a fully free relation, but
  is still greater than for inside supply; while through participation in the
  ownership of specific assets costs have not been fully converted from
  fixed to variable, this is the case for at least a chunk of them.
- By direct involvement in the supplier's firm, made possible by the buyer
  accepting a longer term relation and granting the supplier profit, there
  is improved monitoring of quality, timely delivery, costs, spillover.
- If the supplier is dependent for the potential he offers on technology
  transfer and knowledge from the buyer, he will not switch easily to a
  competitor.

With such arrangements, a virtuous cycle can arise of mutual reinforcement,
trust, commitment, cheap and flexible governance, while maintaining sufficient incentives for ongoing improvement and some scope for flexibility of
relations. One cannot expect competent suppliers to make investments that
tie them down without a perspective of profit. In the short-term advantage
may be obtained in squeezing suppliers, but new partners will turn elsewhere. Ultimately prisoners will escape and if they are unable to do so they
are not the type you would want to keep. It is more efficient and effective
to spend time and money on improvement of competence than on playing
hide and seek on costs, where all the energy leaks away in a tug of war on
price.

But such an approach does require a longer term perspective and the
opportunities for this depend on the wider institutional environment, capital
markets and corporate governance (Groenewegen 1997; Nooteboom 1997b).
In Japan and to a lesser extent Germany, firms can take a longer term
perspective, because for capital they rely less on share markets, with share-
holders and traders demanding short-term profits to maintain share value
and more on industry banks and consortia of firms (*keiretsu*, in Japan).

In Europe we see a tendency towards more cooperative strategies, aimed
at mutual reinforcement, but this has progressed less than in Japan. A marked
difference is that in Japan a 100 per cent share of sales of a supplier is not
abnormal, while in Europe it is quite rare.

An important drawback for the supplier of 100 per cent supply to one customer, apart from becoming too dependent with a view to the risk of hold-
up, is the risk of fluctuations of sales of the single customer. It is preferable to

spread sales risk across multiple customers. A drawback for the buyer is that the supplier's learning is severely constrained without contacts with other customers with different demands, competencies and experiences.

But the downside of having a supplier that also supplies one's competitors is the risk of spillover. Such risk is limited if other supply goes to other industries. If it goes to competitors within the same industry, the problem might be solved with reliable agreements on the secrecy of what has jointly been developed (perhaps until protection by means of patents is achieved). Such agreements are reliable if the partner has a good reputation in this respect and lack of care can be observed and punished. Recall Lamming's (1993) account, discussed in Chapter 4, of how with the appearance of a new car its technological content is 'published' and subject to monitoring for spillover.

Cross-ownership of shares may also serve as a protection device (Mowery 1988, quoted in Lamming 1993). Scher (1996) argued that this can be seen as a hostage mechanism.

All this leads to 'lean supply', where the Japanese system is replaced by one in which buyer and supplier are more equal partners. In terms of our earlier analysis in Chapter 4 (Table 4.3), the Japanese system can be characterized by a combination of 'prettying up' and 'tying down'. In lean supply this shifts to a careful tuning of 'prettying up' and 'setting free'. Both sides accept that the partner deserves profit and cooperate to find ways to achieve the highest possible profit for both. In adversity the burdens are shared. Both also have other partners and take initiatives for ongoing improvement on both sides, based on mutual dependence and commitment with cross-investment, cross-ownership and mutual openness for adjustment, improvement, monitoring and spillover control. Such openness does not imply that all available information is shared, but only what is needed for mutual reinforcement of competencies and monitoring. Spillover risks may be accepted when one is assured of staying ahead of the competition. Risk of premature spillover is covered by controllable agreements. This arrangement is approximated by the 'third way' explored in Appendix 5.2

This type of relation is not based on competitive tendering. When the value of the partner drops behind alternatives, then the first response is to regain the advantage in a joint effort, with pooled resources. It is not until this repeatedly fails that the relation is broken. Then the divorce is prepared, to prevent a destructive cycle of 'devolution and tying down' as analysed in Chapter 4 (Figure 4.9). Partners help each other to limit the damage of breakage and develop alternatives. This goes together with a spirit of loyalty but also contributes to mutual advantage; otherwise it would not be viable.

In view of the effort, time and investment involved in this practice, the relational competence to choose partners well and play this game well will be one of the most important resources for survival and success.

The opportunities for lean supply are not equal for all industries and all countries. They depend on a number of conditions in the social environment, technology, market and industry. Some of these are indicated in Table 5.8.

Table 5.8 Conditions affecting lean supply

In the market
Intensity of competition, entry barriers, demand for product differentiation.

In technology
The extent and type of economies of scale and scope, degree to which investments for cooperation are specific, flexibility of technology, nature of the knowledge involved (tacit or documented), the observability of spillovers, speed of technological development.

In the industry and country
Existing norms and values of conduct, efficiency of reputation mechanisms, the desired duration of cooperation in relation to the size of specific investments, appropriability of innovations, availability of standards for modules to be assembled, opportunities for measuring relative performance ('benchmarking').

As an illustration of the influence of developments in the market, technology, industry and country, consider the building industry.[2] In connection with increasing prosperity and corresponding individualization, there is an increased demand for differentiated housing. Without control of stocks and flows of materials differentiation yields an explosion of costs: every different product form would require its own stocks. Present governmental attempts at deregulation by breaking down cartels is likely to create more competitive pressure hence pressures for efficiency. This will further intensify the tendency to product differentiation in order to mitigate the pressures of pure price competition. In contrast with the building process, technological development in materials, apparatus and communication is fast. Under these conditions cooperation in the building chain is necessary, not only for static efficiency (cost control) but also for dynamic efficiency (innovation, learning), as argued in Chapter 2.

The issue of the duration of cooperation in relation to specificity of investments (Table 5.8) requires discussion. There is a problem if specific investments are required for the sake of differentiated products, but cooperation is too short to recoup the investment. This situation arises especially during project work: cooperation in a consortium of firms that is instituted only for the duration of the project.

Here also the building industry provides an example. For the sake of differentiation, suppliers of building materials and skills must engage in specific investments which they cannot recoup in a single building project. For such investment they require a guarantee of a sequel in a similar project. The builder may not be able to do that due to lack of foresight on the nature of later projects and desires to be free to form novel consortia. This is also connected with the turbulence of entry and exit in the industry: the risk that firms fail and that new, more attractive partners enter the scene. To achieve building which is differentiated and has efficient linkages between elements of the building chain, either the technology has to be made more flexible, so that investments become less specific, or some form of continuity must be achieved for relations to last longer than specific investments.

Under what conditions could a builder provide guarantees for usage of present investments in future projects? In principle, there are several possibilities. One is that the builder knows more about future projects and develops a focused marketing policy, including market research. As already suggested, a second possibility is to make technology and corresponding competencies so flexible that a given investment can be applied to a range of different projects. In view of the complexity and diversity of building, this would require specialization: a typology of building, modules for construction, with different types of technology, with different resources, where different firms specialize in different modules. Then the perspective arises that a builder guarantees that he will contract a supplier again for similar projects, for a given part or module, under the condition that the supplier will remain at the forefront of development, while on the basis of his marketing he is also able to indicate how often and when this is likely to occur.

The builder will to some extent have to stick his neck out on this and the supplier will not have complete certainty, but the risks may be acceptable. To judge the quality of progress that a supplier offers, one may develop criteria of best practice ('benchmarking'). Then the builder can impose controllable conditions to keep suppliers sharp. A second condition is that there are standards for the mutual connection of modules. In both areas industry associations can provide their services.

The problem of spillover also requires attention. As indicated before, this depends on the speed of technological change: when speed is 'radical' there is no fear of spillover. In the building industry it seems difficult to protect innovations from spillover, especially innovation in the building process itself. Is innovation already so fast as to be 'radical' and eliminate the issue? Perhaps presently the most needed innovations are organizational and these cannot easily be copied. One can see what an advanced competitor is doing, but implementation would require organizational change, which is typically slow.

APPENDIX 5.1 SPECIFICATION OF VARIABLES

The specification of variables in the empirical study by Nooteboom *et al.* (1997) which were not yet specified in the main text is as follows:

Value partner

%S: percentage of total sales to the buyer, as a cardinal measure of value of partner

RVA: remaining indicators of value of partner ($\alpha = 0.70$)
- Because we supply to this customer we are able to build up technological know-how that is also useful for other customers.
- Because we supply to this customer we obtain market knowledge that would otherwise be difficult to access.
- Our firm is involved in an early stage in the development of new components for this customer ('early supplier involvement').
- This customer involves us in the testing of components and/or in prototyping.

Switching costs

DA: dedicated assets ($\alpha = 0.83$)
- Our firm employs significantly more people than if we did not supply to this customer.
- Our firm must have people with specific expertise in-house to be able to supply to this customer.
- Our firm has had to create extra capacity to supply to this customer.
- We had to make investments to satisfy the specific supply conditions of this customer (e.g. for 'just in time').

PAS: physical asset specificity ($\alpha = 0.70$)
- In production for this customer highly specific machines, apparatus or instruments are needed.
- Most of the machines, apparatus or instruments needed in production for this customer can also be used for other customers, if necessary.

KAS: knowledge specificity ($\alpha = 0.68$)
- We have had to invest much time in acquiring the procedures desired for this customer (e.g. in the area of logistics and quality control).
- Much specific technological know-how is required effectively to supply to this customer.
- Much knowledge of the internal organization of this customer is required for effective cooperation.

LS: location specificity
- The location of our firm plays an important role in the relation with this customer.

SW: switching costs ego = ASE asset specificity ego ($\alpha = 0.84$) = dedicated assets + physical asset specificity + knowledge specificity + location specificity

Room for opportunism

LO: legal ordering ($\alpha = 0.79$)
- The contract with this customer is as complete as possible.
- The contract forms the core of our relation with this customer.
- In this relationship it is not so important to have a good contract.

PO: private ordering ($\alpha = 0.71$)
- The customer shares in the payment for specific machines and apparatus that we must make in production for him.
- The customer shares in the payment for the investments in specific tools and/or measurement apparatus that we must make in production for him.
- Guarantees are given for minimal custom over an agreed period of time.
- We give guarantees for supply for an agreed period of time.

RO: restriction of room for opportunism ($\alpha = 0.79$) = legal ordering + private ordering

Incentive

VE: value ego ($\alpha = 0.76$)
- Our supply performance to this customer cannot be assessed on its merit if looking only at the price.
- This customer is aware that our supply performance cannot be assessed on its merit if looking only at price.
- Our supply to this customer is clearly custom made.
- We provide an important source of information on new technologies for this customer.
- Our firm is involved in an early stage in the development of new components for this customer ('early supplier involvement').
- This customer involves us in the testing of components and/or in prototyping.

GR: growth ($\alpha = 0.68$)
- The relation between our firm and this customer has continually improved over the course of time.

- Our supply to this customer has increased strongly over the course of time.

FP: future perspective ($\alpha = 0.67$)
- In this relationship it is assumed that contracts will in general be renewed.
- For the foreseeable future we do not expect a break with this customer.
- We see the relationship with this customer as long-term, in which investment should be made, and in which both sides are willing to make concessions if really necessary.

CON: continuity ($\alpha = 0.78$) = growth + future perspective

APPENDIX 5.2 FORMAL ANALYSIS OF GENERIC SYSTEMS OF SUPPLY

Introduction

From the literature, Japanese practice is approximated by the following stereotype, which is characterized here as a 'quality-based' form of contracting and is acknowledged to apply only to selected 'first-tier' suppliers (Kamath and Liker 1994): emphasis on quality and innovation rather than price; high involvement of suppliers in design and development activities; high levels of relation-specific investments; long-term relations; orientation towards mutual gain ('win–win', perception of the game as positive-sum), subject to demands on quality, ongoing improvement, cost, guarantees for recovery of investments; exchange of staff, technology and information on costs; only one first-tier supplier for a given input, for the lifetime of a given model of a given product (which yields multiple suppliers of a given input across different models and products); governance based on mutual commitment, cross-ownership and trust rather than detailed contracts. It is not certain that this is a realistic characterization of Japanese practice. It is based on reports from the literature. The analysis is intended to investigate how viable is this stereotype.

In many respects, past Western practice is the opposite. Currently, in the West, a novel practice is evolving which adopts features from Japan. Traditional Western practice is approximated with the following stereotype, which is characterized as a 'cost-based' form of contracting: oriented primarily at lowest cost of supply; adversarial bargaining on price; no concern for mutual profit ('win–lose': perception of the game as zero-sum); specification, design and even part of the engineering of inputs are performed by the user, as a blueprint for production by the supplier; 'closed' with respect to exchange of information on costs and technology; multiple sourcing (for a given input for a given model of a given product); 'distant' with respect to commitment in terms of investments. For the buyer, control of design, quality and cost takes precedence over utilization of supplier competence.

In the 'quality-based' form, outsourcing is driven primarily by considerations of quality, in the sense of a good fit to requirements for differentiated products, given a maximum price. The user aims to utilize as much as possible the capacities of the supplier. Therefore he leaves part of the design and engineering, as well as production, to the competence and often the initiative of the supplier and invites him to contribute to the determination of optimal specifications. This requires specific investments, particularly on the part of the supplier. To cover for this the user gives certain guarantees (long-term contracts, sufficient minimum volume of purchase), but then requires openness on the part of the user concerning technology used, costs and supply to other customers, in order to control for misuse of such guarantees ('open book contracting'). This openness is also required for effective information exchange for cooperation in development and production. Such openness may have negative effects on the bargaining position of the supplier. To cover for this, the user engages in 'price minus costing'. He grants a profit margin to the supplier, deducts this from the price he can afford to pay, thus arriving at the cost at which the input is to be produced. He transfers knowledge, technology and staff to the user and they jointly invest in development in order to achieve production at this price-minus-profit cost.

For the specification of the model, returns and risks of supply relations are specified as functions of variables that represent the characteristics of a subcontracting relation. The coefficients of those variables range over values that vary between different 'possible worlds'. This allows us to explore the feasibility and efficiency of various relations in such different worlds. Use is made of game theory to identify feasible and stable pairs of strategies for the two sides in the subcontracting relation, in the form of Nash equilibria in different worlds. This allows us to see which generic forms of subcontracting are feasible in which worlds and to compare their efficiency.

The model is based on the following design principles:

- The model specifies discrete alternatives, with binary variables (0–1) indicating whether a given policy or environmental condition obtains or not. This gives a basis to look at extremes that identify the boundaries within which reality appears.
- Net returns are specified in terms of binary variables that characterize the form of contracting, weighted by coefficients that vary across 'possible' worlds and binary variables related to those worlds.
- Boundedness of rationality is taken for granted, under all conditions, so that it need not be indicated. Opportunism, however, although its presence, latency or absence is difficult to identify prior to a relationship, need not always obtain and may be identifiable to some extent on the basis of experience with a relation or public reputation.
- The focus is on the characteristic case of buyer–supplier relations, where the buyer produces a differentiated product and, in order to provide high quality of adjustment to user needs, the supplier conducts more specific investments than the user. Note that the user may also need to make specific adjustments, to receive the product or to contribute to its development. It is assumed that the size of these specific investments is much less than those for the supplier. Note also that even if the user requires no specific investments, specificity of investment on the part of the supplier also makes the user dependent to some extent. If supply is discontinued, the user will incur loss of quality because he has to buy a substitute that conforms less closely to specifications, or has a higher cost because conformance to specifications requires purchase at a more expensive source, or delay because a substitute source first needs to invest to conform to specifications, or some combination of these.

However, typically this risk is smaller than the risk of loss of investment and switching costs faced by the supplier. If symmetry of specific investments does occur, the problem of the risk of hold-up becomes much less because there is a threat of retaliation. So it is both more realistic and more interesting to assume asymmetry in the form of larger specific investments on the part of the supplier.

Variables and returns

The binary variables that define forms of governance and are thus at the discretion of buyers/suppliers indicate whether (1) or not (0):

PMCOS: the user engages in price-minus costing.
OPEN: the supplier engages in open-book contracting.
SPEC: the supplier engages in partner-specific investments.
COV: the user covers the risk of specific assets on the part of the supplier by either participating in their ownership or giving guarantees in terms of duration or total value of purchase, or severance pay.
MULSUP: there are multiple suppliers for the user.
MULCUS: there are multiple customers for the supplier.
UTRAN: the user transfers knowledge to the supplier.
STRAN: vice versa.

An important side condition is the following: one cannot have information transfer without openness. In other words:

$$STRAN = 1 \text{ implies } OPEN = 1. \tag{A5.2.1}$$

Binary variables that represent characteristics of possible worlds are the following:

OPP: agents are opportunistic (yes or no).
SPEED: the speed of product change exceeds the speed of spillover.

The added value or surplus of exchange is normalized at 2 for a standard product, i.e. if it is not tailored to the specific demand of the user and is produced at the volume required for the user. In this case each side will obtain a return of 1 if the surplus is distributed equally. Deviations from this 'focal point' depend on bargaining positions, which are determined by price-minus costing, open-book contracting and access to alternative transaction partners, as will be explained below.

In a world where scale effects obtain and are important, both sides obtain additional benefits when the supplier produces at a larger volume. This requires that assets are non-specific (can be used for production for other customers) (*SPEC* = 0) and that there are multiple users (*MULCUS* = 1). In a world where product quality and differentiation is important, both sides obtain additional benefit when there is specificity of supplier assets (which is assumed to be required for differentiated products) (*SPEC* = 1). In other words: we are creating a choice between specialized production for a differentiated product and large-scale production for a standard product.

Having multiple partners (*MULCUS; MULSUP*) can yield benefits for several reasons: better bargaining position (as already indicated) and greater flexibility, due to opportunities to switch between partners, spread of risks and learning from varied transactions. Note that this form of learning is not based on transfer of competencies from one partner to the other, but internal learning due to dealing with varied partners. Another form of learning obtains when a partner actively contributes to the transfer of competence ('transfer': *STRAN* or *UTRAN* = 1). This requires a certain duration of the relationship. When a variety of sources of competence is important, the utility of a partner for this type of learning is increased to the extent that he has multiple partners ('varied learning': *STRAN.MULCUS* = 1; *UTRAN.-MULSUP* = 1). A yet more intensive form of learning arises when the two partners jointly produce competence ('joint development': *STRAN. UTRAN* = 1). This allows for the mutual transfer of tacit knowledge and the joint development of new knowledge. Next to these positive benefits, transfer of competence carries risk of spillover: the risk that through the partner information or competence spills over to a competitor. This can happen only if the partner has multiple partners ('spillover': *STRAN.MULSUP* = 1; *UTRAN.MULCUS* = 1).

With respect to bargaining position we choose an asymmetrical specification: only the supplier risks loss of bargaining position and hence share of the surplus due to being open ('open book contracting'; *OPEN* = 1). This risk can be eliminated by the user (*U*) granting a profit margin to *S* ('price-minus costing'; *PMCOS* = 1), or by the supplier by keeping access to multiple customers (to create a credible threat of switching to another customer; *MULCUS* = 1). The size of this risk is indicated by the parameter *b*. If *S* has strong and unique competencies to offer, *b* is small or zero.

Hold-up risk as a result of specific investments entails one or more of the following:

- loss of specific assets, to the extent that one participates in their finance;
- payment of guarantees, or loss of hostages committed to protect specific assets of the partner;
- loss due to pressure to compromise on cost, price or quality, due to opportunism which preys on dependence created by unprotected specific assets.

This risk arises only if there is opportunism (*OPP* = 1). The risk for *S* is that if she engages in specific investments (*SPEC* = 1) while her risk is not covered by U either participating in ownership or giving guarantees ($COV = 1$). It arises for U if she participates/guarantees ($COV = 1$), while S does not provide openness for U to control for misuse of ownership or guarantees (OPEN = 0) (in our design principles we assumed that U has no switching costs if she does not give guarantees to cover specific assets, which in this model are assumed only to arise on the part of suppliers).

Concerning the risk of spillover, note that spillover can be blocked by exclusive relations: by requiring the partner not to engage in other contacts for the same product. Note that even when there is no direct linkage of one's partner to one's competitors, information might still spill over to competitors through other linkages, such as through a supplier in a different but related market, or a customer of the customer who is strongly linked to a competitor. But at least direct spillover is blocked. It will take longer for information to reach a competitor and in the longer process of transmission there is more attrition of meaning (i.e. distortion through interpretation in different categorial systems) and a greater chance of obsolescence.

The inclusion of all these effects yields the following specification of returns, under side condition (1).

For the supplier:

$$
\begin{aligned}
SRET = 1 &- b(1\text{-}PMCOS).OPEN.(1\text{-}MULCUS) && \text{bargaining} \\
&+ sS.(1\text{-}SPEC).MULCUS && \text{scale} \\
&+ dS.SPEC && \text{specific product} \\
&+ mS.MULCUS && \text{multiple partners} \\
&+ tS.UTRAN && \text{transfer} \\
&+ vS.UTRAN.MULSUP && \text{varied learning} \\
&+ jS.UTRAN.STRAN && \text{joint development} \\
&- rS.STRAN.MULSUP && \text{spillover risk} \\
&- hS.\{(1\text{-}COV).SPEC\}.OPP && \text{specificity (hold-up) risk}
\end{aligned}
$$

where: $SRET$ = return for the supplier   (A5.2.2)
$b < 1$, sS, dS, mS, tS, vS, jS, rS and $hS > = 0$ are coefficients indicating the weights of the several components of returns to the supplier, which vary between 'possible worlds'.

For the user:

$$
\begin{aligned}
URET = 1 &+ b(1\text{-}PMCOS).OPEN.(1\text{-}MULCUS) && \text{bargaining} \\
&+ sU.(1\text{-}SPEC).MULCUS && \text{scale} \\
&+ dU.SPEC && \text{differentiated product} \\
&+ mU.MULSUP && \text{multiple partners} \\
&+ tU.STRAN && \text{transfer} \\
&+ vU.STRAN.MULCUS && \text{varied learning} \\
&+ jU.UTRAN.STRAN && \text{joint development} \\
&- rU.UTRAN.MULCUS && \text{spillover risk}
\end{aligned}
$$

$$- hU.COV.SPEC.(1-OPEN).OPP \qquad \text{specificity (hold-up) risk}$$

where: $URET$ = return for the user   (A5.2.3)
         The subscript U refers to the user.

When the coefficients are used without subscripts (S, U), they refer to both partners. The items of 'transfer, varied learning and joint development' represent a specification of the concept of 'external economy of cognitive scope' (EECS) discussed in Chapter 1.

Possible worlds and stereotypes

The stereotypes of Western and Japanese contracting are specified in terms of values for the variables that characterize the relation and 'possible worlds' are specified in terms of their coefficients in the specification of returns (A5.2.2, A5.2.3). Subsequently we analyse what Nash equilibria obtain in those worlds and see whether they correspond to Western and Japanese contracting. The reconstruction of the 'Western' and 'Japanese' stereotypes in terms of the variables from the model is as follows:

> *Western contracting*: $PMCOS = OPEN = COV = SPEC = UTRAN = STRAN = 0$; $MULCUS = MULSUP = 1$. In other words: users do not grant margins to suppliers, suppliers do not engage in open-book contracting, users do not supply guarantees to cover specific investments by the supplier, the supplier does not engage in specific investments, there is no transfer of competence between them and they engage in multiple sourcing and multiple supply.

> *Japanese contracting* is characterized as the opposite: $PMCOS = OPEN = COV = SPEC = UTRAN = STRAN = 1$; $MULCUS = MULSUP = 0$. Users and suppliers work closely together, with specific investments, allowing mutual profit, covering for each other's risks and mutually transferring know-how and they engage in exclusive relations (single sourcing; single supply).

To prevent misunderstanding: single sourcing and supply, mean exclusiveness only for the duration of a given model of a given product. For different models, a given input is likely to be sourced from among different suppliers, to maintain incentives for ongoing improvement and to keep monitoring the accomplishments in the market more widely (Kamath and Liker 1994). The proposed possible worlds are the following:

- The world of the *clan* (W1): here there is no opportunism ($SOPP = UOPP = 0$), due to actors being tied together in clans. This eliminates hold-up risk and this world thereby becomes something of a 'degenerate' case. This world can also be used to represent the situation where agents accept hold-up risk even where it is not eliminated by lack of opportunism.

- The *'Fordist world'* (W2): standard products and stable markets and technology. In this world there is no global competition, little need for product differentiation, integrated firms and a focus on price, cost and economy of scale. There is advantage in the flexibility, bargaining position and varied contracting with multiple partners. Due to stability and homogeneity of perceptions there is no great need for learning by transfer from other firms. In terms of the earlier discussion, EECS is not relevant. In terms of model parameters it is characterized as follows: for both U and S: $s > d$; $m > t,v,j$. This world is expected to favour 'Western contracting'.

- The *'world of efficient quality'* (W3): high quality is required in terms of close fit to specifications of differentiated products. Due to differentiated products there is limited economy of scale, a premium on specific inputs and corresponding assets and close cooperation between supplier and user, for optimal use of complementary competencies. Turbulence, in terms of change of markets and technology, is limited, so that learning from many outside partners is not essential. In terms of the model parameters: for U and S: $d > s$; $t,j > m,v$. This world is expected to favour 'Japanese contracting'. Risk of spillover exceeds the benefits of transfer: $r > t + v + j$.

- The world of *'raplex: rapid change and complexity'* (W4): intense competition in global markets, differentiated products (in both input and output markets), fast technological development. In this world, like the previous one, there is a need for specific investments to produce differentiated products, but in addition all forms of learning from outside partners are important (EECS): d, t, m, v, j are all important and the benefits from transfer exceed the risk of spillover: $t + v + j > r$. Within this world we recognize special cases, where the risk of spillover is small from three different causes:

  'radical speed' (W4a): change is so fast, that the life cycle of products is shorter than the development time of new products. Here spillover does not matter: by the time sensitive information reaches a competitor through linkages in the network of one's partner it is obsolete.

  'monitoring against spillover' (W4b): there are technologies to monitor what happens to competence transferred so that their spillover can be controlled.

  'radical differentiation' (W4c): competing producers are so radically differentiated that they cannot greatly benefit from information that spills over from them.

Outcomes

Now Nash equilibria are derived as stable, and in that sense viable outcomes, which are interpreted as 'generic forms of contracting', in each of the possible worlds specified.

A major question in a model of this type is how to weigh risks against returns. As shown, risks of bargaining and spillover were integrated as costs in the functions of net revenue (A5.2.2, A5.2.3). Hold-up risk is treated separately, with risk being either zero or unity; either absent or complete. In this setting, in the determination of equilibria we focus on outcomes in case of risk aversity, where agents first exclude strategies that yield (full) hold-up risk and then go for maximum returns. However, we also discuss what outcomes are under acceptance of risk.

W1 (clan world)

The advantage of W1 is that there can be dedicated products ($SPEC = 1$) without the need for measures of 'governance' to protect against hold-up risk (COV). Also, in this world of mutual trust risks of spillover are likely to be small, either because partnership is restricted ($MULCUS = MULSUP = 0$), or even if there are multiple partners risk of spillover is limited. Spillover may still occur accidentally, but not due to opportunism or the use of sensitive information from the partner as a hostage. But restricted partnership also implies a weakness, because it entails that the scope for learning is limited. The clan regime only works if no one can defect and get out ('hit and run') and there is no outside competition. In due course, this is expected to lead to lack of innovation and backwardness. In this world there are several outcomes, depending on the model parameters, as follows:[3]

> *Clan contracting* is characterized by the following parameter values:
> $SOPP = UOPP = 0$; $PMCOS = OPEN = UTRAN = STRAN = 1$.
> If $s > d$: $SPEC = 0$ and $MULCUS = 1$; $RET = 1 + s + m + t + v + j$, risks are zero.
> If $d > s$: $SPEC = 1$ and $COV = 1$; $RET = 1 + d + m + t + v + j$, risks are zero. Here RET indicates returns for both S and U.

These outcomes also obtain in other worlds in the case that agents accept hold-up risk.

W2 ('Fordist world')

Since scale is more important than product differentiation ($s > d$), the highest returns are reached (according to (A5.2.2) and (A5.2.3)) for: $SPEC = 0$ and $MULCUS = 1$. Since there are no specific investments, there is no need for guarantees: $COV = 0$ and therefore there also is no need for S to be open in order to provide control of such guarantees for U $(OPEN = 0)$. But according to (A5.2.1) this precludes $STRAN = 1$. U will then set $MULSUP = 1$, to obtain benefit m. According to the definition of W2 (m dominates remaining parameters; in particular $mU > vU$) this is higher than the benefit that U would have obtained from $STRAN = 1$ combined with $MULCUS = 1$, so there is no reason for U to get $STRAN = 1$, which would require $OPEN = 1$ (A5.2.1). This applies in spite of the fact that S could afford to do that without losing bargaining position and without needing a margin granted by U $(PMCOS = 0)$, since he can maintain that with the threat of shifting to a different partner $(MULCUS = 1)$ (see (A5.2.2)). Thus the only Nash equilibrium in W2 is:

> *Standard products with multiple partners and no transfer* ('Western form').In model parameters: $PMCOS = OPEN = STRAN = UTRAN = COV = SPEC = 0$ $MULCUS = MULSUP = 1$. $RET = 1 + s + m$.

Note that this is *identical to our reconstruction of the stereotype of 'Western contracting'*, so that we can conclude: in the Fordist world, Western contracting yields an efficient Nash equilibrium.

W4 (raplex: world of rapid change and complexity)

With low risk of spillover relative to the benefits of learning, there is no reason why agents should not set the relevant parameters to achieve 'full learning' ($m + t + v + j$): $STRAN = UTRAN = MULSUP = MULCUS = 1$. By (A5.2.1) this requires $OPEN = 1$, but according to (A5.2.2) the loss of bargaining position by S that this might entail is averted by $MULCUS = 1$ and there is no need for a guaranteed margin for S $(PMCOS = 0)$. To achieve advantages of differentiated product requires $SPEC = 1$, but to eliminate hold-up risk for S this requires $COV = 1$, but to eliminate hold-up risk for U this requires $OPEN = 1$. Thus we arrive at:

> *Cooperation with multiple partners and full learning*: $SPEC = COV = OPEN = SPEC = STRAN = UTRAN = MULSUP = MULCUS = 1$; $PMCOS = 0$.

This form of contracting is called the 'third way', since it presents an alternative to the stereotypes of Western and Japanese contracting. This is a Nash equilibrium: given the conditions of the world considered and the parameters chosen by the partner, no-one can improve his position.

W3 (efficient quality world)

Here we run into problems: the 'Japanese form' does not emerge as a Nash equilibrium and thus our expectation is not fulfilled. We spend a separate paragraph on the issues involved.

Problems with Japanese contracting

In W3 (*efficient quality*), the expectation was that Japanese contracting would constitute an efficient equilibrium. Let us consider that possibility.

Since in this world product differentiation is more important than scale, the aim is $SPEC = 1$. For S to eliminate the hold-up risk involved (A5.2.2), he requires guarantees ($COV = 1$), but (A5.2.3) then U requires the opportunity to monitor S for misuse of such guarantees ($OPEN = 1$). This also opens the possibility for the transfer of competence by S ($STRAN = 1$) that is important in this world. In this world spillover risks dominate the benefits of learning. To eliminate that risk for S, this requires that U does not engage in multiple partnerships ($MULSUP = 0$). In this world the return from joint development (j) dominates the remaining parameters; in particular $j > m$. Therefore $UTRAN = 1$ and to eliminate spillover risk for U, this requires $MULCUS = 0$.

The alternative would have been $UTRAN = 0$ combined with $MULCUS = 1$, which together with $STRAN = 1$ would have yielded U the return v, but would have led S to set $STRAN = 0$, to avoid spillover risk, so that U would lose j and the loss would have exceeded the gain m ($j > m$). Since $OPEN = 1$ and $MULCUS = 0$, not to lose bargaining position S requires U to grant her a margin ($PMCOS = 1$). Thus we arrive at the Japanese form of contracting:

> *Cooperation in exclusive partnerships* ('Japanese form'). $PMCOS = OPEN = SPEC = COV = STRAN = UTRAN = 1$; $MULSUP = MULCUS = 0$; $RET = 1 + d + t + j$.

Given the conditions of world W3, this form of contracting is efficient, but as we will demonstrate below, it does not constitute a Nash equilibrium.

The first problem is that we are in a prisoner's dilemma (PD) situation: from the position indicated both parties are tempted to engage in multiple partnerships, in order to gain additional benefit (m). But this creates risks of spillover (A5.2.2, A5,2.3). To eliminate this, transfer of competence is stopped ($STRAN = UTRAN = 0$) and in W3 the gain (m) is less than the loss (j), so that both sides are worse off. Yet this is what agents will choose, for fear that if one does not and the partner does, one loses too much.

An opportunity to get out of the PD arises in a repeated game, by threatening an end to the relationship if the partner does not maintain an exclusive relation. This may yield mutual cooperation in maintaining exclusiveness by 'tit-for-tat' or some equivalent procedure (Axelrod 1984). But there is another problem that cannot be solved. Why would U accept that she must provide a guaranteed margin to S? Suppose that she does not and puts $PMCOS = 0$? Then returns would be as follows:

$$SRET = 1\text{-}b + dS + tS + jS;\ URET = 1 + b + dU + tU + jU \qquad \text{(A5.2.4)}$$

In an attempt to prevent this, S may threaten to revert to multiple customers ($MULCUS = 0$), to restore bargaining position.[4] But is this a credible threat? To eliminate spillover risk U would set $UTRAN = 0$ to capture benefit m she would set $MULSUP = 1$ and to protect herself against spillover risk S would set $STRAN = 0$. Returns would then be as follows:

$$SRET = 1 + dS + mS;\ URET = 1 + dU + mU \qquad \text{(A5.2.5)}$$

The threat by S to revert to this is credible only if it would make her better off. This is the case only if:

$$b > tS + jS\text{-}mS \qquad \text{(A5.2.6)}$$

(Note that in the present world W3, tS and jS dominate mS.)

But b, which denotes the loss that S may incur as a result of a decrease in bargaining position, can be influenced by U. U could refund S so as to lower b to just below $tS + jS\text{-}mS$. Then condition (A5.2.7) is not satisfied and it is better for S to accept the loss according to (A5.2.4). Substituting $b = tS + jS\text{-}mS$, we then find:

$$SRET = 1 + dS + mS;\ URET = 1 + dU + tU + jU + tS + jS\text{-}mS \quad \text{(A5.2.7)}$$

In other words: U can appropriate all the benefits from transfer (t) and joint production (j) and we wind up at the equilibrium:

> *One-sided benefit in exclusive cooperation,* with $OPEN = SPEC = COV = STRAN = UTRAN = 1$; $PMCOS = MULSUP = MULCUS = 0$; $SRET = 1 + dS + mS$; $URET = 1 + dU + tU + tS + jU + jS\text{-}mS$

Is this, rather than the original reconstruction, the reality of Japanese contracting? Let us call it the 'modified Japanese form'. One way to avoid this result is to assume that $tS + jS < mS$, so that (A5.2.6) is fulfilled. But that means a departure from W3: we no longer have t and $j > m$ for both U and S. At least for S there is less benefit in transfer from U and joint production than from having multiple partners. Let us define world 5 (W5) as one where: $d > s$; $m > t,v,j$. The corresponding equilibrium, in that world, would be:

Differentiated products with multiple partners and no transfer, with *PMCOS* = *UTRAN* = *STRAN* = 0; *OPEN* = *COV* = *SPEC* = *MULCUS* = *MULSUP* = 1; *RET* = 1 + *d* + *m*.

We might consider yet another world (W6), where for U the benefit of transfer and joint production does exceed the benefit from multiple partners, but for S it does not: $d > s$ for U and S; $mS > tS + jS$; $tU + jU > mU$. Since transfer from U to S is of no value to S, S might as well engage in multiple partnerships. That enhances the value of S as a source to U. By offering a side payment e, U could get S to cooperate in transferring competence to U. Then returns would be as follows:

$$SRET = 1 + dS + mS + e; \ URET = 1 + dU + tU + vU\text{-}e \qquad (A5.2.8)$$

How large would the side payment e be? S could threaten not to give the transfer to U ($STRAN = 0$). In that case U would respond by engaging in multiple partnership ($MULSUP = 1$) and returns would be as follows:

$$SRET = 1 + dS + mS; \ URET = 1 + dU + mU \qquad (A5.2.9)$$

As a result, S could push the value of e up to just below the difference in return to U:

$$e = tU + vU\text{-}mU \qquad (A5.2.10)$$

The outcome would thus be:

Differentiated products with leading supplier, with U benefiting from a one-sided transfer from a supplier who is a valuable source of competence and maintains multiple customers, but the supplier appropriating most of that benefit: *PMCOS* = *UTRAN* = *MULSUP* = 0; *OPEN* = *COV* = *SPEC* = *STRAN* = *MULCUS* = 1; *SRET* = 1 + *dS* + *mS* + *tU* + *vU-mU*; *URET* = 1 + *dU* + *mU*

A final possibility to try and 'save' the Japanese form is to assume that there is no risk of the supplier losing bargaining position if he is open to the user ($OPEN = 1$) and has no multiple customers ($MULCUS = 0$): in A5.2.2 and A5.2.3 $b = 0$. We label this world W7. This might be interpreted as a situation where the product or competence offered by the supplier is so strong and unique that he can effectively threaten not to embark upon the relationship, in other words, the supplier has a strong monopoly. But then he would not need a guarantee for margin either and we would still have *PMCOS* = 0, rather than 1, as specified in the original 'Japanese form'. In W7 the outcome would be:

Differentiated products with monopolistic supplier, with $OPEN = SPEC = COV = STRAN = UTRAN = 1$; $MULSUP = MULCUS = PMCOS = 0$. $RET = 1 + d + t + j$

The conclusion is that the 'Japanese' form of contracting in its original reconstruction (picked up from the applied literature) is dubious, in the sense that with our model we have not been able to design a world where a guaranteed margin from the user to supplier is part of an equilibrium. Thereby we have not been able to reconstruct the 'Japanese form' as a viable practice. Cooperative relations in exclusive partnerships with mutual transfer either deteriorate to appropriation of the benefits by the user, or require monopoly on the part of the supplier, or shift to one-sided transfer from a leading and technologically independent supplier.

Discussion

The conclusions are of course only valid within the constraints set in the specification of the model. Two characteristic assumptions in the model are assumptions of asymmetry:

- specific investments arise only on the side of the supplier, if they do at all;
- the supplier runs a risk of loss of bargaining power if he does not satisfy any of the following conditions: unique product offering of high quality, closure to inspection by the user, access to alternative customers.

These features have been chosen because they appear in descriptions in the applied literature (e.g. Lamming 1993; Kamath and Liker 1994).

Another characteristic is a focus on the aversion of (full) risk of 'hold-up'. Perhaps this is a relic from standard TCE, which focuses on hold-up risk, but it does seem in accordance with observations that firms set great value on evading too much dependence and the corresponding risk of hold-up.

The model aims to express all the key issues from the theory of TCE, extended with a perspective of learning of different sorts. Formal reconstructions have been made of the stereotypes of 'Western' and 'Japanese' forms of contracting. Plausible worlds have been specified in which these forms seem relevant.

There are many opportunities for further research:

- Explore alternative specifications of the model: the possibility of symmetry of specific assets between buyer and supplier; the acceptance of some degree of hold-up risk. Perhaps this will lead to a Nash equilibrium for our specification of the Japanese form.
- Exploit the rich source of hypotheses for different worlds, to test them in empirical work.

- Relax the extremes of dichotomous variables in a more continuous analysis.
- In such an analysis, make an explicit trade-off between returns and hold-up risk.
- Extend the analysis of interaction to multiple partners in a network.
- Allow for lack of information on strategies and outcomes.
- Make an explicit model of the development of different forms in different worlds towards evolutionary equilibria.

6 Summary

This book has provided a large amount of detail. In order not to lose sight of the forest in all the attention to the trees, this final chapter pulls together some of the main themes, indicates implications for policy and avenues for further research.

THE BUSINESS ENVIRONMENT

This book analyses interorganizational relations from a perspective which includes innovation and learning. The importance of innovation and learning was shown in a discussion of developments in the business environment in Chapter 2. Several causes lead to 'radical' product differentiation. Pressures of global competition yield an incentive to differentiate products in order to escape from pure price competition and to adapt products to different demands in different countries. Individualization of consumer behaviour, associated with rising prosperity, creates a demand for it. Technology, especially information and communication technology (ICT), enables differentiation by offering the required information and access to customers and flexible methods of development and production. Together with fast development of technology and internationalization of markets, this creates great complexity and turbulence, forcing firms to concentrate on their core competencies and to obtain complementary resources from outside. This is needed to achieve efficiency, speed and quality in differentiated products, but particularly for development and for learning. The importance of alliances cannot be fully appreciated without taking innovation and learning into account.

Thus, increasingly, next to competition between firms there is cooperation. Trade-offs have to be made between the two. On the one hand there is the need to engage in relationships that have sufficient continuity to recoup the specific investments needed for product differentiation and to build and maintain trust-based cooperation. On the other there is the need to maintain flexibility for innovation and variety for learning with openings to novel opportunities from outside.

THEORY

Chapter 1 integrated the resource–competence view, transaction cost theory, a social exchange perspective and a theory of knowledge, to yield a theory of inter-firm relations that incorporates innovation and learning, as well as trust next to opportunism.

In this setting, to paraphrase Hayek: competition and cooperation together form a process of discovery. From this perspective of innovation and learning, the project of this book may be seen as an attempt to contribute to the fulfilment of the original project of Austrian economics. The constructivist theory of knowledge used here aligns with the Austrian notion of subjectivity of both preferences and knowledge. Radical subjectivism may entail relativism, but it is shown how relativism is checked by the fact that cognitive categories develop during interaction between people, so that they are shared to some extent, depending on the intensity and duration of the interaction and the extent to which this takes place in a shared physical and institutional environment.

According to Schumpeter, the entrepreneur has been characterized as being non-adaptive, causing disequilibrium, generating innovation, giving rise to creative destruction and increasing uncertainty. The entrepreneur, according to the Austrian school (Menger, Hayek and more recently Kirzner), is adaptive, reacts to exogenous shocks of change and draws the economy towards equilibrium by realizing present technological opportunities for satisfying demand. He decreases uncertainty. This type of entrepreneur can also be found in Walrasian economics, with the difference that Austrians focus more on the process of equilibration, which may be lengthy, and the problems of information and uncertainty involved, while Walrasians focus on the horizon of equilibrium. One avenue of further theoretical research is to investigate the relation between equilibrating and disequilibrating processes in markets: the utilization of the potential of present knowledge, technology, organization and institutions and the development of new forms on the basis of 'novel combinations' that yield 'creative destruction'. At the firm level, this issue is associated with the relation between realization of the potential of existing resources (exploitation) and development of new ones (exploration). One challenge is to develop some 'logic' which can explain both and can also indicate the relation between the two: between learning by the firm and industrial and technological change. Attempts at this are offered in Nooteboom (1992a,c, 1999).

While Austrian economists have generally used their view of the market as a discovery process to plead for unfettered market mechanisms, the present book yields a different outlook. It provides a basis for assessing the role of government in shaping, maintaining and adapting institutions required as a basis for competition and cooperation. This view follows from the need to have cooperation next to competition, as argued above. Cooperation is more efficient, in the static sense of carrying fewer costs and in the dynamic sense of enhancing innovation, when there is a basis for trust, which is based partly on the institutional environment that constitutes a responsibility for government. But there are dilemmas here which will be considered in a final section on implications for government.

The notion of trust is a slippery one: Different things can be meant, thereby creating a source of potentially dangerous misunderstandings. According to a wide definition it pertains to any reason why one does not expect to be harmed by actions of partners in transaction or cooperation. This includes: legal coercion; power over the partner because she is at least as dependent on you as you are on her; perspectives for profitable future dealings ('shadow of the future'); the keeping of hostages; reputation mechanisms; social coercion; internalized norms and values of conduct; a preference for being trustworthy; feelings of solidarity related to kinship, friendship or empathy. According to a narrower, stronger definition, trust entails that one does not expect to be harmed by a partner even though she has both the opportunity and the incentive to be opportunistic. When the performance of the relationship drops or more attractive alternatives appear, rather than defecting, partners will try to help each other to improve the relation, within certain bounds dictated by pressures of survival. This notion comes closest to what is ordinarily meant by trust, but there can be misunderstandings. When someone says that she can be trusted and assuming she is sincere and not just trying to keep you from setting up safeguards against her opportunism, it is important to know which definition of trust is at play. If different partners entertain different concepts of trust, one of them may be in for unpleasant surprises.

In Chapter 1 it was proposed that trust in the narrow, strong sense does obtain, to a greater or lesser extent, depending on the social–cultural context, the characters and background of the individuals involved, the nature and history of the relationship. It can serve to limit costs of contracts and monitoring, to provide flexibility in the content of cooperation and the basis for the openness needed for mutual learning and innovation. However, it should not be blind: even the most trustworthy may succumb to the temptation of a golden opportunity of defection, or to the pressures of survival. Within the boundaries set by such contingencies, trust can operate as a heuristic; as a routine of conduct that is followed as long as observed actions and conditions stay within certain tolerance limits. Such limits are given by intuitions, based on experience, of where resistance to temptation might be tested too much.

ALLIANCES

Chapter 3 gives an inventory of forms, goals and conditions of alliances. There are many reasons for alliances, next to the core motive of concentrating on core competencies and seeking complementary resources from others. Often, the motive is connected with a strategy of internationalization; hence the importance of international alliances. Underlying motives can be: economy of scale or scope; to share or diversify risk; to prevent transportation costs; to follow customers; to adapt a product to the local market; to circumvent entry barriers (in markets for products or inputs); speed of market entry; political legitimacy; restrictions on the repatriation of profits; to pre-empt the competition from entering first; to attack a competitor in his home market; the need jointly to set a market standard; to limit the competition by instituting a cartel.

When there is a choice between going it alone or employing a partner, the decision depends on: required speed of entry; one's experience, knowledge and access to local resources; availability of partners; need to evade duplication of fixed costs in a saturated, high fixed cost industry. There are many forms of alliance and their choice depends on the motives of the partners and contingencies of market and technology.

The relevant contingencies are many: technological and organizational opportunities for efficiencies of scale or scope; price, quality and accessibility of markets for products and production factors; commercial possibilities to maintain fixed product characteristics across different markets versus the need to adapt the product; the degree to which core competence is subject to spillover (related to the degree to which competence is tacit or embodied in organization and culture); the degree to which technology is dedicated, so that product differentiation requires specific investments; the degree to which technology is systemic or stand-alone and the degree to which standards are available across interfaces between modules; degree and speed of innovation; market pressures to engage in innovation and learning; market pressures to utilize every available opportunity for short-term profit, possibly to the detriment of long-term development; degree to which the institutional environment provides a basis for trust (in the strong sense); degree to which the institutional environment yields adequate property rights, protection against violence and corruption, a stable currency, accounting standards, etc.

Forms of alliance can be distinguished according to at least nine dimensions, but these can, with some distortion, be brought together to two dimensions of integration: of claims to profit and of decision rights. The least integrated form is arm's-length contracting in markets. The most integrated form is integration (merger or acquisition) into a single firm with centralized ownership and decision-making. There are more or less centralized forms of organization connecting formally distinct firms: associations, industrial districts, consortia, franchising, equity joint ventures. Some formally integrated firms allow for extreme decentralization of decisions and claims to profit, with only short-term and partial contracts of engagement: virtual firms. A virtual firm can come close to an industrial district.

As a general rule, the advantage of more integrated forms is better opportunities for efficiencies of scope and better control: of competition, distribution of profit, opportunism, spillover. Disintegrated forms yield more motivation (of autonomous units responsible for their own survival), economy of scale due to specialization; less risk and cost of merging cultures; concentration on core competencies; flexibility of novel combinations, variety of sources for learning. The general rule, confirmed by empirical research, is that mergers and acquisitions are a viable form when partners are close actual or potential competitors, with the same products in the same markets; otherwise more disintegrated forms are superior.

From this perspective it is doubtful, under present conditions of complexity and rapid change, with the resulting need to concentrate on core competencies to maintain flexibility, to innovate and to learn, whether in all cases the new waves of mergers and acquisitions make economic sense and whether the present surge of stock prices is well founded. It seems a lemming phenomenon, with everyone trying to stay ahead of everyone else, in a blind race that is likely to lead to a dip into a cold sea of failure and forced break-up, and a collapse of stock markets to the extent that this happens simultaneously for different firms.

GOVERNANCE

As discussed in Chapter 4, the problems in the governance of inter-firm alliances can be summarized in five dilemmas, as follows: unity and division; contract and cooperation; opportunism and trust; durability and flexibility; openness and closure.

1 *Unity and division.* The most obvious problem is that on the one hand partners must cooperate to achieve maximal joint added value, but the proceeds also need to be divided between them. The problem is most pronounced in a relationship between competitors, when it entails a zero-sum game: the gain of the one is the loss of the other. It is less of a difficulty when partners are complementary rather than competitive. This is why, as argued in Chapter 3, more competitive relations tend to be tackled by integration, by merger and acquisition.

2 *Contract and cooperation.* To reduce risks of dependence some degree of contracting is needed, but too detailed contracts are expensive and impossible to the extent that contingencies are complex and variable. They limit flexibility and can create a self-reinforcing cycle of distrust which necessitates further contractual complexity.

3 *Opportunism and trust.* Trust is indispensable and makes for cheap and flexible governance, but it can cause confusion (it can have diverse meanings) and has its limits, as argued in Chapter 1. We must distinguish competence trust and intentional trust. Intentional trust can be based on hierarchical supervision, contract enforcement, governance by self-interest and governance by trust in the narrow, strong sense: based on prevailing norms of conduct, bonds of friendship or kinship, formation

of routines. It is important to know what is the basis for trust. One should remain aware that apparently loyal partners may succumb to temptation or the pressures of survival when these become too high. Lack of trust yields barren relations, but blind trust is foolish.

4   *Durability and flexibility.* One wants to maintain flexibility to make novel combinations of partnerships which are geared to novel projects or conditions, but the relationship must be of sufficient duration to recover specific investments, to adapt sufficiently to each other (reduce 'cognitive distance'), to understand each other sufficiently to achieve joint production and to build trust.

5   *Openness and closure.* When partners do not share knowledge they cannot cooperate and utilize complementary knowledge and the potential of the relation is not realized. But such openness may carry the danger of loss of core competence due to spillover to competitors via the partner and can jeopardize bargaining position.

Organizations need an instrument to analyse and assess a relation; to deal with the paradoxes of cooperation. They need to assess their position concerning opportunities and threats, to arrive at an evaluation and diagnosis of the relation and actions to improve or redesign it. Chapter 4 developed such an instrument, on the basis of the theory set out in Chapter 1: an integration of the resource–competence perspective and a theory of knowledge, which serves to give a clear view of the purpose of alliances in utilizing and developing complementary resources; an integration of transaction cost economics and a social exchange perspective, which serves to come to grips with behavioural risks in a way that recognizes both opportunism and trust.

According to the scheme used, the damage that can be done in breaking off a relationship is determined by the sum of the relative value of the partner, in excess on one's next best alternative, and switching costs, which are primarily determined by one's share in the ownership of specific assets. That sum of values is what is lost if the relation breaks up. It also determines the maximum to which one can be 'held-up': the partner cannot expropriate more advantage than what one stands to lose if the relationship is severed. Note that if specific investments are one-sided, their switching costs can be divided by sharing their ownership. The probability that such loss occurs, due to opportunistic defection from the relation, or hold-up based on the threat to defect, is determined by the partner's chances for opportunism, her incentives and inclination to utilize them. Chances for opportunism depend on the closure that can be achieved by contracts, which depends on the extent to which contingencies can be foreseen and covered and the effectiveness of monitoring compliance, which can be limited by asymmetry of information. Incentives to utilize chances for opportunism depend on the degree to which the partner is dependent, future perspectives of the relation ('shadow of the future'), hostages and reputation. Inclinations towards opportunism stand for the trust dimension of relations. They are limited to the extent that the partner is not prone to be opportunistic even when he has the opportunity and the incentive. Such trustworthiness can be based on the institutional environment of norms, values and habits of conduct, modified by the degree to which the partner has internalized such norms and is susceptible to ethical appeals, bonds of kinship or friendship, or institutional arrangements developed in the relationship, such as shared norms or routines.

Relative value of a partner can become negative for several reasons. His value can decrease for lack of maintenance and further development, or because his competence spills over so that the value he offers is no longer unique. One's own value may remain the same, while one's relative value declines because new substitutes are mobilized by the partner, or a novel alternative enters the stage and sets a new standard of value. The latter event is a particularly frequent destabilizer of relations and presents a test of loyalty: will the partner defect or will he commit himself to a joint effort to bring the relation up to the new standard.

From these basic variables one can logically derive possible instruments for governance: modify relative value, switching costs, opportunities, incentives or inclinations for opportunism, on one's own side or on the side of the partner. Each instrument has its advantages and drawbacks and the skill of relationship management is to select the right mix for the right conditions.

The drawback of detailed contracts is that they may be impossible due to the inability to foresee and cover all contingencies and monitoring may be limited due to asymmetric information. When feasible they can be costly. They may form a straightjacket that limits flexibility and innovation and can engender distrust. Switching costs can be avoided by evading ownership in specific assets, but such assets may be needed to achieve high quality and differentiated products. Dependence on unique value of the partner can be avoided by entertaining alternative partners, but this multiplies costs of governance, raises spillover risks for the partner (which may prevent him from sharing his knowledge) and may encourage him to engage less in specific investments and to give less information, in order to protect his bargaining position.

Governance by self-interest is perhaps the most efficient. A particularly productive approach is to invest in one's own value to the partner to such an extent that one becomes indispensable and at the same time to mobilize the 'shadow of the future' by offering the perspective for fruitful ongoing collaboration. The weakness of governance by self-interest is that it is not robust under entry of attractive new options for the partner. The advantage of trust is that it is more robust under such contingencies, but how far can trust be trusted? There is likely to be some limit to the partner's resistance to the temptation of defection. But this is still better than no resistance at all. The limitation of trust is that it cannot be simply purchased and installed if it is not already present (on the basis of the institutional environment or prior bonds of kinship or friendship). Then it has to be built up in the relationship, which takes time, effort and discipline.

Experience and empirical research show that firms are not yet sufficiently sophisticated in their governance systematically to take a two-sided approach and look at the relation from the perspective of the partner, to assess what one would do in his place and then to ask what one can do to help the partner to help oneself.

An important topic is not just the design but the development and redesign of alliances. In Chapter 4 an analysis was given, with simple use of game theory, of alternative ways to start and to end a relation. Which method is the best again depends on the conditions. Under a variety of conditions, a good way to start an alliance between strangers is not to begin with detailed contracts, but to aim for small but rapid initial success, with only limited specific investments. This provides an opportunity for the building of both competence trust and intentional trust and to find out more about the potential and risks of the relation. Depending on how the relationship develops, one can later move either to more extended contracts or some form of integration, such as an equity joint venture (which may or may not later evolve into a merger or acquisition), if that need becomes apparent. Alternatively, one can move to some form of extended non-equity alliance with an extension of specific investments on the basis of mutual interest and trust. What form to adopt as the alliance evolves depends on the conditions indicated earlier. More control by contract or integration is desirable only if the need arises due to potential competition, increased specific investments, threat of spillover, lack of trust. A good way to end a relation is often the cooperative mode of giving an early warning of the wish to leave and offering help to the partner in finding ways out: by phasing out specific investments and seeking alternatives. This can be beneficial in evading a mutually destructive 'divorce procedure' and in maintaining reputation as a cooperative and loyal partner. But more research is clearly needed on the management and adaptation of alliances in time, as a function of conditions and the history of the relationship and the partners involved.

SUBCONTRACTING

Chapter 5 focuses on vertical buyer–supplier relations. These tend to involve complementary rather than competitive (substitutive) activities and are therefore more easily governed than horizontal relations between potential competitors. There is less need for integration of buyer and supplier into a single firm. The governance of relations between buyer and supplier can be simple, in the form of ad hoc, arm's-length, price-oriented, impersonal transactions with little information exchange. This is appropriate when the product is a standard one, without uncertainty or substantial innovation and does not require specific investments to tailor it to specific needs (to differentiate the buyer's product). But when there is complexity of product differentiation and innovation, with a perspective for utilizing complementary competencies in joint development ('early supplier involvement') in order to achieve better quality and higher speed of development, and this entails specific investments and information exchange, more sophisticated, durable but not permanent, trust-based relations are required.

Past relations of supply in Europe (and more strongly in the USA) can be described as 'arm's-length' contracting in ad hoc transactions rather than ongoing relations. The evasion of long-term relations is inspired by reluctance towards dependence on a partner and a focus on maintenance of bargaining position for low costs and maximal share of profits. Buyers focus on competitive tendering and suppliers withhold information on their costs, stocks and orders in the pipeline to maintain bargaining position. Given the short-term focus of transactions and the reluctance to engage in transaction-specific investments, there is limited scope for product differentiation and joint innovation. When specific investments do arise, with the need to prolong transactions, and in that sense a relationship rather than isolated transactions arises, there is a tendency towards the use of adversarial strategies. When the commitment of partners on the basis of their self-interest is in doubt, they are tied to the relationship by means of detailed contracts and monitoring of compliance, the demand for partner's participation in the ownership of specific assets and the demand for hostages. When the end of a relationship is envisaged, the adversarial strategy entails attempts to shift the burden of ownership of specific assets to the partner, to exploit asymmetric information by giving little information and demanding much, thus shifting the balance of monitoring and spillover risks to one's advantage, reducing the partner's relative value by developing alternatives and utilizing the resulting bargaining advantage for 'hold-up', i.e. for extorting a larger share in the proceeds of joint added value.

Japanese supply relations are reported to be more cooperative, as follows: the buyer does not go for the lowest price offer, regardless of supplier profit or loss. He acknowledges the supplier's need for profit and turns the issue around in 'price minus costing'. He takes into account a profit margin for the supplier, deducts that from a price that is acceptable to the buyer, to arrive at a cost price at which the supplier should perform. He then makes the commitment to a joint effort, with pooled resources, to achieve that target. The guarantee of a profit margin removes the supplier's need to withhold information in order to maintain bargaining position. Thus an opportunity is created for openness in the exchange of information and knowledge which is necessary for fruitful cooperation. The resulting spillover risk is controlled by exclusiveness: for a given activity there is only one or at most two partners.

In Western countries there is an increasing awareness, for example, in the building industry, that a switch is required from the customary mode of price-oriented contracting to collaborative governance. Price-oriented contracting for the sake of maintaining bargaining position and controlling spillover forecloses the openness needed for pooling resources and joint innovation. The need to maintain bargaining position also entails that dependence due to specific investments is avoided, with a resulting loss of quality in tailormade products. Multiple partners are kept for the same activity, which increases costs of contracting and monitoring and raises spillover risks, which further inhibits collaboration by exchange of knowledge. Finally, in spite of much effort and loss of time in bargaining and contracting, the objective of low costs is frustrated by the fact that unforeseen contingencies arise which allow the partner to restore his share in profits outside the scope of the contract.

Chapter 5 summarizes empirical studies which corroborate the role of trust next to other aspects of governance, such as the specificity of assets. There trust is measured on the basis of shared norms of conduct and 'habituation', which include routinization of conduct. In one study, the extensiveness of contracts had no significant effect on perceived relational risk. This confirms the suspicion that extensive contracts in formal legal governance can have only limited value. Of course this does not imply that there should be no contracts at all, but only that they should not be too extensive. The hypothesized negative effect on perceived risk of information transfer from the buyer to the supplier was confirmed. The theory is that the buyer makes himself more vulnerable, by weakening his bargaining position and by the risk of spillover to competitors (information as hostage), which reassures the supplier with respect to his own perceived dependence. A second study confirmed the earlier results. This also included the possible effect of 'uncertainty avoidance', as a property of the supplier, with the expectation that risk-averse firms have a more gloomy view of risks of dependence. But instead, a significant negative effect on perceived risk came out and this makes sense: more risk averse firms see to it that they select low-risk partners. A second disconfirmation was that a high perceived value offered to the partner did not have the expected negative effect on the perceived probability of loss. A plausible interpretation of this is that firms are not sophisticated enough in their assessment of the situation. They did not take into account the motivations of the partner and did not ask the question what they would do if they stood in his shoes.

Chapter 5 also gives a formal analysis, with simple use of game theory, of the comparative advantages of 'Japanese' and 'Western' modes of governance in different 'possible worlds' and considers whether there might be some 'third way'. The 'Japanese' and 'Western' forms are stylized representations of the modes described above.

Western, arm's-length, price-oriented contracting is found to be an efficient and feasible form in a world of standard products, stable markets and technology. In this world there is no global competition, little need for product differentiation, integrated firms and a focus on price, cost and economy of scale. There is advantage in the flexibility, bargaining position and varied contracting with multiple partners. Due to stability and homogeneity of perceptions there is no great need for learning by knowledge transfer from other firms.

The formalized version of the Japanese form is efficient in a world where high quality is required in terms of close fit to specifications of differentiated products. Due to differentiated products there is limited economy of scale, a premium on specific inputs and corresponding assets and close cooperation between supplier and user, for optimal use of complementary competencies. Turbulence is limited, in terms of change of markets and technology, so that learning from many outside partners is not essential. However, the analysis raises doubts about the viability of this form of governance, in the sense of its stability. There is a temptation for the buyer to renege on his allowance for a reasonable profit margin for the supplier and there is a temptation on both sides to surrender exclusiveness and seek multiple partners.

A 'third way' is more efficient and viable in a world of intense competition in global markets, differentiated products (in both input and output markets) and fast technological development. In this world, like the previous one, there is a need for specific investments to produce differentiated products, but in addition all forms of learning from outside partners are important, and the benefits from knowledge transfer exceed the risk of spillover. The risk of spillover is small for one or more of the following reasons. The first possibility is that change is so fast that the life cycle of products is shorter than the development time of new products. Here, spillover does not matter: by the time sensitive information reaches a competitor, through linkages in the partner's network, it is obsolete. The second possibility is that there are technologies to monitor what happens to transferred competence so that their spillover can be controlled. A third possibility is that competing producers are so radically differentiated that they cannot greatly benefit from information that spills over between them. The 'third way' entails mutual transfer of know-how with multiple partners and full learning. That is needed in this world and is feasible because by assumption spillover risks no longer matter. It resembles 'Western' contracting in its orientation to multiple partnerships and the absence of guarantees for supplier margin (price-minus costing). It resembles Japanese contracting in its orientation towards specific investments with guarantees, open book contracting, mutual transfer of competence and cooperation in development.

EFFECTS OF ICT

Information and communication technology (ICT) is an important contributor to the developments that lead to the need to concentrate on core competencies and thereby engage more in alliances with other firms. It is also an important enabler of such alliances. Generally speaking, ICT reduces transaction costs by reducing costs of coordination. ICT clearly reduces costs of search, yields better opportunities for monitoring (e.g. performance, flow of goods, quality, reputation, financial solidity) and cheaper contracting (by reuse of standard contracts and their flexible adaptation to specific conditions). But it also yields opportunities for more flexible design (by means of computer aided design, virtual prototyping and testing), more flexible production (computer-aided manufacturing, reprogramming of machines, computer-aided adaptation of layouts), low stocks, efficient ordering and just-in-time production, monitoring and optimization of marketing instruments (e.g. on the basis of scanning data from shops).

Since transaction costs are generally higher between than within firms, this is expected to contribute further to a shift from integration to inter-firm relations, thereby also creating a shift from mergers and acquisitions to other more disintegrated forms of alliance. But this general tendency should be qualified by further details.

Given a likely tendency towards more contracting out, a further question is what effect ICT will have on the number of partners. As long as the set-up cost of ICT links or networks is high relative to operating costs and has to be repeated for each partner, this militates against a large number of partners. But this will change if firms start to use some widely shared existing network such as the Internet. There are several other arguments in favour of a smaller number of partners, of more exclusiveness. The most important is that with multiple partners set-up costs of specific investments and bilateral governance are multiplied. However, this effect is less to the extent that ICT lowers asset specificity and set-up costs of contracting and monitoring. Another argument for small numbers is that insofar as there is a risk of spillover (when knowledge is documented and technology is not subject to radical change), then it may be necessary to reduce spillover risk for one's partner by limiting relations with potential competitors. However, ICT may help to control spillover risk. It may also be necessary to keep the number of partners small in order to make oneself more dependent, thereby making it acceptable to the partner to be more dependent by engaging in more specific investments, which may be needed to achieve desired quality and product differentiation.

But there is one important counter-argument. Innovation requires flexibility to make novel combinations and learning requires a diversity of sources; both would be enhanced by a multiplicity of partners. In part, this is the reverse side of spillover. One can have learning without spillover when technology changes so fast as to eliminate its risk. Such speed of change would also enhance the need to use outside sources for learning. Furthermore, we made several qualifications in the above arguments for a small number of partners. ICT tends to reduce the force of the arguments, with widely shared networks and the use of ICT for the reduction of set-up costs of governance and spillover control. Thus, the expectation is that while there are arguments to maintain a small number of partners, ICT will tend to increase it.

A next question concerns the duration of relations. A relation should be sufficiently long to recoup specific investments, including efforts to develop cooperation, to build up trust and to control spillovers, but not too long to inhibit flexibility and innovation. The need for speedy innovation will exert a pressure on the duration of relationships. The greater flexibility of development and production due to ICT and the fact that ICT assets depreciate quickly, will contribute to such shortening of relations.

A further question is what the effect of ICT will be on the geographical distance between partners. Of course, with fax, e-mail, the Internet and telephone conferencing there are more opportunities for coordination at a distance. Does this lead to 'the death of distance'? Distance still matters for the exchange of tacit knowledge: this requires face-to-face interaction with on-line demonstration, imitation and correction. Perhaps virtual reality can make this feasible at a distance. The question then is when this will be economically feasible as a matter of routine. But for as long as distance still matters, it should be noted that knowledge cannot be neatly separated into tacit and documented streams. Rather, any part of knowledge has tacit and documented components that often cannot easily be separated. The question then is what distortions or even disasters might occur when in the application of ICT the tacit component drops out and the documented components get misunderstood and misapplied. However this may work out, distance still matters for other reasons. Face-to-face interaction and mixing of business and personal contact may be needed to develop trust, especially intentional trust which may be required, in learning, to reduce perceived risks of spillover. The mixing of groups of people engaged in related activities, at an appropriate location, may also be needed to enable random encounters that establish opportunities for novel exchange and cooperation which otherwise might not have been detected. The example that comes to mind is the scientific conference: it is likely that, in spite of extensive and intensive use of the Internet and e-mail, such encounters will remain a necessary complement. Finally, proximity of firms in an industrial district may be needed for efficient turnover of staff from failing entrepreneurial firms to successful or start-up firms in a joint pool of labour. In Silicon Valley buses with announcements of recruitment opportunities appear outside failing firms.[1]

Evidence from 'virtual firms' confirms these expectations. They operate on the principle that staff work mostly at home and from there communicate with colleagues worldwide by e-mail. They create efficiencies by sharing successful solutions (exploitation) and cooperate in innovation by novel combinations (exploration). For reasons of social cohesion and probably trust, get-togethers are organized with some frequency, not to work but to engage in social, recreative activities. The trust may be needed for exchange. One of the problems in such a firm is not the technology of ICT but the incentives for people to make their experience available to colleagues who may also be competitors for promotion in the firm. Incentives and trust building have to be developed to solve this problem. There is also evidence that 'work-arounds' are needed to bypass the formal system of knowledge pooling, to allow for personal contact for the exchange of tacit knowledge and to allow sufficient openness of the system for innovative novel combinations.[2]

GOVERNMENT POLICY

There is efficiency in linkages between firms, in network economies, with low transaction costs, mutual adjustment for high quality, differentiated products, joint development, diffusion of innovations and incremental innovation. This requires cooperation based on sufficiently durable and cooperative relations, partly founded on trust. But when networks become too tight and enduring they can obstruct entry, flexibility and radical innovation by novel combinations.

Lack of skill in the governance of inter-firm relations and lack of underlying institutions can block specific investments, to the detriment of the efficiency and quality of supply and innovation, which has repercussions for the competitive advantage of a nation or region. There may be a clear role for government to intervene. One intervention might be to stimulate and facilitate the development of standards for technology and conduct.

An example is the standardization of norms for uniform bar coding of goods, as a basis for the automation of trade, including identification, search, tracking and tracing, ordering, billing, payment.

It is generally acknowledged that government has a task concerning 'infrastructure' and 'external effects'. The question is what we understand by these terms, which are assuming new meanings. This is connected with the new 'techno-economic paradigm' discussed in Chapter 2. The shift from the old to the new paradigm can be seen as a shift from internal to external economies of scale and scope. Efficiencies that used to be achieved by coordination within firms are now achieved in relations between partly autonomous and partly dependent firms, in forms of 'organization between market and hierarchy'. In those linkages flexibility and incentives for independent firms are combined with advantages of scope in relations between them (see the 'external economy of cognitive scope' discussed in Chapter 1). This forms the scientific background to the presently fashionable (at least in the Netherlands) notion of 'clusters' (stimulated by Porter's studies of the competitive advantage of nations). With an industrial or innovation policy oriented towards clusters, government is oriented not towards individual firms but to the enabling of linkages between them.

Such policy is interesting from the perspective of threats that advanced nations are not only losing traditional, but also novel 'high level', employment to emerging nations. If we achieve advantage in complex, systemic, organizational linkages between firms, such risk would be much smaller. Such a complex web of activities is much less easily lost than isolated activities, especially when it is connected with the exchange and joint production of tacit knowledge and is to some extent based on trust. The justification of government intervention is that in such linkages there are often problems of collective action that may need outside arbitration, coaching and the resolution of conflicts.

In the last decades, economics has immersed itself in strategic interactions between firms (by means of game theory), the dynamics of non-linear economic systems (by means of simulation) and the consequences of bounded rationality and asymmetric information. Those lines of thought yield novel insights for government policy. In line with North (1990), the main economic role of government may be conceptualized as the enabler and guardian of institutions to limit transaction costs. More specifically, the roles of government may include:

- arbitrator;
- systems guardian;
- producer and guardian of institutions to contain transaction costs.

In applications of game theory numerous problems of coordination have been explored (e.g. Elster 1979, 1989). Well-known examples are the 'prisoner's dilemma' and the phenomenon of 'free riding'. There are many actions that would be beneficial for all involved and for society at large, but require cooperation which does not get established due to fears of defection. Investment in training, basic research and environmental protection is often feasible only if free riding is contained. There are also coordination problems in the establishment of standards of technology, competence and ethical conduct. Sometimes coordination can occur spontaneously, without outside intervention (Axelrod 1984). But this is highly sensitive to conditions of information flow and stability in the field of players, so that even then government has a task to provide the conditions for cooperation to arise and be maintained. This does not necessarily mean that the government itself has to produce regulation, but that it should act as an intermediary in its production.

Research of non-linear dynamic systems shows that often the system 'hesitates', as it were, between several alternative paths of development ('bifurcations'), which can create obstacles for going back or switching to an alternative trajectory of development ('path dependence'). In this perspective the idea that 'the market' always yields the most efficient outcomes is highly naïve. The selection of paths of development is often the result of a confluence of actions and conditions that no one could foresee, including the government. But in trying to grasp systemic effects the government is not in a worse position and more likely in a better position than business. This suggests a role for government as 'systems guardian', in all due modesty concerning its limited ability of foresight.

The government is responsible for institutions in order to limit transaction costs. The market does not operate in a vacuum but requires an institutional infrastructure, which goes beyond what free market rhetoric suggests. But while institutions are needed to limit transaction costs, they may in fact increase them. The question then is which institutions are needed to limit transaction costs and which in fact increase them, which is seldom simple. What appears to be an obstacle in a static perspective sometimes turns out to be needed from a dynamic perspective: for example, regulation to ensure that there is no free riding in the training of labour inside firms. From a static perspective this may be seen to obstruct the labour market.

An attractive way to categorize tasks of government is perhaps to return to the basic causes of transaction costs, as discussed in Chapter 1: environmental uncertainty, behavioural uncertainty, specific investments:

1   *Environmental uncertainty*: government as enabler and guardian of information flows to govern costs of search. On the one hand government should stimulate the utilization of technical opportunities for the free flow of information. On the other hand there may be a need to allow for the protection of information, in order to control spillovers to encourage innovation.
2   *Behavioral uncertainty*: provide the basis for competence trust and intentional trust (see Chapter 1), by means of property rights (contract law, etc.) and their efficient implementation, norms and values of conduct, reputation mechanisms, certification of skills and professions.
3   *Specific investments*: enabler of standardization of technology and linkages between them.

What government policies should be considered more specifically in the area of buyer–supplier relations? Here also use can be made of the methodology set out in Chapter 4. First, one should be aware that a balanced view is required of the interests and positions of both buyer and supplier industries. It is not simply a matter of improving the technical competencies of supplier industries. It is also and perhaps primarily, an organizational matter of how to achieve balanced governance of buyer–supplier relations, along the lines set out in this book. In the improvement of technical competencies, one should take into account the effects of the distribution of power between partners, resulting from dependencies due to specific investments.

One might consider possible stimuli for financial cross-participation between buyers and suppliers and between suppliers among themselves, to allow for a bundling of strengths. A difficult issue concerning such policy towards clusters or 'industrial districts' is how it can be reconciled with simultaneous attempts to reduce cartels that inhibit economic efficiency.

Take the building industry again. The government quite properly wants to break cartels in this industry. But on the other hand we noted the need to arrive at lean production and supply in that industry, which requires cooperation and mutual adjustment of competencies and joint governance of chains of production and supply. It also requires cooperation to achieve joint standards for linkage in the chain and for benchmarking. Perhaps this problem can be solved: to prevent cartels one must be wary of 'horizontal' collaboration between competitors, and mutual adjustment primarily concerns 'vertical' coordination between buyers and suppliers. But for standards and benchmarking a certain amount of horizontal coordination is required as well.

In buyer–supplier relations, how can a long-term perspective be furthered? How can firms be helped to resist the temptation, in times of adversity, to destroy the basis for cooperation by opportunism for the sake of short-term survival? How can this be done without taking away the challenges of competition? This is related to systems of corporate governance and a discussion of that would go too far for this book (see Groenewegen 1997; Nooteboom 1997b).

Above all, perhaps, it is a task of government to stimulate the establishment of standards: technical, procedural and commercial, reducing transaction costs, especially for small firms and, in particular, reducing the transaction specificity of investments. This applies to a wide range of aspects: technical standards, in production and communication, in standard contracts and in a multitude of systems of certification. Recall the case of CAD (computer aided design) in the car industry. As long as there is no industry standard, suppliers are confronted with switching costs between customers.

Notes

Introduction

1 As discussed in more detail in Chapter 5, the difference between purchasing and contracting out is that in the latter case one could have produced the input oneself, and in the first case not.

1 Theory

1 In fact, the status of the rationality assumption in economics is debatable. To many economists, it is not an assumption concerning the capabilities and inclinations of people, but a purely instrumentalist device for efficient hypothesis formation (Friedman 1953). According to others (Alchian 1950), rationality is the outcome of a market selection process: only efficient behaviour survives.

2 This brings us close to Wittgenstein's (1953) notion of 'meaning as use', and having knowledge as being able to perform a practice according to socially established rules. And this, in turn, is close to the American tradition of pragmatism (Peirce 1957).

3 Clearly, when we talk of the cognition of a firm, in a theory of organizational learning we must indicate how it relates to the cognition of people within the firm (see Nooteboom 1998b).

4 A more abstract argument, taken from the literature on semantics, is the following. It is generally impossible, in ordinary language, to fix the reference of a term regardless of context. That would imply that one could preserve truth while shifting a term with the same reference across all contexts, which is not the case. Meaning is context dependent. To assume a meaning is to assume a context, which often remains unspecified.

5 Socrates is the celebrated master at maieutics; at coaching people to discover their own errors and prejudices.

6 Here I take power in the usual definition of the ability to affect the alternatives of choice for the object of power.

7 This view of causality reflects human activity, and Aristotle's error was to apply it to natural science. The correction of this has led to a reverse error: the application of more simplistic notions of causality derived from natural science, such as mechanical forces, to social science.

2 The context and purpose of alliances

1 See the discussion in Chapter 4 of the possible 'roles of the go-between' in the governance of inter-firm relations.

3 Forms of alliance

1 For such a systematic treatment, on the basis of Porter's 'value chain', see Huyzer *et al.* (1990).

4 Governance

1 The analysis resembles the analysis in the theory of industrial organization concerning strategic manoeuvering in shielding and entering markets. There one finds the typology of 'top dog', 'puppy dog', 'fat cat' and 'lean and hungry look'.

5 Buyer–supplier alliances

1 See McKinsey (1988) The survey had a sample of 1,000 firms in the Netherlands, with a response of 30 per cent. To arrive at sufficient numbers of firms of different size, the sample was stratified in three size classes of firms with more than 10 people engaged. Thereby the large firms are overrepresented, as are commercial services.
2 This contribution to a debate in the building industry was stimulated by a symposium of the industry and scholars in September 1997 about applying principles of lean production and supply in the industry. It was organized by a research group at the Technical University in Delft, led by Professor R.A.F. Smook.
3 I hesitate to discuss these outcomes in terms of Nash equilibria, because it is arguable that they do not apply in this world. Non-cooperative game theory analyses the utilization that agents make of opportunities to take opportunistic action. But in the present 'clan world' trust prevails and trust may be defined as the inclination not to employ opportunities for opportunism, even though one may have a material interest in doing so (see Chapter 1).
4 An alternative is to threaten to close himself off from inspection by U (set $OPEN = 0$). But this is even less credible than setting $MULCUS = 1$, because he would pay a double price for that. The first is that U would withdraw his guarantees ($COV = 0$, and then S would have to stop specific investments ($SPEC = 0$), so that both sides would lose the advantage of differentiated products. The second is that it would prevent transfer ($STRAN = 0$), which would induce U also to withdraw his transfer ($UTRAN = 0$), and both sides would then revert to multiple relations ($MULSUP = MULCUS = 1$), and thereby lose the benefits from transfer.

6 Summary

1 This was pointed out by Wouter van Rossum.
2 This case was communicated by Philip Markovski from Arthur Andersen company.

References

Abernathy, W.J. and J.M. Utterback, 1978, Patterns of industrial innovation, *Technology Review*, 81: 41–47.

Albert, M., 1993, *Capitalism against capitalism* (translated from the 1991 French edition), London: Whurr Publishers.

Alchian, A., 1950, Uncertainty, evolution and economic theory, *Journal of Political Economy*, 43 (1): 211–221.

Amin, A., 1989, Flexible specialisation and small firms in Italy: myths and realities, *Antipode*, 21: 13–34.

Amin, A. and M. Dietrich, 1991, From hierarchy to 'hierarchy': the dynamics of contemporary corporate restructuring in Europe, in A. Amin and M. Dietrich: *Towards a new Europe? Structural change in the European economy*, Aldershot: Edward Elgar: 49–73.

Anderson, E. and H. Gatignon, 1986, Modes of foreign entry: a transaction cost analysis and propositions, *Journal of International Business Studies*, Fall: 1–26.

Argyris, C. and D. Schön, 1978, *Organizational learning*, Reading MA: Addison Wesley.

Arrow, K.J., 1974, *The limits of organization*, New York: W.W. Norton.

Axelrod, R., 1984, *The evolution of cooperation*, New York: Basic Books.

Bakos, J. Y. and E. Brynjolfsson, 1993, Information technology, incentives and the optimal number of suppliers, *Journal of Management Information Systems*, 10 (2): 37–53.

Barber, B., 1983, *The logic and limits of trust*, New Brunswick NJ: Rutgers University Press.

Bateson, G, 1973, *Steps to an ecology of mind*, London: Paladin.

Beamish, P.W., 1985, The characteristics of joint ventures in developed and in developing countries, *Columbia Journal of World Business*, 20 (3): 13–19.

Berger, J., N.G. Noorderhaven and B. Nooteboom, 1995, The determinants of supplier dependence: an empirical study, in J. Groenewegen, C. Pitelis and S.E. Sjöstrand (eds), *On economic institutions: theory and applications*, Aldershot: Edward Elgar: 195–212.

Berger, P.L. and T. Luckmann, 1966, *The social construction of reality*, New York: Doubleday.

Birley, S., S. Cromie and A. Myers, 1991, Entrepreneurial networks: their emergence in Ireland and overseas, *International Small Business Journal*, 9 (4): 56–74.

Blau, P.M., 1964, *Exchange and power in social life*, New York: Wiley.

Bleeke, J. and D. Ernst, 1991, The way to win in cross-border alliances, *Harvard Business Review*, November/December: 127–135.

Boisot, M., 1995, *Information space: a framework for learning in organizations, institutions and culture*, London: Routledge.

Bolwijn, P.T. and T. Kumpe, 1989, What comes after flexibility? (in Dutch), *M&O*, 2.

Bradach, J. and R. Eccles, 1989, Price, authority and trust: From ideal types to plural forms, *Annual Review of Sociology*, 15: 97–118.

Bromiley, Ph. and L.L. Cummings, 1992, *Transaction costs in organizations with trust*, working paper, Carlson School of Management, University of Minnesota, Minneapolis.

Brown, J.S. and P. Duguid, 1991, Organizational learning and communities of practice, *Organization Science*, 2 (1), reprinted in M.D. Cohen and L.S. Sproull (eds), 1996, *Organizational learning*, London: Sage: 58–82.

Buckley, P.J. and M. Casson, 1988, A theory of cooperation in international business, in F. J. Contractor and P. Lorange (eds), *Cooperative strategies in international business*, Lexington MA: Lexington Books.

Burt, R.S., 1982, *Toward a structural theory of action: network models of social structure*, New York: Academic Press.

Burt, R.S., 1987, Social contagion and innovation: cohesion versus structural equivalence, *American Journal of Sociology*, 92: 1297–1335.

Caldwell, B.J. and S. Boehm, 1992, *Austrian economics: tensions and new directions*, Deventer: Kluwer.

Cash, J.I., F.W. McFarlan, J.L. McKenney and L.M. Applegate, 1992, *Corporate Information Systems Management*, Homewood IL: Irwin.

Casson, M., 1991, *The economics of business culture*, Oxford: Clarendon Press.

Casson, M., 1995, *The organization of international business: studies in the economics of trust*, Aldershot: Edward Elgar.

Chesbrough, H.W. and D.J. Teece, 1996, When is virtual virtuous? Organizing for innovation, *Harvard Business Review*, January/February: 65–73.

Chiles, T.H. and J.F. McMackin, 1996, Integrating variable risk preferences, trust, and transaction cost economics, *Academy of Management Review*, 21 (7): 73–99.

Choi, C.J. and S. Lee, 1997, A knowledge based view of cooperative arrangements, in P. Beamish and P. Killing (eds): *Cooperative strategies: European perspectives*, Jossey MA: Bass.

Cohen, M.D., 1991, Individual learning and organizational routine, *Organization Science*, 2 (1), reprinted in M.D. Cohen and L.S. Sproull (eds), 1996, *Organizational learning*, London: Sage: 188–229.

Cohen, M.D. and P. Bacdayan, 1994, Organizational routines are stored as procedural memory, *Organization Science*, 5 (4), reprinted in M.D. Cohen and L.S. Sproull (eds), 1996, *Organizational learning*, London: Sage: 403–430.

Cohen, M.D. and L.S. Sproull (eds), 1996, *Organizational learning*, London: Sage.

Cohen, W.M. and D.A. Levinthal, 1990, Absorptive capacity: a new perspective on learning and innovation, *Administrative Science Quarterly*, 35: 128–152.

Contractor, F.J. and P. Lorange, 1988, *Cooperative strategies in international business*, Lexington MA: Lexington Books.

Cook, S.D.D. and D. Yanow, 1993, Culture and organizational learning, *Journal of Management Enquiry*, 2 (4); reprinted in M.D. Cohen and L.S. Sproull (eds), 1996, *Organizational learning*, London: Sage: 430–459.

Craswell, R. 1993, On the uses of 'trust': comment on Williamson, 'Calculativeness, trust, and economic organization', *Journal of Law and Economics* 36: 487–500.

Cusumano, M.A. and T. Fujimoto, 1991, Supplier relations and management: a survey of Japanese, Japanese-Transplant and U.S. auto plants, *Strategic Management Journal*, 12: 563–588.

Daems, H. 1983, The determinants of hierarchical organization of industry, in A. Francis, J. Turk and P. Willman (eds), *Power, efficiency and institutions*, London: Heinemann.

Daniels, J. and L. Radebaugh, 1995, *International business*, 7th edn, Reading MA: Addison Wesley.

Dasgupta P., 1988, Trust as a commodity, in D. Gambetta (ed.), *Trust: making and breaking of cooperative relations*, Oxford: Blackwell: 49–72.

Deutsch, M., 1962, Cooperation and trust: some theoretical notes, in M.R. Jones (ed.), *Nebraska Symposium on Motivation*, Lincoln, Nebraska: University of Nebraska Press: 275–319.

Deutsch, M., 1973, *The resolution of conflict: constructive and destructive processes*, New Haven: Yale University Press.

Dore, R., 1989, *Taking Japan seriously*, Stanford: Stanford University Press.

Dosi, G., 1984, *Technical change and industrial transformation*, London: Macmillan.

Doz, Y., 1986, *Strategic management in multinational companies*, Oxford: Pergamon.

Dunning, J.H., 1995, Reappraising the eclectic paradigm in an age of alliance capitalism, *Journal of International Business Studies*, 26: 461–491.

Dyer, J.H. and W.G. Ouchi, 1993, Japanese-style partnerships: giving companies a competitive edge, *Sloan Management Review*, 35: 51–63.

Elster, J., 1979, *Ulysses and the sirens*, Cambridge: Cambridge University Press.

Elster, J., 1989, *The cement of society: A study of social order*, Cambridge: Cambridge University Press.

Etzioni, A., 1988, *The moral dimension: towards a new economics*, New York: Free Press.

Faulkner, D., 1995, *International strategic alliances; cooperating to compete*, Maidenhead: McGraw-Hill.

Fiol, C.M. and M.A. Lyles, 1985, Organizational learning, *Academy of Management Review*, 10 (4): 803–813.

Ford, D., 1980 The development of buyer–seller relationships in industrial markets, *European Journal of Marketing*, 14: 339–353.

Foss, N.J., 1994, *The Austrian school and modern economics*, Copenhagen: Munksgaard International Publishers.

Foss, N.J. and C. Knudsen (eds), 1996, *Towards a competence theory of the firm*, London: Routledge.

Frank, R.H., 1988, *Emotions within reason, the strategic role of the emotions*, New York: W.W. Norton.

Franko, L.G., 1971, *Joint venture survival in multinational corporations*, New York: Praeger.

Freeman, C. and C. Perez, 1989, Structural crises of adjustment: business cycles and investment behaviour, in G. Dosi (ed.), *Technical change and economic theory*, London: Pinter.

Friedman, M., 1953, *Essays in positive economics*, Chicago: University of Chicago Press.

Fukuyama, F., 1995, *Trust, the social virtues and the creation of prosperity*, New York: Free Press.

Gambetta, D., 1988a, Can we trust trust? in D. Gambetta (ed.), *Trust: making and breaking of cooperative relations*, Oxford: Blackwell: 213–237.

Gambetta, D., 1988b, The price of distrust, in D. Gambetta (ed.), *Trust, making and breaking of cooperative relations*, Oxford: Blackwell: 158–176.

Geringer, M.J. and L. Hebert, 1989, Control and performance of international joint ventures, *Journal of International Business Studies*, summer: 235–254.

Gilbert, R.J., 1989, Mobility barriers and the value of incumbency, in R. Schmalensee and R.D. Willig, *Handbook of industrial organization*, Amsterdam: North Holland.

Grandori, A., 1997, *An organizational assessment of interfirm coordination modes*, paper presented at the EGOS colloquium, 3–5 July Budapest.

Granovetter, M., 1982, The strength of weak ties, in P. Marsden and N. Lin, *Social structure and network analysis*, Beverly Hills CA: Sage: 105–130.

Griffin, R.W. and M. Pustay, 1996, *International business*, Reading MA: Addison Wesley.

Groenewegen, J., 1997, Institutions of capitalism: US, Europe and Japan compared, *Journal of Economic Issues*, 31/2: 333–348

Gulati, R., 1995, Does familiarity breed trust? The implications of repeated ties for contractual choice in alliances, *Academy of Management Journal*, 30 (1): 85–112.

Hagedoorn, J., 1993, Understanding the rationale of strategic technology partnering: interorganizational modes of cooperation and sectoral differences, *Strategic Management Journal*, 14: 371–385.

Hagedoorn, J. and J. Schakenraad, 1994, The effect of strategic technology alliances on company performance, *Strategic Management Journal*, 15: 291–309.

Hagg, I. and J. Johanson, 1983, *Firms in networks*, Stockholm: Business and Social Research Institute.

Hayek, F., 1978, *New studies in philosophy, economics and the history of ideas*, Chicago: University of Chicago Press.

Håkansson, H. (ed.), 1982, *International marketing and purchasing of industrial goods – an interaction approach*, Chichester: Wiley.

Håkansson, H. (ed.), 1987, *Industrial technological development: a network approach*, London: Croom Helm.

Håkansson, H., 1989, *Corporate technological behaviour; cooperation and networks*, London: Routledge.

Hedberg, B.L.T., P.C. Nystrom and W.H. Starbuck, 1976, Camping on seesaws: prescriptions for a self-designing organization, *Administrative Science Quarterly*, 21: 41–65.

Heide, J.B., 1994, Interorganizational governance in marketing channels, *Journal of Marketing*, 58: 71–85.

Heide, J.B. and A. Miner, 1992 The shadow of the future: effects of anticipated interaction and frequency of contact on buyer–seller cooperation, *Academy of Management Journal*, 35: 265–291.

Helper, S., 1990, Comparative supplier relations in the US and Japanese auto industries: an exit/voice approach, *Business and Economic History*, 19: 1–10.

Helper, S., 1991, Strategy and irreversibility in supplier relations: the case of the U.S. automobile industry, *Business History Review*, 65: 781–824.

Helper, S. and D.I. Levine, 1992, Long-term supplier relations and product-market structure, *Journal of Law, Economics and Organization*, 8 (3): 561–581.

Hennart, J-F., 1988, A transaction costs theory of equity joint ventures, *Strategic Management Journal*, 9: 361–374.

Herrigel, G., 1994, Industry as a form of order, in J.R. Holligsworth, P.C. Schmitter and W. Streeck, *Governing capitalist economies*, Oxford: Oxford University Press: 97–128.

Hill, C.W.L., 1990, Cooperation, opportunism and the invisible hand: implications for transaction cost theory, *Academy of Management Review*, 15 (3): 500–513.

Hirschman, A.O., 1970, *Exit, voice and loyalty: responses to decline in firms, organisations and states*, Cambridge MA: Harvard University Press

Hirschman, A.O., 1984, Against parsimony: three easy ways of complicating some categories of economic discourse, *American Economic Review*, 74: 88–96.

Holland, J.H., 1975, *Adaptation in natural and artificial systems*, Ann Arbor: University of Michigan.

Huyzer, S.E., W. Luimes and M.G.M. Spitholt, 1992, *Strategic cooperation: orientation and implementation*, Alphen a/d Rijn: Coopers and Lybrand Dijker van Dien/ Samson.

Itami, H., 1987, *Mobilizing invisible assets*, Cambridge MA: Harvard University Press.

Jacobs, D. and A.P. de Man, 1996, Clusters, industrial policy and firm strategy: a menu approach, *Technology Analysis and Strategic Management*, 8 (4): 425–437.

Jarillo, J.C., 1988, On strategic networks, *Strategic Management Journal*, 9: 31–41.

Johannisson, B., 1986, Network strategies, management technology for entrepreneurship and change, *International Small Business Journal*, 5 (1): 19–30.

Johanson, J. and L.G. Mattson, 1987, Interorganisational relations in industrial systems – a network approach compared with the transaction cost approach, *International Studies of Management and Organization*, 17 (1): 34–48.

Johnson, J.L. and R. Kuehn, 1987, The small business owner/manager's search for external information', *Journal of Small Business Management*, July: 53–60.

Kamath, R.R. and J.K. Liker, 1994, A second look at Japanese product development, *Harvard Business Review*, November–December: 154–170.

Kay, J., 1993, *Foundations of corporate success: how business strategies add value*, Oxford: Oxford University Press.

Kee, H.W. and R.E. Knox, 1970, Conceptual and methodological considerations in the study of trust and suspicion, *Journal of Conflict Resolution*, 14: 357–366.

Kets de Vries, M.F.R., 1977, The entrepreneurial personality: a person at the crossroads, *Journal of Management Studies*, February: 34–57.

Killing, J.P., 1983, *Strategies for joint ventures*, New York: Praeger.

Killing, J.P., 1988, Understanding alliances: the role of task and organizational complexity, *Strategic Management Journal*, 9: 319–332.

Kirzner, I.M., 1973, *Competition and entrepreneurship*, Chicago: University of Chicago Press.

Klein Woolthuis, R., 1997, *Entrepreneurial activity through inter-organisational relationships*, Faculty of Technology and Management, University of Twente, paper RENT X, Research in Entrepreneurship and Small Business, Brussels, 20–23 November.

Kogut, B., 1988, A study of the life cycle of joint ventures, in F.J. Contractor and P. Lorange (eds), *Cooperative strategies in international business*, Lexington MA: Lexington Books: 169–240.

Kogut, B. and H. Singh, 1988, Entering the US by joint venture: competitive rivalry and industry structure, in F.J. Contractor and P. Lorange (eds), *Cooperative strategies in international business*, Lexington MA: Lexington Books: 241–246.

Laat, P.B. de, 1996, *Dangerous liaisons: sharing knowledge within R&D alliances*, paper presented at the EMOT workshop (European Management and Organization in Transition, van de European Science Foundation), 6–8 September, Modena; Faculty of Philosophy, University of Groningen.

Lamming, R., 1993, *Beyond partnership*, New York: Prentice Hall.

Lane, C., 1997, *International networks in a changing global environment*, paper presented at the EGOS conference, Budapest, July.

Lane, C. and R. Bachmann, 1996, The social constitution of trust: supplier relations in Britain and Germany, *Organization Studies*, 17: 365–213.

Langlois, R.N. and P.L. Robertson, 1990, Innovation in a modular system: lessons from the microcomputer and stereo component industries, paper presented at the conference International Joseph. A. Schumpeter Society, Airlie House, Virginia, USA.

Langlois, R.N. and P.L. Robertson, 1995, *Firms, markets and economic change*, London: Routledge.

Lei, D. and J.W. Slocum, 1990, Global strategic alliances: payoffs and pitfalls, *Organizational Dynamics*, 3: 44–62.

Lippman, S. and R.P. Rumelt, 1982, Uncertain imitability: an analysis of interfirm differences in efficiency under competition, *Bell Journal of Economics*, 13: 418–438.

Lorange, P. and J. Roos, 1992, *Strategic alliances*, Cambridge: Blackwell.

Lorenz, E.H., 1988 Neither friends nor strangers: Informal networks of subcontracting in French industry, in D. Gambetta, (ed.), *Trust: making and breaking cooperative relations*, Oxford: Blackwell: 194–210.

Lorenzini, G. and C. Baden-Fuller, 1993, Creating a strategic centre to manage a web of partners, paper presented at the IMP conference, Bath, England, September.

Luhmann, N., 1988, Familiarity, confidence, trust, in D. Gambetta (ed.), *Trust; making and breaking of cooperative relations*, Oxford: Blackwell: 94–108.

McAllister, D.J., 1995, Affect and cognition based trust as foundations for interpersonal cooperation in organizations, *Academy of Management Journal*, 38 (1): 24–59.

Macauley, S., 1963, Non-contractual relations in business: a preliminary study, *American Sociological Review*, 28: 55–67.

McKinsey and Company, 1988, *Making choices for the eighties*, (in Dutch), Amsterdam: North Holland.

Makhija, M.V. and U. Ganesh, 1997, The relationship between control and partner learning in learning-related joint ventures, *Organization Science*, 8 (5): 508–527.

March, J., 1991, Exploration and exploitation in organizational learning, *Organization Science*, 2 (1): 71–87.

Mayer, R.C., J.H. Davis and F. D. Schoorman, 1995, An integrative model of organizational trust, *Academy of Management Review*, 20: 709–734.

Milgrom, P. and J. Roberts, 1989, Bargaining costs, influence costs and the organisation of economic activity, in J. Alt and K. Shepsle (eds), *The Foundation of Political Economy*, Cambridge MA: Harvard University Press.

Ministry of Economic Affairs, 1991, *Partners in production; subcontracting in innovation* (in Dutch), The Hague.

Mody, A., 1993, Learning through alliances, *Journal of Economic Behavior and Organization*, 20: 151–170.

Mokyr, J., 1990, *The lever of riches: technological creativity and economic progress*, Oxford: Oxford University Press.

Mowery, D.C., 1988, *International collaborative ventures in US manufacturing*, Cambridge MA: Ballinger.

Mueller, D.C., 1989, Mergers: causes, effects and policies, *International Journal of Industrial Organization*, 7 (1): 1–11.

Murakami, Y. and T.P. Rohlen, 1992, Social-exchange aspects of the Japanese political economy: culture, efficiency and change, in S. Kumon and H. Rosorsky (eds), *The political economy of Japan, vol. 3, Cultural and social dynamics*, Stanford CA: Stanford University Press: 63–105.

Nelson, R.R. and S.G. Winter, 1982, *An evolutionary theory of economic change*, Harvard: Belknap Press.

Nonaka, I. and H. Takeuchi, 1995, *The knowledge creating company*, New York: Oxford University Press.

Noorderhaven, N.G., 1995, Trust and transactions: towards transaction cost analysis with a differential behavioral assumption, *Tijdschrift voor Economie en Management*, 15: 5–18.

Noorderhaven, N.G., 1996, Opportunism and trust in transaction cost economics, in J. Groenewegen (ed.), *Transaction cost economics and beyond*, Boston: Kluwer: 105–128.

Nooteboom, B., 1984, Innovation, life cycle and the share of independents: cases from retailing, *International Small Business Journal*, 3 (1): 21–33.

Nooteboom, B., 1992a, Towards a dynamic theory of transactions, *Journal of Evolutionary Economics*, 2: 281–299.

Nooteboom, B., 1992b, Information technology, transaction costs and the decision to 'make or buy', *Technology Analysis and Strategic Management*, 4: 339–350.

Nooteboom, B., 1992c, Agent, context and innovation: a Saussurian view of markets, in W. Blaas and J. Foster (ed.), *Mixed economies in Europe: an evolutionary perspective on their emergence, transition and regulation*, Aldershot: Edward Elgar: 33–52.

Nooteboom, B., 1993a, An analysis of specificity in transaction cost economics, *Organization Studies*, 14 (3): 443–451.

Nooteboom, B., 1993b, Firm size effects on transaction costs, *Small Business Economics*, 5: 283–295.

Nooteboom, B., 1994, Innovation and diffusion in small business: theory and empirical evidence, *Small Business Economics*, 6: 327–347.

Nooteboom, B., 1996, Trust, opportunism and governance: a process and control model, *Organization Studies*, 17 (6): 985–1010.

Nooteboom, B., 1997a, *Will opportunism go away?*, research report, Faculty of Management and Organization, Groningen University.

Nooteboom, B., 1997b, *Voice and exit based forms of corporate control*, Paper presented at the EAEPE conference, Athens.

Nooteboom, B., 1998a, Roles of the go-between, in S.M. Gabbay and R. Leenders (eds), *Corporate social capital*, Deventer: Kluwer.

Nooteboom, B., 1998b, *Organizational learning: how to combine exploitation and exploration*, research paper, Faculty of Management and Organization, Groningen University.

Nooteboom, B., 1998c, Cost, quality and learning based governance of transactions, in M. Colombo (ed.), *The changing boundaries of the firm*, London: Routledge.

Nooteboom, B., 1998d, *Trust as a governance device: theory and empirical evidence*, paper for a symposium on Cultural Factors in Economic Growth, Marienrode, Germany, 3–5 April.

Nooteboom, B., 1999, Innovation, learning and industrial organization, *Cambridge Journal of Economics*, forthcoming.

Nooteboom, B., J. Berger and N.G. Noorderhaven, 1997, Effects of trust and governance on relational risk, *Academy of Management Journal*, 40 (2): 308–338.

North, D.C., 1990, *Institutions, institutional change and economic performance*, Cambridge: Cambridge University Press.

North, D. and R. Thomas, 1973, *The rise of the new world: a new economic history*, Cambridge: Cambridge University Press.

Ohmae, K., 1989, Global logic of strategic alliances, *Harvard Business Review*, March/April: 143–154.

Osborn, R.N. and C.C. Baughn, 1990, Forms of interorganizational governance for multinational alliances, *Academy of Management Journal*, 33 (3): 503–519.

Ouchi, W.G., 1980, Markets, bureaucracies, clans, *Administrative Science Quarterly*, 25: 129–141.

Pagden, A., 1988, The destruction of trust and its economic consequences in the case of eighteenth-century Naples, in D. Gambetta (ed.), *Trust: making and breaking cooperative relations*, Oxford: Blackwell.

Palay, Th. M., 1984, Comparative institutional economics: the governance of rail freight contracting, *Journal of Legal Studies*, 13: 265–287.

Parkhe, A., 1993, Strategic alliance structuring: a game theoretic and transaction cost examination of inter-firm cooperation, *Academy of Management Journal*, 36: 794–829.

Pavitt, K., 1984, Sectoral patterns of technical change: towards a taxonomy and a theory, *Research Policy*, 13: 343–373.

Peirce, C.S., 1957, *Essays in the philosophy of science*, Indianapolis: Bobbs Merrill.

Penrose, E., 1959, *The theory of the growth of the firm*, New York: Wiley.

Piaget, J., 1970, *Psychologie et epistémologie*, Paris: Denoël.

Piaget, J., 1974, *Introduction a l'epistémologie génétique*, Paris: Presses Universitaires de France.

Piore, M. and C. Sabel, 1983, Italian small business development: lessons for US industrial policy, in J. Zysman and L. Tyson (eds), *American industry in international competition: government policies and corporate strategies*, Ithaca: Cornell University Press.

Piore M.J. and C.F. Sabel, 1984, *The second industrial divide*, New York: Basic Books.

Polanyi, M., 1962, *Personal knowledge*, London: Routledge.

Polanyi, M., 1966, *The tacit dimension*, London: Routledge.

Polanyi, M., 1969, *Knowing and being*, London: Routledge.

Porter, M., 1985, *Competitive advantage*, New York: Free Press.

Porter, M.E., 1990, *The competitive advantage of nations*, London: Macmillan.

Porter, M.E. and M.B. Fuller, 1986, Coalitions and global strategies, in M.E. Porter (ed.), *Competition in global industries*, Boston MA: Harvard Business School Press: 315–344.

Powell, W.W., 1990, Neither market nor hierarchy: Network forms of organization, in B.M. Staw and L.L. Cummings (eds), *Research in organizational behavior 12*, Greenwich, CT: JAI Press: 295–336.

Prahalad, C. and G. Hamel, 1990 The core competences of the corporation, *Harvard Business Review*, May-June: 79–83.

Ravenscraft, D.J. and F.M. Scherer, 1986, Life after takeover, *Journal of Industrial Economics*, 7 (1): 101–117.

Reitman, V., 1997, To the rescue: Toyota's fast rebound after fire at supplier shows why it is tough, *Wall Street Journal*, 8 May: A15–16.

Ring, P.S. and A. van de Ven, 1992, Structuring cooperative relations between organizations, *Strategic Management Journal*, 13: 483–498.

Ring, P.S. and A.H. Van de Ven, 1994, Developmental processes of cooperative interorganizational relationships, *Academy of Management Review*, 19 (1): 90–118.

Rogers, E.M., 1983, *Diffusion of innovations*, 3rd edn, New York: Free Press.

Ruigrok, W. and R. van Tulder, 1995, *The logic of international restructuring*, London: Routledge.

Sako, M., 1994, Neither markets nor hierarchies: a comparative study of the printed circuit board industry in Britain and Japan, in J.R. Hollingsworth, P.C. Schmitter and W. Streeck, *Governing capitalist economies*, Oxford: Oxford University Press: 17–42.

Schenk. H., 1997, *Mergers, efficient choice and international competitiveness*, Aldershot: Edward Elgar.

Scher, M.J., 1996, The relational access paradigm and Japanese interfirm networks: why outsiders seldom win: outcomes and policy implications, paper presented at the EMOT workshop (European Management and Organization in Transition, of the European Science Foundation), Turin, 15–16 November.

Scherer, F.M., 1988, Corporate takeovers: the efficiency arguments, *Journal of Economic Perspectives*, 2 (1): 68–83.

Seabright, M.A., D.A. Levinthal and M. Fichman, 1992, Role of individual attachments in the dissolution of interorganizational relationships, *Academy of Management Journal*, 35: 122–160.

Semlinger, K., 1991, New developments in subcontracting: mixing market and hierarchy, in: A. Amin and M. Dietrich, *Towards a new Europe? Structural change in the European economy*, Aldershot: Edward Elgar: 96–115.

Simon, H.A., 1983, *Reason in human affairs* Oxford: Blackwell.

Smith Ring, P. and A.H. Van de Ven, 1994, Developmental processes of cooperative interorganizational relationships, *Academy of Management Review*, 19 (1): 90–118.

Stoelhorst, J.W., 1997, *In search of a dynamic theory of the firm*, doctoral dissertation, Twente University, Netherlands.

Sydow, J., 1996, *Understanding the constitution of inter-organizational trust*, paper presented at the SASE conference, University of Geneva, 12–14 July.

Teece, D.J., 1986, Profiting from technological innovation: implications for integration, collaboration, licensing and public policy, *Research Policy*, 15: 285–305.

Teece, D.J., 1988, Technological change and the nature of the firm, in G. Dosi, C. Freeman, R. Nelson, G. Silverberg and L. Soete (eds), *Technical change and economic theory*, London: Pinter.

Telser, L.G., 1980, A theory of self-enforcing agreements, *Journal of Business*, 53: 27–44.

Uzzi, B., 1997, Social structure and competition in interfirm netwoks: the paradox of embeddedness, *Administrative Science Quarterly*, 42: 35–67.

Vaughn, K.I., 1994, *Austrian economics in America*, Cambridge: Cambridge University Press.

Walker, G. and L. Poppo, 1991, Profit centers, single-source suppliers and transaction costs, *Administrative Science Quarterly*, 36: 66–87.

Walker, G. and D. Weber, 1987, Supplier competition, uncertainty and make-or-buy decisions, *Academy of Management Journal*, 30: 589–596.

Weigelt, K., and C. Camerer, 1988, Reputation and corporate strategy: a review of recent theory and applications, *Strategic Management Journal*, 9: 443–454.

Williams, B., 1988, Formal structures and social reality, in D. Gambetta (ed.), *Trust: making and breaking of cooperative relations*, Oxford: Blackwell: 3–13.

Williamson, O.E., 1975, *Markets and hierarchies*, New York: Free Press.

Williamson, O.E., 1985, *The economic institutions of capitalism: firms markets, relational contracting*, New York: Free Press.

Williamson, O.E., 1991, Comparative economic organization: the analysis of discrete structural alternatives, *Administrative Science Quarterly*, 36: 269–296.

Williamson, O.E., 1993, Calculativeness, trust, and economic organization, *Journal of Law and Economics*, 36: 453–486.

Willinger, M. and E. Zuscovitch, 1988, Towards the economics of information-intensive production systems: the case of advanced materials, in G. Dosi, C. Freeman, R. Nelson, G. Silverberg and L. Soete, *Technical change and economic theory*, London: Pinter: 239–255.

Wittgenstein, L., 1953, *Philosophical investigations*, Oxford: Blackwell.

Womack, J., D. Jones and D. Roos, 1990, *The machine that changed the world*, New York: Rawson.

Woodside, A.G. and K. Möller, 1992, Middle range theories of industrial purchasing strategies, *Advances in Marketing and Purchasing*, 5: 21–59.

Zand, D.E., 1972, Trust and managerial problem solving, *Administrative Science Quarterly*, 17 (2): 229–239.

Zucker, L.G., 1986, Production of trust: institutional sources of economic structure 1840–1920, in Barry, Staw and Cummings, *Research in organisational behaviour*, 8: 53–111.

Zuscovitch, E., 1994, *Sustainable differentiation: economic dynamism and social norms*, paper presented at the J.A. Schumpeter conference, Münster, 19–21 August.

Index of authors cited

General index

absorptive capacity 12, 15, 54, 100
accountancy firms 90–1, 118
acquisitions *see* mergers and
     acquisitions
adaptability of alliances 135
adversarial orientation 130–1, 172, 187,
     209
adverse selection 169
aircraft manufacture 52, 83
airline reservation systems 169
airline takeovers 87
alertness, entrepreneurial 9
alimony 149, 151
alliances: dimensions of 66–8, 204;
     forms of 1, 6, 64–70, 99; purpose and
     role of 4–5, 16, 110, 203–6;
     specifying limits of 137–8; *see also*
     goals
aluminium, supply of 58–9
American Hospital Supplies 169
arbitration 123, 141, 215; between
     supply and demand 9
'architecture' of firms' relationships 7
'arms'-length' relationships 172, 204,
     208–10
assembly lines 45
associations 66, 68, 84, 127
asymmetric information 1, 17, 95, 113,
     124, 173, 206–9, 215; in marriage
     150–1
asymmetry in alliances 97, 139, 179,
     199
'atmosphere' 23, 31, 125, 127, 129,
     136
auditing of firms' relations 4
Austrian economics 11, 202
automobile industry 7, 49, 74, 78, 118,
     120, 122, 135, 154, 157–9, 168,
     172–5, 181, 217

bandwagon effect 38
banking 85, 87, 90
bar codes 44, 55, 167, 214
behavioural trust 26–8
behavioural uncertainty 216
benchmarking 122, 182–3
Benetton 65
Bessemer, Sir Henry 62
bifurcations 215
'binding' strategy 95–6, 130–1, 136,
     172–3
bluffing 132
BMW (company) 135
Bosch (company) 154, 157
boundaries of the firm 51
bounded rationality 17, 188, 215
brand names 46, 58–9, 86–90
breakdown of alliances 2, 140, 144,
     181, 206, 208
Bridgestone (company) 59
building industry 4, 182–3, 209, 217
business process engineering 45
buyer profiles 44
buyer–supplier relations (BSR) 4, 49,
     67, 95, 152–9, 188, 208, 216; generic
     types of 152

'capabilities' view of the firm *see*
     'resource' view
captiveness 109, 112–14, 121, 125–6
car industry *see* automobile industry
cartels 217
causal ambiguity 10, 20, 50, 101
cause: 'efficient', 'material', 'final',
     'formal', 'exemplary' and
     'conditional' 36–9, 57, 69, 120
chance encounters 55, 213
children 149, 151
chips *see* semiconductors